Praise for Rogue States

"World-famous MIT linguist [Noam] Chomsky has long kept up a second career as a cogent voice of the hard left, excoriating American imperialism, critiquing blinkered journalists and attacking global economic injustice.... [In *Rogue States*] Chomsky has delivered another impressive argument that the U.S. flouts international law when it finds it convenient to do so."

—*Publishers Weekly*

"Noam Chomsky is like a medic attempting to cure a national epidemic of selective amnesia.... [*Rogue States* is] a timely guide to the tactics that the powerful employ to keep power concentrated and people compliant.... Chomsky's work is crucial at a time when our empire perpetually disguises its pursuit of power under the banners of 'aid,' 'humanitarian intervention,' and now 'globalization.' Americans have to begin deciphering the rhetoric. Chomsky's a good place to start."

—*Village Voice*

"Nothing escapes [Chomsky's] attention... [*Rogue States* is] wonderfully lucid."

—*PeaceWork*

On Noam Chomsky

"An exploder of received truths."

—*New York Times*

"Reading Chomsky is like standing in a wind tunnel. With relentless logic, Chomsky bids us to listen closely to what our leaders tell us—and to discern what they are leaving out.... The questions Chomsky raises will eventually have to be answered. Agree with him or not, we lose out by not listening."

—*Business Week*

Rogue States

The Rule of Force in World Affairs

Noam Chomsky

Pluto Press

First published in the United Kingdom 2000 by
Pluto Press
345 Archway Road
London N6 5AA

www.plutobooks.com

British Library Cataloguing in Publication Data
A catalogue record for this book is available from the British Library.

ISBN 0 7453 1709 X hardback
ISBN 0 7453 1708 1 paperback

10 9 8 7 6 5 4 3
Typeset in the United States of America
Printed in the European Union by
Antony Rowe, Chippenham and Eastbourne, England

Contents

1

Rogues' Gallery
Who Qualifies?

Like many other terms of political discourse, the term "rogue state" has two uses: a propagandistic use, applied to assorted enemies, and a literal use that applies to states that do not regard themselves as bound by international norms. Logic suggests that the most powerful states should tend to fall into the latter category unless internally constrained, an expectation that history confirms.

Though international norms are not rigidly determined, there is a measure of agreement on general guidelines. In the post–World War II period, these norms are partially codified in the UN Charter, International Court of Justice decisions, and various conventions and treaties. The US regards itself as exempt from these conditions, increasingly so since the Cold War ended, leaving US dominance so overwhelming that pretense can be largely dropped. The fact has not gone unnoticed. The newsletter of the American Society of International Law (ASIL) observed in March 1999 that "international law is today probably less highly regarded in our country than at any time" in the century; the editor of its professional journal had warned shortly before of the "alarming exacerbation" of Washington's dismissal of treaty obligations.[1]

The operative principle was articulated by Dean Acheson in 1963 when he informed the ASIL that the "propriety" of a response to a "challenge ... [to the] ... power, position, and prestige of the United States ... is not a legal issue." International law, he had observed earlier, is useful "to gild our positions with an ethos derived from very general moral principles which have affected legal doctrines." But the US is not bound by it.[2]

Acheson was referring specifically to the Cuba blockade. Cuba has

1

been one of the main targets of US terror and economic warfare for 40 years, even before the secret decision of March 1960 to overthrow the government. The Cuban threat was identified by Arthur Schlesinger, reporting the conclusions of Kennedy's Latin American mission to the incoming president: It is "the spread of the Castro idea of taking matters into one's own hands," which might stimulate the "poor and underprivileged" elsewhere, who "are now demanding opportunities for a decent living," Schlesinger later elaborated — the "virus" or "rotten apple" effect, as it is sometimes called. There was a Cold War connection: "The Soviet Union hovers in the wings, flourishing large development loans and presenting itself as the model for achieving modernization in a single generation."[3]

Unsurprisingly, the US assault became considerably harsher after the USSR disappeared from the scene. The measures have been near-universally condemned: by the UN, the European Union, the Organization of American States (OAS) and its judicial body, the Inter-American Juridical Committee, which ruled unanimously that they violate international law, as did the Inter-American Commission on Human Rights. Few doubt that they would also be condemned by the World Trade Organization (WTO), but Washington has made it clear that it would disregard any WTO ruling, keeping to the rogue state principle.

To mention another illustration of contemporary relevance, when Indonesia invaded East Timor in 1975 it was ordered to withdraw at once by the UN Security Council, but to no avail. The reasons were explained in his 1978 memoirs by UN Ambassador Daniel Patrick Moynihan:

> The United States wished things to turn out as they did, and worked to bring this about. The Department of State desired that the United Nations prove utterly ineffective in whatever measures it undertook. This task was given to me, and I carried it forward with no inconsiderable success.[4]

He goes on to report that within two months some 60,000 people had been killed. The numbers reached about 200,000 within a few years, thanks to increasing military support from the US, joined by Britain as atrocities peaked in 1978. Their support continued through 1999, as Kopassus commandoes, armed and trained by the US, organized "Operation Clean Sweep" from January, killing 3,000 to 5,000 people by August, according to credible Church sources, and later expelling 750,000 people — 85 percent of the population — and virtually destroying the country. Throughout, the Clinton administration kept to its stand that "it is the responsibility of the government of Indonesia, and we don't want to take it away from them." Under mounting domestic and international (primarily Australian) pressure, Washington finally indicated to the Indonesian generals that the game was over. They quickly reversed course, announcing their withdrawal, an indication of the latent power that had always been available.

US support for Indonesian aggression and slaughter was almost reflexive. The murderous and corrupt General Suharto was "our kind of guy," the Clinton administration explained, as he had been ever since he supervised a Rwanda-style massacre in 1965 that elicited unrestrained euphoria in the US. So he remained, while compiling one of the worst human rights records of the modern era, though he fell from grace in 1997 when he lost control and was dragging his feet on harsh International Monetary Fund (IMF) austerity programs. The pattern is familiar: another grand killer, Saddam Hussein, was also supported through his worst atrocities, changing status only when he disobeyed (or misunderstood) orders. There is a long series of similar illustrations: Trujillo, Mobutu, Marcos, Duvalier, Noriega, and many others. Crimes are not of great consequence; disobedience is.

The 1965 mass murders, mostly of landless peasants, ensured that Indonesia would not be a threat of the Cuban variety — an "infection" that "would sweep westward" through South Asia, as George Kennan had warned in 1948 when he took "the problem of Indonesia" to be the "most crucial" issue in "the struggle with the Kremlin," which was scarcely visible. The massacre was also taken to be a justification of Washington's wars in Indochina, which had strengthened the resolve of the generals to cleanse their society.[5]

Rendering the UN "utterly ineffective" has been routine procedure since the organization fell out of control with decolonization. One index is Security Council vetoes, covering a wide range of issues: from the 1960s, the US has been far in the lead, Britain second, France a distant third. General Assembly votes are similar. The more general principle is that if an international organization does not serve the interests that govern US policy, there is little reason to allow it to survive.

The reasons for dismissing international norms were elaborated by the Reagan administration when the World Court was considering Nicaragua's charges against the US. Secretary of State George Shultz derided those who advocate "utopian, legalistic means like outside mediation, the United Nations, and the World Court, while ignoring the power element of the equation." State Department legal advisor Abraham Sofaer explained that most of the world cannot "be counted on to share our view," and the "majority often opposes the United States on important international questions." Accordingly, we must "reserve to ourselves the power to determine" how we will act and which matters fall "essentially within the domestic jurisdiction of the United States, as determined by the United States" — in this case, the actions that the Court condemned as the "unlawful use of force" against Nicaragua.[6]

The Court called on Washington to desist and pay substantial reparations, also ruling that all aid to the mercenary forces attacking Nicaragua was military, not humanitarian. Accordingly, the Court was dismissed as a "hostile forum" (*New York Times*) that had discredited itself by condemning the US, which reacted by escalating the war and dismissing the call for reparations. The US then vetoed a UN Security Council resolution calling on all states to observe international law, and voted in virtual isolation against similar General Assembly resolutions. All of this was considered so insignificant that it was barely reported, just as the official reactions have been ignored. Aid was called "humanitarian" until the US victory.[7]

The rogue state doctrine remained in force when the Democrats returned to the White House. President Clinton informed the United Nations in 1993 that the US will act "multilaterally when possible, but unilaterally when necessary," a position reiterated a year later by UN Ambassador Madeleine Albright and in 1999 by Secretary of Defense William Cohen, who declared that the US is committed to "unilateral use of military power" to defend vital interests, which include "ensuring uninhibited access to key markets, energy supplies, and strategic resources," and indeed anything that Washington might determine to be within its "domestic jurisdiction."[8]

The only novelty in these positions is that they are public. In the internal record, they are assumed from the earliest days of the post-war order. The first memorandum of the newly formed National Security Council (NSC 1/3) called for military support for underground operations in Italy, along with national mobilization in the United States, "in the event the Communists obtain domination of the Italian government by legal means"; subversion of democracy in Italy remained a major project at least into the 1970s.[9] The record elsewhere is too rich to sample. It includes not only direct aggression, subversion, and terror, but also support for the same practices on the part of client states: for example, regular Israeli attacks on Lebanon that have left tens of thousands dead and have repeatedly driven hundreds of thousands from their homes; and massive ethnic cleansing and other large-scale atrocities conducted by Turkey, within NATO, abetted by a huge flow of arms from the Clinton administration that escalated as atrocities peaked.[10]

The record also includes incitement of atrocities. An illustration is the state that has just replaced Turkey as the leading recipient of US military aid (Israel and Egypt are in a separate category), now that Clinton-backed Turkish terror has succeeded, at least temporarily. The new champion, Colombia, had the worst human rights record in the hemisphere in the '90s, and — conforming to a well-substantiated regularity — has been the leading recipient of US military aid and training, now scheduled to increase sharply.

The US contributions to the Colombian tale of horrors date back to the Kennedy administration. One of the most significant legacies of the Kennedy administration was its 1962 decision to shift the mission of the Latin American military from "hemispheric defense" to "internal security," while providing the means and training to carry out the task. As described by Charles Maechling, who led counterinsurgency and internal defense planning from 1961 to 1966, that historic decision led to a change from toleration "of the rapacity and cruelty of the Latin American military" to "direct complicity" in "the methods of Heinrich Himmler's extermination squads." The aftermath need not be reviewed. The consequences persist even after state terror has achieved its immediate goals. A Jesuit-sponsored conference in San Salvador in 1994 took particular note of the efficacy of the residual "culture of terror in domesticating the expectations of the majority vis-à-vis alternatives different to those of the powerful," a powerful force, buttressed with ample historical memory and current evidence.[11]

Much the same has been true in other parts of the "South." In 1958, President Eisenhower supervised one of the major US clandestine operations in an effort to break up Indonesia, meanwhile dismantling its parliamentary institutions and setting the stage for the massive terror of the next 40 years. At the same time, Washington subverted the first (and last) free election in Laos, supported an attack on Cambodia, undermined the Burmese government, and intensified the terror of its client regime in South Vietnam, escalated to direct US aggression by JFK a few years later. In each case, the long-term effects have been disastrous.[12]

To ensure that its writ is law, a rogue superpower must maintain "credibility": failure to respect its power carries severe penalties. The concept is invoked regularly in justification of state violence. The regular appeal to "credibility" was the only plausible argument advanced for the preference for war over other means in the case of Kosovo in early 1999; the standard cover phrase was "credibility of NATO," but no one believed that it was the credibility of Belgium or Italy that had to be established in the minds of potentially disobedient elements — "rogues" in the technical propagandistic usage: "the defiant, the indolent, and the miscreant," the "disorderly" elements of the world who reject the right of the self-anointed "enlightened states" to resort to violence when, where, and as they "believe it to be just," discarding "the restrictive old rules" and obeying "modern notions of justice" that they fashion for the occasion.[13]

The need for "credibility" is also a leading factor in long-term planning. It is stressed, for example, in a 1995 study of "Post–Cold War Deterrence" by the US Strategic Command (STRATCOM): Washington's "deterrence statement" must be "convincing" and "immediately discernible" by leaders of "rogue states." The US should have available "the full range of responses," primarily nuclear weapons, because "unlike chemical or biological weapons, the extreme destruction from a nuclear explosion is immediate, with few if any palliatives to reduce its effect." Bioterrorism may be a weapon of the weak, but the powerful rogue states prefer more efficient means of terror, intimidation, and devastation. "Although we are not likely [sic] to use nuclear weapons in less than matters of the greatest national importance, or in less than extreme circumstances, nuclear weapons always cast a shadow over any crisis or conflict." Furthermore, "planners should not be too rational about determining ... what the opponent values the most," all of which must be targeted. "It hurts to portray ourselves as too fully rational and cool-headed." "That the US may become irrational and vindictive if its vital interests are attacked should be a part of the national persona we project." It is "beneficial" for our strategic posture if "some elements may appear to be potentially 'out of control.' "

While the vast destruction of nuclear weapons is the preferred mode of "cast[ing] a shadow" over crisis and conflict, low-tech options should not be overlooked. STRATCOM also advises "creative deterrence": "an insightful tailoring of what is valued within a culture, and its weaving into a deterrence message." One illustration is provided, and suggested as a model: When Soviet citizens were kidnapped and killed in Lebanon, "the Soviets had delivered to the leader of the revolutionary activity a package containing a single testicle — that of his eldest son." With skillful intermingling of creative deterrence and the threat of nuclear destruction, against the background of many examples of the residual "culture of terror" described by the Salvadoran Jesuits, the "defiant" and "miscreant" who might disturb good order should be effectively controlled.

The reasoning would be familiar to any mafia don. In one or another form, it finds its natural place in any system of power and domination, and one should hardly be surprised to find that an appropriate version is crafted by the global enforcer, and applied where necessary. This is the rational way to advance towards the ideal outlined by Winston Churchill in his reflections on the shape of the post–World War II world:

> The government of the world must be entrusted to satisfied nations, who wished nothing more for themselves than what they had. If the world-government were in the hands of hungry nations, there would always be danger. But none of us had any reason to seek for anything more. The peace would be kept by peoples who lived in their own way and were not ambitious. Our power placed us above the rest. We were like rich men dwelling at peace within their habitations.[14]

In the post–Cold War world, the Pentagon elaborated, "deterrence strategy" shifted from the "weapon-rich environment" of the super-power enemy to the "target-rich environment" of the South — in reality, the primary target of aggression and terror throughout the Cold War. Nuclear weapons "seem destined to be the centerpiece of US strategic deterrence for the foreseeable future," the STRATCOM report concludes. The US should therefore reject a "no-first-use policy," and should make it clear to adversaries that its "reaction" may "either be response or preemptive." It should also reject the stated goal of the Non-Proliferation Treaty and should not agree to "Negative Security

Assurances" that ban use of nuclear weapons against non-nuclear states that are parties to the Treaty. A Negative Security Assurance of 1995 was overridden by internal planning and other presidential directives, leaving Cold War strategy pretty much on course, apart from the broader range of targets.[15]

It is perhaps of interest that none of this elicits concern or even commentary.

During the Cold War years, the standard pretext for terror and aggression was "communism," a highly flexible notion, as the victims recognize. Inspection of the internal record reveals that leading concerns were commonly the threat of independence and "infection." In Indonesia, as in Italy, a prime concern was that the government was too democratic, even permitting participation of a party of the left, the PKI, which "had won widespread support not as a revolutionary party but as an organization defending the interests of the poor within the existing system," developing a "mass base among the peasantry" through its "vigor in defending the interests of the ... poor," Australian Indonesia specialist Harold Crouch observes. There was no Russian connection, as Eisenhower stressed "vociferously" in internal discussion.[16]

The PKI was pro-Chinese, but by 1965, when it was demolished by mass slaughter, Russia and China were hardly allies. The way the fear of China was invoked illustrates well the opportunistic character of Cold War propaganda. Thus, when the State Department decided to support French efforts to reconquer its former colony, US intelligence was instructed to "prove" that Ho Chi Minh was an agent of the Kremlin or "Peiping"; either would do, and when it turned out that no evidence could be found, that was taken as proof that the targeted enemy was a mere slave of its foreign masters, in one of the more comical episodes of the history of intelligence.[17] Moynihan's explanation of why the US had to render the Security Council "utterly ineffective" and support Indonesian slaughter in East Timor was that the resistance was supported by China — outlandish, but it reflected the understanding that some Cold War element is required by the doctrinal system.

The significance of Moynihan's invocation of China was illuminated by events four years earlier and four years later, the US reactions to the two major (perhaps only) examples of post–World War II military interventions that had highly beneficial humanitarian consequences: India's invasion of East Pakistan (Bangladesh) in 1971, and Vietnam's overthrow of the Pol Pot regime eight years later. Both interventions were bitterly opposed by Washington, and in both cases its friendly relations with China were a leading factor. An apparent reason for the furious reaction to India's termination of huge atrocities was that it might have interfered with the PR operation planned for Kissinger's surprise visit to China; Vietnam's crime of terminating the atrocities of Pol Pot was punished by a US-backed Chinese invasion, while the US turned to overt diplomatic and military support for the displaced Pol Pot regime (Democratic Kampuchea).

Cold War pretexts were always available, and sometimes had a modicum of plausibility; and, of course, great power interactions are always in the background. But a close look commonly reveals that other factors are the operative ones, as in the case of Indochina, Cuba, and Indonesia — a fact sometimes conceded when Cold War pretexts faded. Thus, in its first post–Cold War request for Pentagon funding in March 1990, the Bush administration called for maintaining the major US intervention forces, targeting the Middle East, where the "threats to our interests ... could not be laid at the Kremlin's door," contrary to decades of propaganda.[18]

Similarly, when the US terminated Guatemala's brief democratic experiment with a military invasion, setting off 40 years of horror, the concern voiced internally (though not publicly) was that the "social and economic programs of the elected government met the aspirations" of labor and the peasantry and "inspired the loyalty and conformed to the self-interest of most politically conscious Guatemalans."[19] More dangerous still, Guatemala's

> agrarian reform is a powerful propaganda weapon; its broad social program of aiding the workers and peasants in a victorious struggle against the upper classes and large foreign enterprises has a strong appeal to the populations of Central American neighbors where similar conditions prevail.[20]

The threat to order was suppressed with 40 years of brutal violence and massacres.

These are constant refrains in the internal record. Accordingly, the policies continue with only tactical modification when the Cold War can no longer be invoked, as in 1991, when Washington moved at once to reverse Haiti's hopeful democratic experiment, then undermined the OAS embargo while the military junta tortured and murdered, and finally restored the elected president on the condition that he adopt the policies of Washington's defeated candidate in the 1990 elections, who had received 14 percent of the vote. Subsequent debate focuses on the question of whether this "humanitarian intervention" in defense of democracy was well-advised.[21]

Against the background of large-scale aggression and terror, actions that would be considered major crimes if perpetrated by others are mere footnotes: for example, the murder of 80 Lebanese in the worst terrorist atrocity of 1985, at the peak of fury about "international terrorism," a CIA-initiated car-bombing targeting a Muslim leader. Or the destruction of half the pharmaceutical supplies of a poor African country (Sudan) in 1998, with a death toll that is unknown, and uninvestigated: Washington blocked a UN inquiry. The bombing was legitimate, the editors of the *New York Times* explained, because the US "has the right to use military force against factories and training camps where terrorist attacks against American targets are being prepared" (or perhaps are not).[22] The reaction would presumably be different if, say, Islamic terrorists were to destroy half the pharmaceutical supplies in the US, Israel, or some other favored state.

These and other examples of retail terror may fall under the category of "creative deterrence."

The human toll is too vast to try to calculate, but for rogue states with tremendous power, crimes do not matter. They are eliminated from history or transmuted into benign intent that sometimes goes awry. Thus, at the outer limits of admissible critique, the war against South Vietnam, then all of Indochina, began with "blundering efforts to do good," though "by 1969" it had become clear "that the intervention had been a disastrous mistake" because the US "could not impose a solution except at a price too costly to itself." Robert McNamara's apology for the war was addressed to Americans, and was either condemned as treachery (by hawks) or considered highly meritorious and courageous (by doves): If millions of dead litter the ruins of the countries devastated by our assault, and still die from unexploded ordnance and the lingering effects of chemical warfare, that is not our concern, and calls for no apology, let alone reparations or war crimes trials.[23]

Quite the contrary. The US is hailed as the leader of the "enlightened states" that are entitled to resort to violence as they see fit. In the Clinton years its foreign policy has ascended to a "noble phase" with a "saintly glow" (according to the *New York Times*), as America is "at the height of its glory," with a record unsullied by international crimes, only a few of which have been mentioned.[24]

Rogue states that are internally free — and the US is at the outer limits in this respect — must rely on the willingness of the educated classes to produce accolades and to tolerate or deny terrible crimes. On this matter too there is a rich record, reviewed extensively elsewhere. It should not elicit much pride.

2

Rogue States

The concept of "rogue state" plays a preeminent role today in policy planning and analysis. The April 1998 Iraq crisis is only one of the most recent examples. Washington and London have declared Iraq a "rogue state," a threat to its neighbors and to the entire world, an "outlaw nation" led by a reincarnation of Hitler who must be contained by the guardians of world order, the United States and its "junior partner," to adopt the term ruefully employed by the British foreign office half a century ago.[1]

The concept merits a close look. But first, let's consider its application in the current crisis.

The Iraq Crisis

The most interesting feature of the debate over the Iraq crisis is that it never took place. True, many words flowed, and there was dispute about how to proceed. But discussion kept within rigid bounds that excluded the obvious answer: the US and UK should act in accord with their laws and treaty obligations.

The relevant legal framework is formulated in the Charter of the United Nations, a "solemn treaty" recognized as the foundation of international law and world order, and under the US Constitution, "the supreme law of the land."

The Charter states that "the Security Council shall determine the existence of any threat to the peace, breach of the peace, or act of aggression, and shall make recommendations, or decide what measures shall be taken in accordance with Articles 41 and 42," which detail the preferred "measures not involving the use of armed force" and permit the Security Council to take further action if it finds such measures inadequate.

The only exception is Article 51, which permits the "right of individual or collective self-defense" against "armed attack ... until the Security Council has taken the measures necessary to maintain international peace and security." Apart from these exceptions, member states "shall refrain in their international relations from the threat or use of force."

There are legitimate ways to react to the many threats to world peace. If Iraq's neighbors feel threatened, they can approach the Security Council to authorize appropriate measures to respond to the threat. If the US and Britain feel threatened, they can do the same. But no state has the authority to make its own determinations on these matters and to act as it chooses; the US and UK would have no such authority even if their own hands were clean — hardly the case.

Outlaw states do not accept these conditions: Saddam's Iraq, for example, or the United States. The US position was forthrightly articulated by Secretary of State Madeleine Albright, then UN ambassador, when she informed the Security Council during an earlier US confrontation with Iraq that the US will act "multilaterally when we can, and unilaterally as we must," because "we recognize this area as vital to US national interests" and therefore accept no external constraints. Albright reiterated that stand when UN Secretary-General Kofi Annan undertook his February 1998 diplomatic mission: "We wish him well," she stated, "and when he comes back we will see what he has brought and how it fits with our national interest," which will determine how we respond. When Annan announced that an agreement had been reached, Albright repeated the doctrine: "It is possible that he will come with something we don't like, in which case we will pursue our national interest." President Clinton announced that if Iraq failed the test of conformity (as determined by Washington), "everyone would understand that then the United States and hopefully all of our allies would have the unilateral right to respond at a time, place, and manner of our own choosing," in the manner of other violent and lawless states.[2]

The Security Council unanimously endorsed Annan's agreement, rejecting US/UK demands that it authorize their use of force in the event of non-compliance. The resolution warned of "severest consequences," but with no further specification. In the crucial final paragraph, the Council "DECIDES, in accordance with its responsibilities under the Charter, to remain actively seized of the matter, in order to ensure imple-

mentation of this resolution and to ensure peace and security in the
area" — the Council, no one else; in accordance with the Charter.

The facts were clear and unambiguous. Headlines read: "An Automatic Strike Isn't Endorsed" *(Wall Street Journal)*, "UN Rebuffs US on
Threat to Iraq If It Breaks Pact" *(New York Times)*, etc. Britain's UN ambassador "privately assured his colleagues on the Council that the resolution does not grant the United States and Britain an 'automatic trigger'
to launch strikes against Iraq if it impedes" UN searches for chemical
weapons. "It has to be the Security Council who determines when to use
armed force," the ambassador of Costa Rica declared, expressing the position of the Security Council.

Washington's reaction was different. US Ambassador Bill Richardson asserted that the agreement "did not preclude the unilateral use of
force" and that the US retains its legal right to attack Baghdad at will.
State Department spokesperson James Rubin dismissed the wording of
the resolution as "not as relevant as the kind of private discussions that
we've had": "I am not saying that we don't care about that resolution,"
but "we've made clear that we don't see the need to return to the Security
Council if there is a violation of the agreement." The president stated
that the resolution "provides authority to act" if the US is dissatisfied
with Iraqi compliance; his press secretary made clear that that means
military action. "US Insists It Retains Right to Punish Iraq," the *New
York Times* headline read, accurately. The US has the unilateral right to
use force at will. Period.

Some felt that even this stand strayed too close to our solemn obligations under international and domestic law. Senate majority leader
Trent Lott denounced the administration for having "subcontracted" its
foreign policy "to others" — to the UN Security Council. Senator John
McCain warned that "the United States may be subordinating its power
to the United Nations," an obligation only for law-abiding states. Senator John Kerry added that it would be "legitimate" for the US to invade
Iraq outright if Saddam "remains obdurate and in violation of the United
Nations resolutions, and in a position of threat to the world community,"
whether the Security Council so determines or not. Such unilateral US
action would be "within the framework of international law," as Kerry
conceives it. A liberal dove who reached national prominence as an opponent of the Vietnam War, Kerry explained that his current stand was con-

sistent with his earlier views. Vietnam taught him that force should be used only if the objective is "achievable and it meets the needs of your country." Saddam's invasion of Kuwait was therefore wrong for only one reason: it was not "achievable," as matters turned out.[3]

At the liberal-dovish end of the spectrum, Annan's agreement was welcomed, but within the narrow framework that barred the central issues. In a typical reaction, the *Boston Globe* stated that had Saddam not backed down, "the United States would not only have been justified in attacking Iraq — it would have been irresponsible not to," with no further questions asked. The editors also called for "a universal consensus of opprobrium" against "weapons of mass destruction" as "the best chance the world has of keeping perverted science from inflicting hitherto unimagined harm." A sensible proposal; one can think of easy ways to start, without the threat of force, but these are not what are intended.

Political analyst William Pfaff deplored Washington's unwillingness to consult "theological or philosophical opinion" (the views of Thomas Aquinas and Renaissance theologian Francisco Suarez), as "a part of the analytical community" in the US and UK had done "during the 1950s and 1960s," but not the foundations of contemporary international and domestic law, which are clear and explicit, though irrelevant to the intellectual culture. Another liberal analyst urged the US to face the fact that if its incomparable power "is really being exercised for mankind's sake, mankind demands some say in its use," which would not be permitted by "the Constitution, the Congress, nor television's Sunday pundits"; "the other nations of the world have not assigned Washington the right to decide when, where, and how their interests should be served" (Ronald Steel).

The Constitution does happen to provide such mechanisms, namely, by declaring valid treaties "the supreme law of the land," particularly the most fundamental of them, the UN Charter. It further authorizes Congress to "define and punish ... offenses against the law of nations," undergirded by the Charter in the contemporary era. It is, furthermore, a bit of an understatement to say that other nations "have not assigned Washington the right"; they have forcefully denied it that right, following the (at least rhetorical) lead of Washington, which largely crafted the Charter.[4]

Reference to Iraq's violation of UN resolutions was regularly taken to imply that the two warrior states have the right to use force unilaterally, taking the role of "world policemen" — an insult to the police, who in principle are supposed to enforce the law, not tear it to shreds. There was criticism of Washington's "arrogance of power" and the like — not quite the proper terms for a self-designated violent outlaw state.

One might contrive a tortured legal argument to support US/UK claims, though no one has really tried. Step One would be that Iraq has violated UN Resolution 687 of April 3, 1991, which declares a cease-fire "upon official notification by Iraq" that it accepts the provisions that are spelled out (destruction of weapons, inspection, etc.). This is probably the longest and most detailed Security Council resolution on record, but it mentions no enforcement mechanism. Step Two of the argument, then, would be that Iraq's non-compliance "reinvokes" Resolution 678.[5] That resolution authorizes member states "to use all necessary means to uphold and implement Resolution 660,"[6] which calls on Iraq to withdraw at once from Kuwait and for Iraq and Kuwait "to begin immediately intensive negotiations for the resolution of their differences," recommending the framework of the Arab League. Resolution 678 also invokes "all subsequent relevant resolutions" (listing them: 662, 664); these are "relevant" in that they refer to the occupation of Kuwait and Iraqi actions relating to it. Reinvoking 678 thus leaves matters as they were: with no authorization to use force to implement the later Resolution 687, which brings up completely different issues, authorizing nothing beyond sanctions.

There is no need to debate the matter. The US and UK could readily have settled all doubts by calling on the Security Council to authorize their "threat and use of force," as required by the Charter. Britain did take some steps in that direction, but abandoned them when it became obvious, at once, that the Security Council would not go along. Blair's initiative, quickly withdrawn, was a "mistake" because it "weakened the Anglo-American position," a *Financial Times* editorial concluded.[7] But these considerations have little relevance in a world dominated by rogue states that reject the rule of law.

Suppose that the Security Council were to authorize the use of force to punish Iraq for violating the cease-fire resolution (UN 687). That authorization would apply to *all* states: for example, to Iran, which would therefore be entitled to invade southern Iraq to sponsor a rebellion. Iran is a neighbor and the victim of US-backed Iraqi aggression and chemical warfare, and could claim, not implausibly, that its invasion would have some local support; the US and UK can make no such claim. Such Iranian actions, if imaginable, would never be tolerated, but would be far less outrageous than the plans of the self-appointed enforcers. It is hard to imagine such elementary observations entering public discussion in the US and UK.

Open Contempt

Contempt for the rule of law is deeply rooted in US practice and intellectual culture. Recall, for example, the reaction to the judgment of the World Court in 1986 condemning the US for "unlawful use of force" against Nicaragua, demanding that it desist and pay extensive reparations, and declaring all US aid to the contras, whatever its character, to be "military aid," not "humanitarian aid." The Court was denounced on all sides for having discredited itself. The terms of the judgment were not considered fit to print, and were ignored.

The Democrat-controlled Congress immediately authorized new funds to step up the unlawful use of force. Washington vetoed a Security Council resolution calling on all states to respect international law — not mentioning anyone, though the intent was clear. When the General Assembly passed a similar resolution, the US voted against it, joined only by Israel and El Salvador, effectively vetoing it; the following year, only the automatic Israeli vote could be garnered. Little of this, let alone what it signifies, received mention in the media or journals of opinion.

Secretary of State George Shultz meanwhile explained that "negotiations are a euphemism for capitulation if the shadow of power is not cast across the bargaining table."[8] He condemned those who advocate "utopian, legalistic means like outside mediation, the United Nations, and the World Court, while ignoring the power element of the equation" — sentiments not without precedent in modern history.[9]

The open contempt for Article 51 is particularly revealing. It was demonstrated with remarkable clarity immediately after the 1954 Geneva accords on a peaceful settlement for Indochina, regarded as a "disaster" by Washington, which moved at once to undermine them. The National Security Council secretly decreed that even in the case of "local Communist subversion or rebellion *not constituting armed attack,*" the US would consider the use of military force, including an attack on China if it is "determined to be the source" of the "subversion."[10] The wording, repeated verbatim annually in planning documents, was chosen so as to make explicit the US right to violate Article 51. The same document called for remilitarizing Japan, converting Thailand into "the focal point of US covert and psychological operations in Southeast Asia," undertaking "covert operations on a large and effective scale" throughout Indochina, and in general, acting forcefully to undermine the accords and the UN Charter. This critically important document was grossly falsified by the Pentagon Papers historians, and has largely disappeared from history.

The US proceeded to define "aggression" to include "political warfare, or subversion" (by someone else, that is) — what Adlai Stevenson called "internal aggression" while defending JFK's escalation to a full-scale attack against South Vietnam. When the US bombed Libyan cities in 1986, the official justification was "self-defense against future attack." *New York Times* legal specialist Anthony Lewis praised the administration for relying "on a legal argument that violence [in this case] is justified as an act of self-defense" under this creative interpretation of Article 51 of the Charter, which would have embarrassed a literate high school student. The US invasion of Panama was defended in the Security Council by Ambassador Thomas Pickering by appeal to Article 51, which, he declared, "provides for the use of armed force to defend a country, to defend our interests and our people," and entitles the US to invade Panama to prevent its "territory from being used as a base for smuggling drugs into the United States." Educated opinion nodded sagely in assent.

In June 1993, Clinton ordered a missile attack on Iraq, killing civilians and greatly cheering the president, congressional doves, and the press, who found the attack "appropriate, reasonable, and necessary." Commentators were particularly impressed by Ambassador Albright's appeal to Article 51. The bombing, she explained, was in "self-defense against armed attack" — namely, an alleged attempt to assassinate former president Bush two months earlier, an appeal that would have scarcely risen to the level of absurdity even if the US had been able to demonstrate Iraqi involvement; "administration officials, speaking anonymously," informed the press "that the judgment of Iraq's guilt was based on circumstantial evidence and analysis rather than ironclad intelligence," the *New York Times* reported, dismissing the matter. The press assured elite opinion that the circumstances "plainly fit" Article 51 (*Washington Post*). "Any president has a duty to use military force to protect the nation's interests" (*New York Times*, while expressing some skepticism about the case in hand). "Diplomatically, this was the proper rationale to invoke," and "Clinton's reference to the UN Charter conveyed an American desire to respect international law" (*Boston Globe*). Article 51 "permits states to respond militarily if they are threatened by a hostile power" (*Christian Science Monitor*). Article 51 entitles a state to use force "in self-defense against threats to one's nationals," British Foreign Secretary Douglas Hurd instructed Parliament, supporting Clinton's "justified and proportionate exercise of the right of self-defense." There would be a "dangerous state of paralysis" in the world, Hurd continued, if the US were required to gain Security Council approval before launching missiles against an enemy that might — or might not — have ordered a failed attempt to kill an ex-president two months earlier.[11]

The record lends considerable support to the concern widely voiced about "rogue states" that are dedicated to the rule of force, acting in the "national interest" as defined by domestic power — most ominously, rogue states that anoint themselves global judge and executioner.

Rogue States: The Narrow Construction

It is also interesting to review the issues that did enter the non-debate on the Iraq crisis. But first a word about the concept "rogue state."

The basic conception is that although the Cold War is over, the US still has the responsibility to protect the world — but from what? Plainly it cannot be from the threat of "radical nationalism" — that is, unwillingness to submit to the will of the powerful. Such ideas are fit only for internal planning documents, not the general public. From the early 1980s, it was clear that the conventional techniques for mass mobilization — the appeal to JFK's "monolithic and ruthless conspiracy," Reagan's "evil empire"— were losing their effectiveness: New enemies were needed.

At home, fear of crime — particularly drugs — was stimulated by "a variety of factors that have little or nothing to do with crime itself," the National Criminal Justice Commission concluded, including media practices and "the role of government and private industry in stoking citizen fear," "exploiting latent racial tension for political purposes" with racial bias in enforcement and sentencing that is devastating black communities, creating a "racial abyss," and putting "the nation at risk of a social catastrophe." The results have been described by criminologists as "the American Gulag," "the new American Apartheid," with African Americans now a majority of prisoners for the first time in US history, imprisoned at well over seven times the rate of whites, completely out of the range of arrest rates, which themselves target blacks far out of proportion to drug use or trafficking.[12]

Abroad, the threats were to be "international terrorism," "Hispanic narcotraffickers," and most serious of all, "rogue states." A secret 1995 study of the Strategic Command, which is responsible for the strategic nuclear arsenal, outlines the basic thinking. Released through the Freedom of Information Act, the study, *Essentials of Post–Cold War Deterrence*, "shows how the United States shifted its deterrent strategy from the defunct Soviet Union to so-called rogue states such as Iraq, Libya, Cuba, and North Korea," the Associated Press reports. The study advocates that the US exploit its nuclear arsenal to portray itself as "irrational and vindictive if its vital interests are attacked." That "should be a part of the national persona we project to all adversaries," in particular the "rogue states." "It hurts to portray ourselves as too fully rational and cool-headed," let alone committed to such silliness as international law and treaty obligations. "The fact that some elements" of the US government "may appear to be potentially 'out of control' can be beneficial to creating and reinforcing fears and doubts within the minds of an adversary's decision-makers." The report resurrects Nixon's "madman theory": our enemies should recognize that we are crazed and unpredictable, with extraordinary destructive force at our command, so they will bend to our will in fear. The concept was apparently devised in Israel in the 1950s by the governing Labor Party, whose leaders "preached in favor of acts of madness," Prime Minister Moshe Sharett records in his diary, warning that "we will go crazy" ("*nishtagea*") if crossed, a "secret weapon" aimed in part against the US, not considered sufficiently reliable at the time. In the hands of the world's sole superpower, which regards itself as an outlaw state and is subject to few constraints from elites within, that

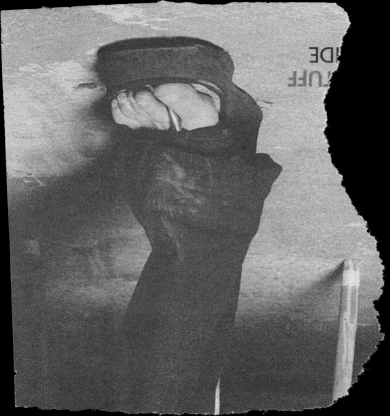

stance poses no small problem for the world.[13]

Libya was a favorite choice as "rogue state" from the earliest days of the Reagan administration. Vulnerable and defenseless, it is a perfect punching bag when needed: for example, in 1986, when the first bombing in history orchestrated for prime-time TV was used by the Great Communicator's speechwriters to muster support for Washington's terrorist forces attacking Nicaragua, on grounds that the "archterrorist" Qaddafi "has sent $400 million and an arsenal of weapons and advisors into Nicaragua to bring his war home to the United States," which was then exercising its right of self-defense against the armed attack of the Nicaraguan rogue state.

Immediately after the Berlin Wall fell, ending any resort to the Soviet threat, the Bush administration submitted its annual call to Congress for a huge Pentagon budget. It explained that "in a new era, we foresee that our military power will remain an essential underpinning of the global balance, but ... the more likely demands for the use of our military forces may not involve the Soviet Union and may be in the Third World, where new capabilities and approaches may be required," as "when President Reagan directed American naval and air forces to return to [Libya] in 1986" to bombard civilian urban targets, guided by the goal of "contributing to an international environment of peace, freedom, and progress within which our democracy — and other free nations — can flourish." The primary threat we face is the "growing technological sophistication" of the Third World. We must therefore strengthen "the defense industrial base" — a.k.a. high-tech industry — creating incentives "to invest in new facilities and equipment as well as in research and development." And we must maintain intervention forces, particularly those targeting the Middle East, where the "threats to our interests" that have required direct military engagement "could not be laid at the Kremlin's door" — contrary to endless fabrication, now put to rest. As had occasionally been recognized in earlier years, sometimes in secret, the "threat" is now conceded officially to be indigenous to the region, the "radical nationalism" that has always been a primary concern, not only in the Middle East.[14]

At the time, the "threats to our interests" could not be laid at Iraq's door either. Saddam was then a favored friend and trading partner. His status changed only a few months later, when he misinterpreted US willingness to allow him to modify the border with Kuwait by force as authorization to take the country over — or, from the perspective of the Bush administration, to duplicate what the US had just done in Panama. At a high-level meeting immediately after Saddam's invasion of Kuwait, President Bush articulated the basic problem: "My worry about the Saudis is that they're ... going to bug out at the last minute and accept a puppet regime in Kuwait." Chair of the Joint Chiefs Colin Powell posed the problem sharply: "[In] the next few days Iraq will withdraw," putting "his puppet in," and "everyone in the Arab world will be happy."[15]

Historical parallels are never exact, of course. When Washington partially withdrew from Panama after putting its puppet in, there was great anger throughout the hemisphere, including Panama — indeed, throughout much of the world — compelling Washington to veto two Security Council resolutions and to vote against a General Assembly resolution condemning Washington's "flagrant violation of international law and of the independence, sovereignty, and territorial integrity of states" and calling for the withdrawal of the "US armed invasion forces from Panama." Iraq's invasion of Kuwait was treated differently, in ways remote from the standard version, but readily discovered in print.

The inexpressible facts shed interesting light on the commentary of political analysts: Ronald Steel, for example, who muses on the "conundrum" faced by the US, which, "as the world's most powerful nation, faces greater constraints on its freedom to use force than does any other country" — hence Saddam's success in Kuwait as compared with Washington's inability to exert its will in Panama.[16]

It is worth recalling that debate was effectively foreclosed in 1990–91 as well. There was much discussion of whether sanctions would work, but none of whether they already had worked, perhaps shortly after Resolution 660 was passed. Fear that sanctions might have worked animated Washington's refusal to test Iraqi withdrawal offers from August 1990 to early January 1991. With the rarest of exceptions, the information system kept tight discipline on the matter. Polls a few days before the January 1991 bombing showed 2 to 1 support for a peaceful settlement based on Iraqi withdrawal along with an international conference on the Israel-Arab conflict. Few among those who expressed this position could have heard any public advocacy of it; the media had loyally followed the president's lead, dismissing "linkage" as unthinkable — in this unique case. It is unlikely that any respondents knew that their views were shared by the Iraqi democratic opposition, barred from mainstream media. Or that an Iraqi proposal in the terms they advocated had been released a week earlier by US officials, who found it reasonable, and had been flatly rejected by Washington. Or that an Iraqi withdrawal offer had been considered by the National Security Council as early as mid-August but dismissed, and effectively suppressed, apparently because it was feared that unmentioned Iraqi initiatives might "defuse the crisis," as the *New York Times* diplomatic correspondent obliquely reported administration concerns.

Since then, Iraq has displaced Iran and Libya as the leading "rogue state." Others have never entered the ranks. Perhaps the most relevant case is Indonesia, which shifted from enemy to friend when General Suharto took power in 1965, presiding over a Rwanda-style slaughter that elicited great satisfaction in the West. Since then Suharto has been "our kind of guy," as the Clinton administration described him, while carrying out murderous aggression and endless atrocities against his own people — killing 10,000 Indonesians just in the 1980s, according to the personal testimony of "our guy," who wrote that "the corpses were left lying around as a form of shock therapy."[17] In December 1975 the UN Security Council unanimously ordered Indonesia to withdraw its invading forces from East Timor "without delay" and called upon "all States to respect the territorial integrity of East Timor as well as the inalienable right of its people to self-determination." The US responded by (secretly) increasing shipments of arms to the aggressors; Carter accelerated the arms flow once again as the attack reached near-genocidal levels in 1978. In his memoirs, UN Ambassador Daniel Patrick Moynihan takes pride in his success in rendering the UN "utterly ineffective in whatever measures it undertook," following the instructions of the State Department, which "wished things to turn out as they did, and worked to bring this about." The US also happily accepts the robbery of East Timor's oil (with participation of a US company), in violation of any reasonable interpretation of international agreements.[18]

The analogy to Iraq/Kuwait is close, though there are differences: to mention only the most obvious, US-sponsored atrocities in East Timor were vastly beyond anything attributed to Saddam Hussein in Kuwait.

There are many other examples, though some of those commonly invoked should be treated with caution, particularly concerning Israel. The civilian toll of Israel's US-backed invasion of Lebanon in 1982 exceeded Saddam's in Kuwait, and it remains in violation of a 1978 Security Council resolution ordering it to withdraw forthwith from Lebanon, along with numerous other resolutions regarding Jerusalem, the Golan Heights, and other matters; and there would be far more such resolutions if the US did not regularly veto them. But the common charge that Israel, particularly its current government, is violating UN 242 and the Oslo accords, and that the US exhibits a "double standard" by tolerating those violations, is dubious at best, based on serious misunderstanding of these agreements. From the outset, the Madrid–Oslo process was designed and implemented by US-Israeli power to impose a Bantustan-style settlement. The Arab world has chosen to delude itself about the matter, as have many others, but it is clear in the actual documents, and particularly in the US-supported projects of the Rabin-Peres governments, including those for which Netanyahu's Likud government has been denounced.[19]

It is clearly untrue to claim that "Israel is not demonstrably in violation of Security Council decrees,"[20] but the reasons often given should be examined carefully.

Returning to Iraq, it surely qualifies as a leading criminal state. Defending the US plan to attack Iraq at a televised public meeting on February 18, 1998, Secretaries Albright and Cohen repeatedly invoked the ultimate atrocity: Saddam was guilty of "using weapons of mass destruction against his neighbors as well as his own people," his most awesome crime. "It is very important for us to make clear that the United States and the civilized world cannot deal with somebody who is willing to use those weapons of mass destruction on his own people, not to speak of his neighbors," Albright emphasized in an angry response to a questioner who asked about US support for Suharto. Shortly after, Senator Lott condemned Kofi Annan for seeking to cultivate a "human relationship with a mass murderer," and denounced the administration for trusting a person who would sink so low.

Ringing words. Putting aside their evasion of the question raised, Albright and Cohen only forgot to mention — and commentators have been kind enough not to point out — that the acts that they now find so horrifying did not turn Iraq into a "rogue state." And Lott failed to note that his heroes Reagan and Bush forged unusually warm relations with the "mass murderer." There were no passionate calls for a military strike after Saddam's gassing of Kurds at Halabja in March 1988; on the contrary, the US and UK extended their strong support for the mass murderer, then also "our kind of guy." When ABC TV correspondent Charles Glass revealed the site of one of Saddam's biological warfare programs 10 months after Halabja, the State Department denied the facts, and the story died; the department "now issues briefings on the same site," Glass observes.

The two guardians of global order also expedited Saddam's other atrocities — including his use of cyanide, nerve gas, and other barbarous weapons — with intelligence, technology, and supplies, joining with many others. The Senate Banking Committee reported in 1994 that the US Commerce Department had traced shipments of "biological materials" identical to those later found and destroyed by UN inspectors, Bill Blum recalls. These shipments continued at least until November 1989. A month later, Bush authorized new loans for his friend Saddam, to achieve the "goal of increasing US exports and [to] put us in a better position to deal with Iraq regarding its human rights record," the State Department announced with a straight face, facing no criticism (or even report) in the mainstream.

Britain's record was exposed, at least in part, in an official inquiry (the Scott Inquiry). The British government has just now been compelled to concede that it continued to grant licenses to British firms to export materials usable for biological weapons after the Scott Inquiry Report was published, at least until December 1996.

In a February 28, 1998, review of Western sales of materials usable for germ warfare and other weapons of mass destruction, the *New York Times* mentions one example of US sales in the 1980s that included "deadly pathogens," with government approval — some from the army's center for germ research in Fort Detrick. Just the tip of the iceberg, however.[21]

A common current pretense is that Saddam's crimes were unknown, so we are now properly shocked at the discovery and must "make clear" that we civilized folk "cannot deal with" the perpetrator of such crimes (in Albright's words). The posture is cynical fraud. UN reports of 1986 and 1987 condemned Iraq's use of chemical weapons. US Embassy staffers in Turkey interviewed Kurdish survivors of chemical warfare attacks, and the CIA reported them to the State Department. Human rights groups reported the atrocities at Halabja and elsewhere at once. Secretary of State George Shultz conceded that the US had evidence on the matter. An investigative team sent by the Senate Foreign Relations Committee in 1988 found "overwhelming evidence of extensive use of chemical weapons against civilians," charging that Western acquiescence in Iraqi use of such weapons against Iran had emboldened Saddam to believe — correctly — that he could use them against his own people with impunity — actually against Kurds, hardly "the people" of this tribal-based thug. The chair of the committee, Claiborne Pell, introduced the Prevention of Genocide Act of 1988, denouncing silence "while people are gassed" as "complicity," much as when "the world was silent as Hitler began a campaign that culminated in the near extermination of Europe's Jews," and warning that "we cannot be silent to genocide again." The Reagan administration strongly opposed sanctions and insisted that the matter be silenced, while extending its support for the mass murderer. In the Arab world, "the Kuwait press was amongst the most enthusiastic of the Arab media in supporting Baghdad's crusade against the Kurds," journalist Adel Darwish reports.

In January 1991, while the war drums were beating, the International Commission of Jurists observed to the UN Human Rights Commission that "after having perpetrated the most flagrant abuses on its own population without a word of reproach from the UN, Iraq must have concluded it could do whatever it pleased"; UN in this context means US and UK, primarily. That truth must be buried along with international law and other "utopian" distractions.[22]

An unkind commentator might remark that recent US/UK toleration for poison gas and chemical warfare is not too surprising. The British used chemical weapons in their 1919 intervention in North Russia against the Bolsheviks, with great success, according to the British command. As Secretary of State at the War Office in 1919, Winston Churchill was enthusiastic about the prospects of "using poisoned gas against uncivilized tribes" — Kurds and Afghans — and authorized the RAF Middle East command to use chemical weapons "against recalcitrant Arabs as [an] experiment," dismissing objections by the India office as "unreasonable" and deploring the "squeamishness about the use of gas": "We cannot in any circumstances acquiesce in the non-utilization of any weapons which are available to procure a speedy termination of the disorder which prevails on the frontier," he explained; chemical weapons are merely "the application of western science to modern warfare."[23]

The Kennedy administration pioneered the massive use of chemical weapons against civilians as it launched its attack against South Vietnam in 1961–62. There has been much rightful concern about the effects on US soldiers, but not the incomparably worse effects on civilians. Here, at least. In an Israeli mass-circulation daily, the respected journalist Amnon Kapeliouk reported on his 1988 visit to Vietnam, where he found that "thousands of Vietnamese still die from the effects of American chemical warfare," citing estimates of one-quarter of a million victims in South Vietnam and describing the "terrifying" scenes in hospitals in the South, where children were dying of cancer and hideous birth deformities. It was South Vietnam that was targeted for chemical warfare, not the North, where these consequences are not found, he reports. There is also substantial evidence of US use of biological weapons against Cuba, reported as minor news in 1977, and at worst only a small component of continuing US terror.[24]

These precedents aside, the US and UK are now engaged in a deadly form of biological warfare in Iraq. The destruction of infrastructure and banning of imports to repair it has caused disease, malnutrition, and early death on a huge scale, including more than 500,000 children, according to UNICEF investigations — an average of 5,000 children dying each month. In a bitter condemnation of the sanctions on January 20, 1998, 54 Catholic bishops quoted the archbishop of the southern region of Iraq, who reports that "epidemics rage, taking away infants and the sick by the thousands," while "those children who survive disease succumb to malnutrition." The bishops' statement, reported in full in Stanley Heller's journal *The Struggle*, received scant mention in the press. The US and Britain have taken the lead in blocking aid programs — for example, delaying approval for ambulances on the grounds that they could be used to transport troops, and barring insecticides for preventing the spread of disease and spare parts for sanitation systems. Meanwhile, Western diplomats point out, "The US had directly benefited from [the humanitarian] operation as much, if not more, than the Russians and the

French," for example, by purchase of $600 million worth of Iraqi oil (second only to Russia) and sale by US companies of $200 million in humanitarian goods to Iraq. They also report that most of the oil bought by Russian companies ends up in the US.[25]

Washington's support for Saddam reached such an extreme that it was even willing to overlook an Iraqi air force attack on the USS *Stark*, killing 37 crewmen, a privilege otherwise enjoyed only by Israel (in the case of the USS *Liberty*). It was Washington's decisive support for Saddam, well after the crimes that now so shock the administration and Congress, that led to Iranian capitulation to "Baghdad and Washington," Dilip Hiro concludes in his history of the Iran-Iraq war. The two allies had "co-ordinate[d] their military operations against Teheran." The shooting down of an Iranian civilian airliner by the guided-missile cruiser USS *Vincennes* was the culmination of Washington's "diplomatic, military, and economic campaign" in support of Saddam, he writes.[26]

Saddam was also called upon to perform the usual services of a client state: for example, to train several hundred Libyans sent to Iraq by the US so they could overthrow the Qaddafi government, former Reagan White House aide Howard Teicher revealed.[27]

It was not his massive crimes that elevated Saddam to the rank of "Beast of Baghdad." Rather, it was his stepping out of line, much as in the case of the far more minor criminal Noriega, whose major crimes were also committed while he was a US client.

Exempt Rogue States

The qualifications of "rogue state" are illuminated further by Washington's reaction to the uprisings in Iraq in March 1991, immediately after the cessation of hostilities. The State Department formally reiterated its refusal to have any dealings with the Iraqi democratic opposition, and just as before the Gulf War, they were virtually denied access to the major US media. "Political meetings with them would not be appropriate for our policy at this time," State Department spokesperson Richard Boucher stated. "This time" happened to be March 14, 1991, while Saddam was decimating the southern opposition under the eyes of General Schwarzkopf, who refused even to permit rebelling military officers access to captured Iraqi arms. Had it not been for unexpected public reaction,

Washington probably would not have extended even tepid support to rebelling Kurds, subjected to the same treatment shortly after.

Iraqi opposition leaders got the message. Leith Kubba, head of the London-based Iraqi Democratic Reform Movement, alleged that the US favors a military dictatorship, insisting that "changes in the regime must come from within, from people already in power." London-based banker Ahmed Chalabi, head of the Iraqi National Congress, said that "the United States, covered by the fig leaf of non-interference in Iraqi affairs, is waiting for Saddam to butcher the insurgents in the hope that he can be overthrown later by a suitable officer," an attitude rooted in the US policy of "supporting dictatorships to maintain stability."

Administration reasoning was outlined by *New York Times* chief diplomatic correspondent Thomas Friedman. While opposing a popular rebellion, Washington did hope that a military coup might remove Saddam, "and then Washington would have the best of all worlds: an iron-fisted Iraqi junta without Saddam Hussein," a return to the days when Saddam's "iron fist ... held Iraq together, much to the satisfaction of the American allies Turkey and Saudi Arabia," not to speak of Washington. Two years later, in another useful recognition of reality, he observed that "it has always been American policy that the iron-fisted Mr. Hussein plays a useful role in holding Iraq together," maintaining "stability." There is little reason to believe that Washington has modified the preference for dictatorship over democracy deplored by the ignored Iraqi democratic opposition, though it doubtless would prefer a different "iron fist" at this point. If not, Saddam will have to do.[28]

The concept "rogue state" is highly nuanced. Thus, Cuba qualifies as a leading "rogue state" because of its alleged involvement in international terrorism, but the US does not fall into the category despite its terrorist attacks against Cuba for close to 40 years, apparently continuing through 1997, according to important investigative reporting of the *Miami Herald*, which failed to reach the national press (here; it did in Europe). Cuba was a "rogue state" when its military forces were in Angola, backing the government against South African attacks supported by the US. South Africa, in contrast, was not a rogue state then, nor during the Reagan years, when it caused more than $60 billion in damage and 1.5 million deaths in neighboring states, according to a UN commission, not to speak of some events at home — and with ample US/UK support. The same exemption applies to Indonesia and many others.

The criteria are fairly clear: a "rogue state" is not simply a criminal state, but one that defies the orders of the powerful — who are, of course, exempt.

More on "The Debate"

That Saddam is a criminal is undoubtedly true, and one should be pleased, I suppose, that the US and UK, and the mainstream doctrinal institutions have at last joined those who "prematurely" condemned US/UK support for the mass murderer. It is also true that he poses a threat to anyone within his reach. On the comparison of the threat with others, there is little unanimity outside the US and UK, after their (ambiguous) transformation from August 1990. Their 1998 plan to use force was justified in terms of Saddam's threat to the region, but there was no way to conceal the fact that the people of the region objected to their salvation, so strenuously that governments were compelled to join in opposition.

Bahrein refused to allow US/UK forces to use bases there. The president of the United Arab Emirates described US threats of military action as "bad and loathsome," and declared that Iraq does not pose a threat to its neighbors. Saudi Defense Minister Prince Sultan had already stated that "we'll not agree, and we are against striking Iraq as a people and as a nation," causing Washington to refrain from a request to use Saudi bases. After Annan's mission, long-serving Saudi Foreign Minister Prince Saud al-Faisal reaffirmed that any use of Saudi air bases "has to be a UN, not a US, issue."

An editorial in Egypt's quasi-official journal *Al-Ahram* described Washington's stand as "coercive, aggressive, unwise, and uncaring about the lives of Iraqis, who are unnecessarily subjected to sanctions and humiliation," and denounced the planned US "aggression against Iraq." Jordan's Parliament condemned "any aggression against Iraq's territory and any harm that might come to the Iraqi people"; the Jordanian army was forced to seal off the city of Maan after two days of pro-Iraq rioting. A political science professor at Kuwait University warned that "Saddam has come to represent the voice of the voiceless in the Arab world," expressing popular frustration over the "New World

Order" and Washington's advocacy of Israeli interests.

Even in Kuwait, support for the US stance was at best "tepid" and "cynical over US motives," the press recognized. "Voices in the streets of the Arab world, from Cairo's teeming slums to the Arabian Peninsula's shiny capitals, have been rising in anger as the American drumbeat of war against Iraq grows louder," *Boston Globe* correspondent Charles Sennott reported.[29]

The Iraqi democratic opposition was granted slight exposure in the mainstream, breaking the previous pattern. In a telephone interview with the *New York Times*, Ahmed Chalabi reiterated the position that had been reported in greater detail in London weeks earlier: "Without a political plan to remove Saddam's regime, military strikes will be counterproductive," he argued, killing thousands of Iraqis, perhaps even leaving Saddam strengthened along with his weapons of mass destruction, and with "an excuse to throw out UNSCOM [the UN weapons inspectors]," who have in fact destroyed vastly more weapons and production facilities than the 1991 bombing. US/UK plans would "be worse than nothing." Interviews with opposition leaders from several groups found "near unanimity" in opposing military action that did not lay the basis for an uprising to overthrow Saddam. Speaking to a parliamentary committee, Chalabi held that it was "morally indefensible to strike Iraq without a strategy" for removing Saddam.

In London, the opposition also outlined an alternative program: (1) declare Saddam a war criminal; (2) recognize a provisional Iraqi government formed by the opposition; (3) unfreeze hundreds of millions of dollars of Iraqi assets abroad; and (4) restrict Saddam's forces by a "no-drive zone," or extend the "no-flight zone" to cover the whole country. The US should "help the Iraqi people remove Saddam from power," Chalabi told the Senate Armed Services Committee. Along with other opposition leaders, he "rejected assassination, covert US operations, or US ground troops," Reuters reported, calling instead for "a popular insurgency." Similar proposals have occasionally appeared in the US. Washington claims to have attempted support for opposition groups, but their own interpretation is different. Chalabi's view, published in England, is much as it was years earlier: "Everyone says Saddam is boxed in, but it is the Americans and British who are boxed in by their refusal to support the idea of political change."[30]

Regional opposition was regarded as a problem to be evaded, not a factor to be taken into account any more than international law. The same was true of warnings by senior UN and other international relief officials in Iraq that the planned bombing might have a "catastrophic" effect on people already suffering miserably, and might terminate the humanitarian operations that have brought at least some relief.[31] What matters is to establish that "what we say goes," as President Bush triumphantly proclaimed, announcing the New World Order as bombs and missiles were falling in 1991.

As Kofi Annan was preparing to go to Baghdad, former Iranian president Rafsanjani, "still a pivotal figure in Teheran, was given an audience by the ailing King Fahd in Saudi Arabia," British Middle East correspondent David Gardner reported, "in contrast to the treatment experienced by Madeleine Albright ... on her recent trips to Riyadh seeking support from America's main Gulf ally." As Rafsanjani's 10-day visit ended on March 2, 1998, Foreign Minister Prince Saud described it as "one more step in the right direction towards improving relations," reiterating that "the greatest destabilizing element in the Middle East and the cause of all other problems in the region" is Israel's policy towards the Palestinians and US support for it, which might activate popular forces that Saudi Arabia greatly fears, as well as undermine its legitimacy as "guardian" of Islamic holy places, including the Dome of the Rock in East Jerusalem (now effectively annexed by US/Israeli programs as part of their intent to extend "greater Jerusalem" virtually to the Jordan Valley, to be retained by Israel). Shortly before, the Arab states had boycotted a US-sponsored economic summit in Qatar that was intended to advance the "New Middle East" project of Clinton and Peres. Instead, they attended an Islamic conference in Teheran in December, joined even by Iraq.[32]

These are tendencies of considerable import, relating to the background concerns that motivate US policy in the region: its insistence, since World War II, on controlling the world's major energy reserves. As many have observed, in the Arab world there is growing fear and resentment of the long-standing Israel-Turkey alliance that was formalized in 1996, now greatly strengthened. For some years, it had been a component of the US strategy of controlling the region with "local cops on the beat," as Nixon's defense secretary put the matter. There is apparently a growing appreciation of the Iranian advocacy of regional security arrangements to replace US domination. A related matter is the intensifying conflict over pipelines to bring Central Asian oil to the rich countries, one natural outlet being via Iran. And US energy corporations will not be happy to see foreign rivals — now including China and Russia — gain privileged access to Iraqi oil reserves, second only to Saudi Arabia's in scale, or to Iran's natural gas, oil, and other resources.

For the present, Clinton planners may well be relieved to have escaped temporarily from the "box" they had constructed, which was leaving them no option but a bombing of Iraq that could have been harmful even to the interests they represent. The respite is temporary. It offers opportunities to citizens of the warrior states to bring about changes of consciousness and commitment that could make a great difference in the not-too-distant future.

3

Crisis in the Balkans

On March 24, 1999, US-led NATO forces launched cruise missiles and bombs at targets in the Federal Republic of Yugoslavia, "plunging America into a military conflict that President Clinton said was necessary to stop ethnic cleansing and bring stability to Eastern Europe," lead stories in the press reported. In a televised address, Clinton explained that by bombing Yugoslavia, "we are upholding our values, protecting our interests, and advancing the cause of peace."[1]

In the preceding year, according to Western sources, about 2,000 people had been killed in the Yugoslav province of Kosovo, and there were several hundred thousand internal refugees. The humanitarian catastrophe was overwhelmingly attributable to Yugoslav military and police forces, the main victims being ethnic Albanian Kosovars, commonly said to constitute about 90 percent of the population (estimates vary). After three days of bombing, according to the UN High Commissioner for Refugees, several thousand refugees had been expelled to Albania and Macedonia, two of the neighboring countries. Refugees reported that the terror had reached the capital city of Pristina, largely spared before, and provided credible accounts of large-scale destruction of villages, assassinations, and a radical increase in the generation of refugees — perhaps an effort to expel a good part of the Albanian population. Within two weeks the flood of refugees had reached some 350,000, mostly from the southern sections of Kosovo adjoining Macedonia and Albania, while unknown numbers of Serbs fled north to Serbia to escape the increased violence from the air and on the ground.

On March 27, US-NATO Commanding General Wesley Clark declared that it was "entirely predictable" that Serbian terror and violence would intensify after the NATO bombing. On the same day, State Department spokesperson James Rubin said that "the United States is extremely alarmed by reports of an escalating pattern of Serbian attacks on Kosovar Albanian civilians," now attributed in large part to paramilitary forces mobilized after the bombing.[2] General Clark's phrase "entirely predictable" is an overstatement. Nothing is "entirely predictable," surely not the effects of extreme violence. But he is surely correct in implying that what happened at once was highly likely. As observed by Carnes Lord of the Fletcher School of Law and Diplomacy, formerly a Bush administration national security advisor, "enemies often react when shot at," and "though western officials continue to deny it, there can be little doubt that the bombing campaign has provided both motive and opportunity for a wider and more savage Serbian operation than what was first envisioned."[3]

In the preceding months, the threat of NATO bombing was reportedly followed by an increase in atrocities; the departure of international observers under the threat of bombing predictably had the same consequence. The bombing was then undertaken under the rational expectation that killing and refugee generation would escalate as a result, as indeed happened, even if the scale may have come as a surprise to some, though apparently not the commanding general.

Under Tito, Kosovars had had a considerable measure of self-rule. So matters remained until 1989, when Kosovo's autonomy was rescinded by Slobodan Milosevic, who established direct Serbian rule and imposed "a Serbian version of Apartheid," in the words of former US government specialist on the Balkans James Hooper, no dove: he advocated direct NATO invasion of Kosovo. The Kosovars "confounded the international community," Hooper continues, "by eschewing a war of national liberation, embracing instead the nonviolent approach espoused by leading Kosovo intellectual Ibrahim Rugova and constructing a parallel civil society," an impressive achievement, for which they were rewarded by "polite audiences and rhetorical encouragement from western governments." The nonviolent strategy "lost its credibility" at the Dayton accords in November 1995, Hooper observes. At Dayton, the US effectively partitioned Bosnia-Herzegovina between an eventual greater Croatia and greater Serbia, after having roughly equalized the balance of terror by providing arms and training for the forces of Croatian dictator Tudjman and supporting his violent expulsion of Serbs from Krajina and elsewhere. With the sides more or less balanced, and exhausted, the US took over, displacing the Europeans who had been assigned the dirty work — much to their annoyance. "In deference to Milosevic," Hooper writes, the US "excluded Kosovo Albanian delegates" from the Dayton negotiations and "avoided discussion of the Kosovo problem." "The reward for nonviolence was international neglect"; more accurately, US neglect.[4]

Recognition that the US understands only force led to "the rise of the guerrilla Kosovo Liberation Army (KLA) and expansion of popular support for an armed independence struggle."[5] By February 1998, KLA attacks against Serbian police stations led to a "Serbian crackdown" and retaliation against civilians, another standard pattern: Israeli atrocities in Lebanon, particularly under Nobel Peace laureate Shimon Peres, are — or should be — a familiar example, though one that is not entirely appropriate. These Israeli atrocities are typically in response to attacks on its military forces occupying foreign territory in violation of long-standing Security Council orders to withdraw. Many Israeli attacks are not retaliatory at all, including the 1982 invasion that devastated much of Lebanon and left 20,000 civilians dead (a different story is preferred in US commentary, though the truth is familiar in Israel). We scarcely need imagine how the US would respond to attacks on police stations by a guerrilla force with foreign bases and supplies.

Fighting in Kosovo escalated, the scale of atrocities corresponding roughly to the resources of violence. An October 1998 cease-fire made possible the deployment of 2,000 OSCE (Organization for Security and Cooperation in Europe) monitors. The breakdown of US-Milosevic negotiations led to renewed fighting, which increased with the threat of NATO bombing and the withdrawal of the monitors, again as predicted. Officials of the UN refugee agency and Catholic Relief Services had warned that the threat of bombing "would imperil the lives of tens of thousands of refugees believed to be hiding in the woods," predicting "tragic" consequences if "NATO made it impossible for us to be here."[6]

Atrocities then sharply escalated as the late March 1999 bombing provided "motive and opportunity," as was surely "predictable," if not "entirely" so.

The bombing was undertaken, under US initiative, after Milosevic had refused to sign the proposals worked out by the NATO powers at Rambouillet in February. There were disagreements within NATO, captured in a *New York Times* headline that read: "Trickiest Divides Are Among Big Powers at Kosovo Talks." One problem had to do with deployment of NATO peacekeepers. The European powers wanted to ask the Security Council to authorize the deployment, in accord with treaty obligations and international law. Washington, however, refused to allow the "neuralgic word 'authorize,' " the *New York Times* reported, though it did finally permit "endorse." The Clinton administration "was sticking to its stand that NATO should be able to act independently of the United Nations."

The discord within NATO continued. Apart from Britain (by now about as much of an independent actor as the Ukraine was in pre-Gorbachev years), NATO countries were skeptical of Washington's preference for force and annoyed by Secretary of State Albright's "saber-rattling," which they regarded as "unhelpful when negotiations were at such a sensitive stage," though "US officials were unapologetic about the hard line."[7]

Turning from generally uncontested fact to speculation, we may ask why events proceeded as they did, focusing on the decisions of US planners — the factor that must be our primary concern on elementary moral grounds, and that is a leading, if not decisive, factor on grounds of equally elementary considerations of power.

We may note at first that the dismissal of Kosovar democrats "in deference to Milosevic" is hardly surprising. To mention another example, after Saddam Hussein's repeated gassing of Kurds in 1988, in deference to its friend and ally the US barred official contacts with Kurdish leaders and Iraqi democratic dissidents, who were largely excluded from the media as well. The official ban was renewed immediately after the Gulf War, in March 1991, when Saddam was tacitly authorized to conduct a massacre of rebelling Shi'ites in the south and then Kurds in the north. The massacre proceeded under the steely gaze of "Stormin' " Norman Schwarzkopf, who explained that he was "suckered" by Saddam, not anticipating that Saddam might carry out military actions with the helicopters he was authorized by Washington to use. The Bush administration explained that support for Saddam was necessary to preserve "stability," and its preference for a military dictatorship that would

rule Iraq with an "iron fist" just as Saddam had done was sagely endorsed by respected US commentators.[8]

Tacitly acknowledging past policy, Secretary of State Albright announced in December 1998 that "we have come to the determination
that the Iraqi people would benefit if they had a government that really
represented them." Months earlier, on May 20, Albright had informed
Indonesian President Suharto that he was no longer "our kind of guy,"
having lost control and disobeyed IMF orders, so that he must resign and
provide for "a democratic transition." A few hours later, Suharto transferred formal authority to his hand-picked vice president. We celebrated
the May 1999 elections in Indonesia, hailed by Washington and the
press as the first democratic elections in 40 years — but without a re-
minder of the major US clandestine military operation 40 years earlier
that brought Indonesian democracy to an end, undertaken in large measure because the democratic system was unacceptably open, even allowing participation of the left.[9]

We need not tarry on the plausibility of Washington's discovery of
the merits of democracy; the fact that the words can be articulated, eliciting no comment, is informative enough. In any event, there is no reason
to be surprised at the disdain for nonviolent democratic forces in
Kosovo, or at the fact that the bombing was undertaken with the likely
prospect that it would undermine a courageous and growing democratic
movement in Belgrade, now probably demolished as Serbs are "unified
from heaven — but by the bombs, not by God," in the words of Aleksa
Djilas, the historian son of Yugoslav dissident Milovan Djilas. "The
bombing has jeopardized the lives of more than 10 million people and
set back the fledgling forces of democracy in Kosovo and Serbia," having "blasted ... [its] germinating seeds and insured they will not sprout
again for a very long time," according to Serbian dissident Veran Matic,
editor in chief of the independent station Radio B-92 (now banned). Former *Boston Globe* editor Randolph Ryan, who has been working for
years in the Balkans and living in Belgrade, writes that "now, thanks to
NATO, Serbia has overnight become a totalitarian state in a frenzy of
wartime mobilization," as NATO must have expected, just as it "had to
know that Milosevic would take immediate revenge by redoubling his
attacks in Kosovo," which NATO would have no way to stop.[10]

As to what planners "envisioned," Carnes Lord's confidence is hard to share. If the documentary record of past actions is any guide, planners probably were doing what comes naturally to those with a strong card — in this case, violence. Namely, play it, and then see what happens.

With the basic facts in mind, one may speculate about how Washington's decisions were made. Turbulence in the Balkans qualifies as a "humanitarian crisis," in the technical sense: it might harm the interests of rich and privileged people, unlike slaughters in Sierra Leone or Angola, or crimes we support or conduct ourselves. The question, then, is how to control the authentic crisis. The US will not tolerate the institutions of world order, so the problems have to be handled by NATO, which the US pretty much dominates. The divisions within NATO are understandable: violence is Washington's strong card. It is necessary to guarantee the "credibility of NATO" — meaning, of US violence: others must have proper fear of the global hegemon. "One unappealing aspect of nearly any alternative" to bombing, Barton Gellman observed in a *Washington Post* review of "the events that led to the confrontation in Kosovo," "was the humiliation of NATO and the United States."[11] National Security Advisor Samuel Berger "listed among the principal purposes of bombing 'to demonstrate that NATO is serious.' " A European diplomat concurred: "Inaction would have involved 'a major cost in credibility, particularly at this time as we approach the NATO summit in celebration of its 50th anniversary.' " "To walk away now would destroy NATO's credibility," Prime Minister Tony Blair informed Parliament.

Violence may fail, but planners can be confident that there is always more in reserve. Side benefits include an escalation of arms production and sales — the cover for the massive state role in the high-tech economy for years. And just as bombing unites Serbs behind Milosevic, it unites Americans behind Our Leaders. These are standard effects of violence; they may not last for long, but planning is for the short term.

These are speculations, but perhaps reasonable ones.

The Issues

There are two fundamental issues: What are the accepted and applicable "rules of world order"? How do these or other considerations apply in the case of Kosovo?

There is a regime of international law and international order, binding on all states, based on the UN Charter and subsequent resolutions and World Court decisions. In brief, the threat or use of force is banned unless explicitly authorized by the Security Council after it has determined that peaceful means have failed, or in self-defense against "armed attack" (a narrow concept) until the Security Council acts.

There is, of course, more to say. Thus, there is at least a tension, if not an outright contradiction, between the rules of world order laid down in the UN Charter and the rights articulated in the Universal Declaration of Human Rights (UD), a second pillar of the world order established under US initiative after World War II. The Charter bans force that violates state sovereignty; the UD guarantees the rights of individuals against oppressive states. The issue of "humanitarian intervention" arises from this tension. It is the right of "humanitarian intervention" that is claimed by the US/NATO in Kosovo, with the general support of editorial opinion and news reports.

The question was addressed at once in a *New York Times* report headed: "Legal Scholars Support Case for Using Force." One example is offered: Allen Gersoń, former counsel to the US mission to the UN. Two other legal scholars are cited. One, Ted Galen Carpenter, "scoffed at the administration argument" and dismissed the alleged right of intervention. The other is Jack Goldsmith, a specialist on international law at Chicago Law School. He says that critics of the NATO bombing "have a pretty good legal argument," but "many people think [an exception for humanitarian intervention] does exist as a matter of custom and practice."[12] That summarizes the evidence offered to justify the favored conclusion stated in the headline.

Goldsmith's observation is reasonable, at least if we agree that facts are relevant to the determination of "custom and practice." We may also bear in mind a truism: the right of humanitarian intervention, if it exists, is premised on the "good faith" of those intervening, and that assumption is based not on their rhetoric but on their record, in particular their record of adherence to the principles of international law, World Court decisions, and so on. That is indeed a truism, at least with regard to others. Consider, for example, Iranian offers to intervene in Bosnia to prevent massacres at a time when the West would not do so. These were dismissed with ridicule (and were, in fact, generally ignored); if there was a reason beyond subordination to power, it was because Iranian good faith could not be assumed. A rational person then asks obvious questions: is the Iranian record of intervention and terror worse than that of the US? And other questions, for example: How should we assess the "good faith" of the only country to have vetoed a Security Council resolution calling on all states to obey international law? What about its historical record? Unless such questions are prominent on the agenda of discourse, an honest person will dismiss it as mere allegiance to doctrine. A useful exercise is to determine how much of the literature — media or other — survives such elementary conditions as these.

When the decision was made to bomb, there had been a serious humanitarian crisis in Kosovo for a year. In such cases, outsiders have three choices:

I. try to escalate the catastrophe,

II. do nothing, or

III. try to mitigate the catastrophe.

The choices are illustrated by other contemporary cases. Let's keep to a few of approximately the same scale, and ask where Kosovo fits into the pattern.

Colombia. In Colombia, according to State Department estimates, the annual level of political killing by the government and its paramilitary associates is about at the level of Kosovo, and refugee flight primarily from their atrocities is well over a million. Colombia was the leading western hemisphere recipient of US arms and training as violence increased through the '90s, and that assistance is now increasing, under a "drug war" pretext dismissed by almost all serious observers. The Clinton administration was particularly enthusiastic in its praise for President Gaviria, whose tenure in office was responsible for "appalling levels of violence," according to human rights organizations, even surpassing his predecessors. Details are readily available.[13]

In this case, the US reaction is (I): escalate the atrocities.

Turkey. For years, Turkish repression of Kurds has been a major scandal. It peaked in the '90s; one index is the flight of more than a million Kurds from the countryside to the unofficial Kurdish capital Diyarbakir from 1990 to 1994, as the Turkish army was devastating the countryside. Two million were left homeless, according to the Turkish state minister for human rights, a result of "state terrorism" in part, he acknowledged. "Mystery killings" of Kurds (assumed to be death squad killings) alone amounted to 3,200 in 1993 and 1994, along with torture, destruction of thousands of villages, bombing with napalm, and an unknown number of casualties, generally estimated in the tens of thousands; no one was counting. The killings are attributed to Kurdish terror in Turkish propaganda, generally adopted in the US as well. Presumably Serbian propaganda follows the same practice. Nineteen ninety-four marked two records in Turkey: it was "the year of the worst repression in the Kurdish provinces," Jonathan Randal reported from the scene, and the year when Turkey became

> the biggest single importer of American military hardware and thus the world's largest arms purchaser. Its arsenal, 80 percent American, included M-60 tanks, F-16 fighter-bombers, Cobra gunships, and Blackhawk "slick" helicopters, all of which were eventually used against the Kurds.[14]

When human rights groups exposed Turkey's use of US jets to bomb villages, the Clinton administration found ways to evade laws requiring suspension of arms deliveries, much as it was doing in Indonesia and elsewhere.

Colombia and Turkey explain their (US-supported) atrocities on grounds that they are defending their countries from the threat of terrorist guerrillas. As does the government of Yugoslavia.

Again, the example illustrates (I): act to escalate the atrocities.

Laos. Every year thousands of people, mostly children and poor farmers, are killed in the Plain of Jars in Northern Laos, the scene of the heaviest bombing of civilian targets in history, it appears, and arguably the most cruel: Washington's furious assault on a poor peasant society had little to do with its wars in the region. The worst period was after 1968, when Washington was compelled to undertake negotiations (under popular and business pressure), ending the regular bombardment of North Vietnam. Kissinger and Nixon then shifted the planes to the task of bombarding Laos and Cambodia.

The deaths are from "bombies," tiny anti-personnel weapons, far worse than land mines: they are designed specifically to kill and maim, and have no effect on trucks, buildings, etc. The Plain was saturated with hundreds of millions of these criminal devices, which have a failure-to-explode rate of 20–30 percent, according to the manufacturer,

Honeywell. The numbers suggest either remarkably poor quality control or a rational policy of murdering civilians by delayed action. This was only a fraction of the technology deployed, which also included advanced missiles to penetrate caves where families sought shelter. Current annual casualties from "bombies" are estimated from hundreds a year to "an annual nationwide casualty rate of 20,000," more than half of them deaths, according to the veteran Asia reporter Barry Wain of the *Wall Street Journal* — in its Asia edition. A conservative estimate, then, is that the crisis this year is approximately comparable to Kosovo, though deaths are far more highly concentrated among children — over half, according to studies reported by the Mennonite Central Committee, which has been working in Laos since 1977 to alleviate the continuing atrocities.

There have been efforts to publicize and deal with the humanitarian catastrophe. A British-based Mine Advisory Group (MAG) is trying to remove the lethal objects, but the US is "conspicuously missing from the handful of western organizations that have followed MAG," the British press reports, though it has finally agreed to train some Laotian civilians. The British press also reports, with some annoyance, the allegation of MAG specialists that the US refuses to provide them with "render harmless procedures" that would make their work "a lot quicker and a lot safer." These remain a state secret, as does the whole affair in the United States. The Bangkok press reports a very similar situation in Cambodia, particularly the eastern region, where US bombardment after early 1969 was most intense.[15]

In this case, the US reaction is (II): do nothing. And the reaction of the media and commentators is to keep silent, following the norms under which the war against Laos was designated a "secret war" — meaning well-known, but suppressed, as was also in the case of Cambodia from March 1969. The level of self-censorship was extraordinary then, as is the current phase. The relevance of this shocking example should be obvious without further comment.

President Clinton explained to the nation that "there are times when looking away simply is not an option"; "we can't respond to every tragedy in every corner of the world," but that doesn't mean that "we should do nothing for no one."[16] But the president, and commentators, failed to add that the "times" are well defined. The principle applies to "humanitarian crises," in the technical sense discussed earlier: when the interests of rich and privileged people are endangered. Accordingly, the examples just mentioned do not qualify as "humanitarian crises," so looking away and not responding are definitely options, if not obligatory. On similar grounds, Clinton's policies on Africa are understood by Western diplomats to be "leaving Africa to solve its own crises," for example, in the Republic of Congo, scene of a major war and huge atrocities: here Clinton refused a UN request for $100,000 for a battalion of peacekeepers, according to the UN's senior Africa envoy, the highly respected diplomat Mohamed Sahnoun, a refusal that "torpedoed" the UN proposal. In the case of Sierra Leone, "Washington dragged out discussions on a British proposal to deploy peacekeepers" in 1997, paving the way for another major disaster, but also of the kind for which "looking away" is the preferred option. In other cases too, "the United States has actively thwarted efforts by the United Nations to take on peacekeeping operations that might have prevented some of Africa's wars, according to European and UN diplomats," correspondent Colum Lynch reported as the plans to bomb Kosovo were reaching their final stages.[17]

I will skip other examples of (I) and (II), which abound, and also contemporary atrocities of a different kind, such as the slaughter of Iraqi civilians by means of a vicious form of what amounts to biological warfare — "a very hard choice," Madeleine Albright commented on national TV in 1996 when asked for her reaction to the killing of half a million Iraqi children in five years, but "we think the price is worth it." Current estimates remain at about 5,000 children killed every month, and the price is still "worth it."[18] These and other examples might be kept in mind when we read admiring accounts of how the "moral compass" of the Clinton administration is at last functioning properly, in Kosovo.[19]

Kosovo is another illustration of (I): act in such a way as to escalate the violence, with exactly that expectation.

"Humanitarian Intervention"

To find examples illustrating (III) is all too easy, at least if we keep to official rhetoric. The most extensive recent academic study of "humanitarian intervention" is by Sean Murphy, now counselor for legal affairs at the US Embassy in the Hague. He reviews the record after the

Kellogg-Briand pact of 1928, which outlawed war, and then after the UN Charter, which strengthened and articulated these provisions. In the first phase, he writes, the most prominent examples of "humanitarian intervention" were Japan's attack on Manchuria, Mussolini's invasion of Ethiopia, and Hitler's occupation of parts of Czechoslovakia, all accompanied by uplifting humanitarian rhetoric and factual justifications as well. Japan was going to establish an "earthly paradise" as it defended Manchurians from "Chinese bandits," with the support of a leading Chinese nationalist, a far more credible figure than anyone the US was able to conjure up during its attack on South Vietnam. Mussolini was liberating thousands of slaves as he carried forth the Western "civilizing mission." Hitler announced Germany's intention to end ethnic tensions and violence, and to "safeguard the national individuality of the German and Czech peoples," in an operation "filled with earnest desire to serve the true interests of the peoples dwelling in the area," in accordance with their will; the Slovakian president asked Hitler to declare Slovakia a protectorate.[20]

Another useful intellectual exercise is to compare those obscene justifications with those offered for interventions, including "humanitarian interventions," in the post–UN Charter period.

In that period, perhaps the most compelling example of (III) is the Vietnamese invasion of Cambodia in December 1978, terminating Pol Pot's atrocities, which were then peaking. Vietnam pleaded the right of self-defense against armed attack, one of the few post-Charter examples when the plea is plausible: the Khmer Rouge regime (Democratic Kampuchea, DK) was carrying out murderous attacks against Vietnam in border areas. The US reaction is instructive. The press condemned the "Prussians" of Asia for their outrageous violation of international law. They were harshly punished for the crime of having ended Pol Pot's slaughters, first by a (US-backed) Chinese invasion, then by the US imposition of extremely harsh sanctions. The US recognized the expelled DK as the official government of Cambodia, because of its "continuity" with the Pol Pot regime, the State Department explained. Not too subtly, the US supported the Khmer Rouge in its continuing attacks in Cambodia.

The example tells us more about the "custom and practice" that underlies "the emerging legal norms of humanitarian intervention."

Another illustration of (III) is India's invasion of East Pakistan in 1971, which terminated an enormous massacre and refugee flight (more than 10 million, according to estimates at the time). The US condemned India for aggression; Kissinger was particularly infuriated by India's action, in part, it seems, because it was interfering with a carefully staged secret trip to China. Perhaps this is one of the examples that historian John Lewis Gaddis had in mind in his fawning review of the latest volume of Kissinger's memoirs, when he reports admiringly that Kissinger "acknowledges here, more clearly than in the past, the influence of his upbringing in Nazi Germany, the examples set by his parents, and the consequent impossibility, for him, of operating outside a moral framework."[21] The logic is overpowering, as are the illustrations, too well known to record.

Again, the same lessons.

Despite the desperate efforts of ideologues to prove that circles are square, there is no serious doubt that the NATO bombings further undermine what remains of the fragile structure of international law. The US made that clear in the debates that led to the NATO decision, as already discussed. The more closely one approaches the conflicted region, the greater the opposition to Washington's insistence on force, even within NATO (in Greece and Italy). Again, that is not an unusual phenomenon: another recent example is the US/UK bombing of Iraq, undertaken in December 1998 with unusually brazen gestures of contempt for the Security Council — even the timing, which coincided with an emergency session to deal with the crisis. Still another illustration, minor in context, is the destruction of half the pharmaceutical production of a poor African country (Sudan) a few months earlier, another event that does not indicate that the "moral compass" is straying from righteousness, though comparable destruction of US facilities by Islamic terrorists might evoke a slightly different reaction. It is unnecessary to emphasize that there is a far more extensive record that would be prominently reviewed right now if facts were considered relevant to determining "custom and practice."

The Rules of World Order

It could be argued, rather plausibly, that further demolition of the rules of world order is by now of no significance, as in the late 1930s. The contempt of the world's leading power for the framework of world order has become so extreme that there is little left to discuss.[22] While the Reaganites broke new ground, under Clinton the defiance of world order has become so extreme as to be of concern even to hawkish policy analysts. In the leading establishment journal *Foreign Affairs*, Samuel Huntington warns that Washington is treading a dangerous course. In the eyes of much of the world — probably most of the world, he suggests — the US is "becoming the rogue superpower," considered "the single greatest external threat to their societies." Realist "international relations theory," he argues, predicts that coalitions may arise to counterbalance the rogue superpower.[23] On pragmatic grounds, then, the stance should be reconsidered. Americans who prefer a different image of their society might have other grounds for concern over these tendencies, but they are probably of little concern to planners, with their narrower focus and immersion in ideology.

Where does that leave the question of what to do in Kosovo? It leaves it unanswered. The US has chosen a course of action that, as it explicitly recognizes, escalates atrocities and violence; a course that strikes yet another blow against the regime of international order, which does offer the weak at least some limited protection from predatory states; a course that undermines — perhaps destroys — promising democratic developments within Yugoslavia, probably Macedonia as well. As for the longer term, consequences are unpredictable.

One plausible observation is that "every bomb that falls on Serbia and every ethnic killing in Kosovo suggests that it will scarcely be possible for Serbs and Albanians to live beside each other in some sort of peace."[24] Other possible long-term outcomes are not pleasant to contemplate. The resort to violence has, again predictably, narrowed the options. Perhaps the least ugly that remains is an eventual partition of Kosovo, with Serbia taking the northern areas that are rich in resources and have the main historical monuments, and the southern sector becoming a NATO protectorate where some Albanians can live in misery. Another possibility is that with much of the population gone, the US might turn to the Carthaginian solution. If that happens, it would again be nothing new, as large areas of Indochina can testify.

A standard argument is that we had to do something: we could not simply stand by as atrocities continued. The argument is so absurd that it is rather surprising to hear it voiced. Suppose you see a crime in the streets, and feel that you can't just stand by silently, so you pick up an assault rifle and kill everyone involved: criminal, victim, bystanders. Are we to understand that to be the rational and moral response?

One choice, always available, is to follow the Hippocratic principle: "First, do no harm." If you can think of no way to adhere to that elementary principle, then do nothing; at least that is preferable to causing harm. But there are always other ways that can be considered. Diplomacy and negotiations are never at an end. That was true right before the bombing, when the Serb Parliament, responding to Clinton's ultimatum, condemned the withdrawal of the monitors and called for negotiations leading "toward the reaching of a political agreement on a wide-ranging autonomy" for Kosovo and on "the size and character of the international presence" in Kosovo for carrying out the accord.[25] The proposal was immediately available on international wire services, but scarcely reported in the US and generally unknown. Just what the proposal might have meant we cannot know, since the two warrior states preferred to reject the diplomatic path in favor of violence.

Another argument, if one can call it that, has been advanced most prominently by Henry Kissinger. He believes that intervention was a mistake ("open-ended," quagmire, etc.). That aside, it is futile. "Through the centuries, these conflicts [in the Balkans] have been fought with unparalleled ferocity because none of the populations has any experience with — and essentially no belief in — western concepts of toleration." At last we understand why Europeans have treated each other with such gentle solicitude "through the centuries," and have tried so hard over many centuries to bring to others their message of nonviolence, toleration, and loving kindness.[26]

One can always count on K. for some comic relief, though in reality, he is not alone. He is joined by those who ponder "Balkan logic" as contrasted with the Western record of humane rationality, and those who remind us of the "distaste for war or for intervention in the affairs of others" that is "our inherent weakness," of our dismay over the "repeated violations of norms and rules established by international treaty [and] human rights conventions."[27] We are to consider Kosovo as "a

New Collision of East and West," a *New York Times* think-piece is head-lined, a clear illustration of Samuel Huntington's "Clash of Civiliza-tions": "a democratic West, its humanitarian instincts repelled by the barbarous inhumanity of Orthodox Serbs," all of this "clear to Ameri-cans" but not to others, a fact that Americans fail to comprehend.[28]

Or we may listen to the inspiring words of Secretary of Defense William Cohen, introducing the president at Norfolk Naval Air Station. He opened by quoting Theodore Roosevelt, speaking "at the dawn of this century, as America was awakening into its new place in the world." President Roosevelt said, "Unless you're willing to fight for great ideals, those ideals will vanish." Cohen added, "Today, at the dawn of the next century, we're joined by President Bill Clinton," who understands as well as Roosevelt that "standing on the sidelines ... as a witness to the unspeakable horror that was about to take place, that would in fact affect the peace and stability of NATO countries, was simply unacceptable."[29] One has to wonder what must pass through the mind of someone invok-ing this famous racist fanatic and raving jingoist as a model of American values, along with the events that illustrated his cherished "great ideals": the slaughter of hundreds of thousands of Filipinos who had sought lib-eration from Spain, shortly after Roosevelt's own contribution to pre-venting Cubans from achieving the same goal.

Wiser commentators will wait until Washington settles on an official story. After two weeks of bombing, the story was that they both knew and didn't know that a catastrophe would follow. On March 28, 1999, "when a reporter asked if the bombing was accelerating the atrocities, [Presi-dent Clinton] replied, 'absolutely not.' "[30] He reiterated that stand in his April 1 speech at Norfolk: "Had we not acted, the Serbian offensive would have been carried out with impunity." The following day, Penta-gon spokesman Kenneth Bacon announced that the opposite was true: "I don't think anyone could have foreseen the breadth of this brutality,"[31] the "first acknowledgment" by the administration that "it was not fully prepared for the crisis," the press reported — a crisis that was "entirely predictable," as the commanding general had informed the press a week earlier. From the start, reports from the scene were that "the administra-tion had been caught off guard" by the Serbian military reaction.[32]

The right of "humanitarian intervention" is likely to be more fre-quently invoked in coming years — maybe with justification, maybe not — now that Cold War pretexts have lost their efficacy. In such an era, it may be worthwhile to pay attention to the views of highly respected commentators — not to speak of the World Court, which ruled on the matter of intervention and "humanitarian aid" in a decision rejected by the United States, its essentials not even reported.

In the scholarly disciplines of international affairs and international law it would be hard to find more respected voices than Hedley Bull or Louis Henkin. Bull warned 15 years ago that "particular states or groups of states that set themselves up as the authoritative judges of the world common good, in disregard of the views of others, are in fact a menace to international order, and thus to effective action in this field." Henkin, in a standard work on world order, writes:

> [T]he pressures eroding the prohibition on the use of force are deplorable, and the arguments to legitimize the use of force in those circumstances are unpersuasive and dangerous.... Violations of human rights are indeed all too common, and if it were permissible to remedy them by external use of force, there would be no law to forbid the use of force by almost any state against almost any other. Human rights, I believe, will have to be vindicated, and other injustices remedied, by other, peaceful means, not by opening the door to aggression and destroying the principal advance in international law: the outlawing of war and the prohibition of force.[33]

Recognized principles of international law and world order, treaty obligations, decisions by the World Court, considered pronouncements by the most respected commentators — these do not automatically yield solutions to particular problems. Each has to be considered on its merits. For those who do not adopt the standards of Saddam Hussein, there is a heavy burden of proof to meet in undertaking the threat or use of force in violation of the principles of international order. Perhaps the burden can be met, but that has to be shown, not merely proclaimed with passionate rhetoric. The consequences of such violations have to be assessed carefully — in particular, what we take to be "predictable." And for those who are minimally serious, the reasons for the actions also have to be assessed — on rational grounds, with attention to historical fact and the documentary record, not simply by adulation of our leaders and their "moral compass."

4

East Timor Retrospective

It is not easy to write with feigned calm and dispassion about the events that have been unfolding in East Timor. Horror and shame are compounded by the fact that the crimes are so familiar and could so easily have been terminated. That has been true ever since Indonesia invaded in December 1975, relying on US diplomatic support and arms — used illegally, but with secret authorization, and even new arms shipments sent under the cover of an official "embargo." There has been no need to threaten bombing or even sanctions. It would have sufficed for the US and its allies to withdraw their active participation, and to inform their close associates in the Indonesian military command that the atrocities must be terminated and the territory granted the right of self-determination that has been upheld by the United Nations and the International Court of Justice. We cannot undo the past, but we should at least be willing to recognize what we have done, and to face the moral responsibility of saving the remnants and providing ample reparations, a pathetic gesture of compensation for terrible crimes.

The latest chapter in this painful story of betrayal and complicity opened right after the referendum of August 30, 1999, when the population voted overwhelmingly for independence. At once, atrocities mounted sharply, organized and directed by the Indonesian military (TNI). The UN Mission (UNAMET) gave its appraisal on September 11:

> The evidence for a direct link between the militia and the military is beyond any dispute and has been overwhelmingly documented by UNAMET over the last four months. But the scale and thoroughness of the destruction of East Timor in the past week has demonstrated a new level of open participation of the military in the implementation of what was previously a more veiled operation.

The Mission warned that "the worst may be yet to come.... It cannot be ruled out that these are the first stages of a genocidal campaign to stamp out the East Timorese problem by force."[1]

Indonesia historian John Roosa, an official observer of the vote, described the situation starkly:

> Given that the pogrom was so predictable, it was easily preventable.... But in the weeks before the ballot, the Clinton administration refused to discuss with Australia and other countries the formation of [an international force]. Even after the violence erupted, the administration dithered for days,[2]

until compelled by international (primarily Australian) and domestic pressure to make some timid gestures. Even these ambiguous messages sufficed to induce the Indonesian generals to reverse course and to accept an international presence, illustrating the latent power that has always been at hand.

The same power relations ensure that the UN can do nothing without Washington consent and initiative. While Clinton "dithered," almost half the population were expelled from their homes, according to UN estimates, and thousands murdered.[3] The Air Force that excels in pinpoint destruction of civilian targets in Novi Sad, Belgrade, and Pancevo apparently lacked the capacity to drop food to people facing starvation in the mountains to which they were driven by the terror of the TNI forces armed and trained by the United States and its no less cynical allies.

The recent events will evoke bitter memories among those who do not prefer "intentional ignorance." We are witnessing a shameful replay of events of 20 years ago. After carrying out a huge slaughter in 1977–78 with the decisive support of the Carter administration, Indonesia felt confident enough to permit a brief visit by members of the Jakarta diplomatic corps, among them US Ambassador Edward Masters. They recognized that an enormous humanitarian catastrophe had been created. The aftermath was described by Benedict Anderson, one of the most distinguished Indonesia scholars. "For nine long months" of starvation and terror, Anderson testified at the United Nations, "Ambassador Masters deliberately refrained, even within the walls of the State Department, from proposing humanitarian aid to East Timor," waiting "until the generals in Jakarta gave him the green light" — until they felt "secure enough to permit foreign visitors," as an internal State Department document recorded. Only then did Washington consider taking some steps to deal with the consequences of its actions.[4]

As TNI forces and their paramilitaries were burning down the capital city of Dili in September 1999, murdering and rampaging with renewed intensity, the Pentagon announced that "a US-Indonesian training exercise focused on humanitarian and disaster relief activities concluded August 25," five days before the referendum that elicited the sharp escalation in crimes — precisely as the political leadership in Washington expected, at least if they were reading their own intelligence reports.[5] The lessons of this cooperation were applied within days in the standard way, as all but the voluntarily blind must understand after many years of the same tales, the same outcomes.

One gruesome illustration was the coup that brought General Suharto to power in 1965. Army-led massacres slaughtered hundreds of thousands, mostly landless peasants, in a few months, destroying the mass-based political party of the left, the PKI. The achievement elicited unrestrained euphoria in the West and fulsome praise for the Indonesian "moderates," Suharto and his military accomplices, who had cleansed the society and opened it to foreign plunder. Secretary of Defense Robert McNamara informed Congress that US military aid and training had "paid dividends" — including half a million corpses — "enormous dividends," a congressional report concluded. McNamara informed President Johnson that US military assistance "encouraged [the army] to move against the PKI when the opportunity was presented." Contacts with Indonesian military officers, including university programs, were "very significant factors in determining the favorable orientation of the new Indonesian political elite" (the army).[6]

The degree of cooperation between Washington and Jakarta is impressive. US weapons sales to Indonesia amount to over $1 billion since the 1975 invasion. Military aid during the Clinton years is at about $150 million.

Through the 1990s, the US continued support for "our kind of guy," as General Suharto was described by the Clinton administration before he fell from grace by losing control and failing to implement harsh IMF orders with sufficient ardor. After the 1991 Dili massacre, Congress restricted arms sales and banned US training of the Indonesian military, but Clinton found devious ways to evade the ban. Congress expressed its "outrage," reiterating that "it was and is the intent of Congress to prohibit US military training for Indonesia," as readers of the *Far Eastern Economic Review* and dissident publications here could learn. But to no avail.

Inquiries about Clinton's programs received the routine response from the State Department: US military training serves the positive function of exposing foreign militaries to US values. These values were exhibited as military aid to Indonesia flowed and government-licensed sales of armaments increased fivefold from fiscal year 1997 to 1998. In April 1999, shortly after the massacre of dozens of refugees who had taken shelter in a church in Liquica, Admiral Dennis Blair, US Pacific commander, assured TNI commander General Wiranto of US support and assistance, proposing a new US training mission.[7]

On September 19, 1999, the *London Observer* international news service reported Clinton's "Iron Balance" program, which trained the Indonesian military into 1998, in violation of congressional restrictions. Included were Kopassus units, the murderous forces that organized and directed the "militias," and participated directly in their atrocities, as Washington was well aware. "Iron Balance" provided these forces with more training in counterinsurgency and "psychological operations," expertise that they put to use effectively at once.

All of this found its way to the memory hole that contains the past record of the crucial US support for the atrocities, granted the same (null) coverage as many other events of the past year; for example, the unanimous Senate vote on June 30, 1999, calling on the Clinton administration to link Indonesian military actions in East Timor to "any loan or financial assistance to Indonesia," as readers could learn from the *Irish Times*.

In the face of this record, only briefly sampled, and duplicated repeatedly elsewhere, the government lauds "the value of the years of training given to Indonesia's future military leaders in the United States and the millions of dollars in military aid for Indonesia," urging more of the same for Indonesia and throughout the world.[8]

"The Dilemma" of East Timor

The reasons for the disgraceful record have sometimes been honestly recognized. During the latest phase of atrocities, a senior diplomat in Jakarta described "the dilemma" faced by the great powers: "Indonesia matters, and East Timor doesn't."[9] It is therefore understandable that Washington should keep to ineffectual gestures of disapproval while insisting that internal security in East Timor "is the responsibility of the government of Indonesia, and we don't want to take that responsibility away from them" — the official stance a few days before the August referendum, repeated in full knowledge of how that "responsibility" had been carried out, and maintained as the most dire predictions were quickly fulfilled.[10]

The reasoning of the senior diplomat was spelled out more fully by two Asia specialists of the *New York Times*: the Clinton administration, they write, "has made the calculation that the United States must put its relationship with Indonesia, a mineral-rich nation of more than 200 million people, ahead of its concern over the political fate of East Timor, a tiny impoverished territory of 800,000 people that is seeking independence." The second national journal quotes Douglas Paal, president of the Asia Pacific Policy Center, stating the facts of life: "Timor is a speed bump on the road to dealing with Jakarta, and we've got to get over it safely. Indonesia is such a big place and so central to the stability of the region."[11]

The term "stability" has long served as a code word, referring to a "favorable orientation of the political elite" — favorable not to their populations, but to foreign investors and global managers.

In the rhetoric of official Washington, "We don't have a dog running in the East Timor race." Accordingly, what happens there is not our business. But after intensive Australian pressure, the calculations shifted: "We have a very big dog running down there called Australia, and we have to support it," a senior government official concluded.[12] The survivors of US-backed crimes in a "tiny impoverished territory" are not even a "small dog."

The guiding principles were well understood by those responsible for Indonesia's 1975 invasion. They were articulated by UN Ambassador Daniel Patrick Moynihan, in words that should be committed to memory by anyone with a serious interest in international affairs, human rights, and the rule of law. The Security Council condemned the invasion and ordered Indonesia to withdraw, but to no avail. In his 1978 memoirs, Moynihan explains why:

The United States wished things to turn out as they did, and worked to bring this about. The Department of State desired that the United Nations prove utterly ineffective in whatever measures it undertook. This task was given to me, and I carried it forward with no inconsiderable success. [13]

Success was indeed considerable. Moynihan cites reports that within two months some 60,000 people had been killed, "10 percent of the population, almost the proportion of casualties experienced by the Soviet Union during the Second World War." A sign of the success, he adds, is that within a year "the subject disappeared from the press." So it did, as the invaders intensified their assault. Atrocities peaked as Moynihan was writing in 1977–78. Relying on a new flow of advanced military equipment from the Human Rights Administration, the Indonesian military carried out a devastating attack against the hundreds of thousands who had fled to the mountains, driving the survivors to Indonesian control. It was then that highly credible Church sources in East Timor sought to make public the estimates of 200,000 deaths that came to be accepted years later, after constant denial. The US reaction to the carnage has already been described.

As the slaughter reached near-genocidal levels, Britain and France joined in, providing arms and diplomatic support. Other powers too sought to participate in the lucrative aggression and massacre, always following the principles that have been lucidly enunciated.

The story does not begin in 1975. East Timor had not been overlooked by the planners of the post-war world. The territory should be granted independence, Roosevelt's senior advisor Sumner Welles mused, but "it would certainly take a thousand years." With an awe-inspiring display of courage and fortitude, the people of East Timor have struggled to confound that cynical prediction, enduring monstrous disasters. Perhaps 50,000 lost their lives protecting a small contingent of Australian commandoes fighting the Japanese; their heroism may have saved Australia from Japanese invasion. Almost a third of the population were victims of the first years of the 1975 Indonesian invasion, many more since.

Nineteen ninety-nine opened with a moment of hope. Indonesia's interim president Habibie opened the possibility for a referendum with a choice between incorporation within Indonesia ("autonomy") or independence. The army moved at once to prevent the latter outcome by terror and intimidation. In the months leading to the August referendum, 3,000 to 5,000 were killed, according to highly credible Church sources — twice the number of deaths prior to the NATO bombing in Kosovo, more than four times the number relative to population. The terror was widespread and sadistic, intended as a warning of the fate awaiting those foolhardy enough to disregard the orders of the occupying army.[14]

Braving violence and threats, almost the entire population voted, many emerging from hiding to do so. Close to 80 percent chose independence. Then followed the latest phase of TNI atrocities in an effort to reverse the outcome by slaughter and expulsion, while reducing much of the country to ashes. Within two weeks more than 10,000 might have been killed, according to Bishop Carlos Filipe Belo, the Nobel Peace laureate who was driven from his country under a hail of bullets, his house burned down and the refugees sheltering there dispatched to an uncertain fate.[15]

To Destroy a Nation

Even before Habibie's surprise call for a referendum, the army anticipated threats to its rule, including its control over East Timor's resources, and undertook careful planning with "the aim, quite simply, ... to destroy a nation." The plans were known to Western intelligence, as has been the case from the outset. TNI recruited thousands of West Timorese and brought in forces from Java. More ominously, the military command sent units of its dread US-trained Kopassus special forces and, as senior military advisor, General Makarim, a US-trained intelligence specialist with experience in East Timor and "a reputation for callous violence."[16]

Terror and destruction began early in the year. The TNI forces responsible have been described as "rogue elements" in the West, a questionable judgment. There is good reason to accept Bishop Belo's assignment of direct responsibility to commanding General Wiranto in Jakarta.[17] It appears that the militias have been managed by elite units of Kopassus, the "crack special forces unit" that had "been training regularly with US and Australian forces until their behavior became too much of an embarrassment for their foreign friends," veteran Asia correspondent David Jenkins reports. These forces are "legendary for their cruelty," Benedict Anderson observes: in East Timor they "became the pioneer and exemplar for every kind of atrocity," including systematic rapes, tortures, and executions, and the organization of hooded gangsters. They adopted the tactics of the US Phoenix program in South Vietnam that killed tens of thousands of peasants and much of the indigenous South Vietnamese leadership, Jenkins writes, as well as "the tactics employed by the Contras" in Nicaragua, following lessons taught by their CIA mentors. The state terrorists were "not simply going after the most radical pro-independence people but going after the moderates, the people who have influence in their community." "It's Phoenix," a well-placed source in Jakarta reported: the aim is "to terrorize everyone" — the NGOs, the Red Cross, the UN, the journalists.[18]

Well before the referendum, the commander of the Indonesian military in Dili, Colonel Tono Suratman, had warned of what was to come: "I would like to convey the following," he said: "if the pro-independents do win ... all will be destroyed.... It will be worse than 23 years ago."[19] An army document of early May, when international agreement on the referendum was reached, ordered that "massacres should be carried out from village to village after the announcement of the ballot if the pro-independence supporters win." The independence movement "should be eliminated from its leadership down to its roots."[20] Citing diplomatic, Church, and militia sources, the Australian press reported "that hundreds of modern assault rifles, grenades, and mortars are being stockpiled, ready for use if the autonomy option is rejected at the ballot box."[21] It warned that the army-run militias might be planning a violent takeover of much of the territory if, despite the terror, the popular will was expressed.

All of this was understood by the "foreign friends," who knew how to bring the terror to an end, but preferred evasive and ambiguous reactions that the Indonesian generals could easily interpret as a "green light" to carry out their work.

The sordid history must be viewed against the background of US-Indonesia relations in the post-war era. The rich resources of the archipelago, and its critical strategic location, guaranteed it the central role in US global planning. These factors lie behind US efforts 40 years ago to dismantle Indonesia, perceived as too independent and too democratic, even permitting participation of the leftist, peasant-based PKI.

The same factors account for Western support for the regime of killers and torturers who brought about a "favorable orientation" in 1965. Their achievements were, furthermore, understood to be a vindication of Washington's wars in Indochina, motivated in large part by concerns that the "virus" of independent nationalism might "infect" Indonesia, to borrow Kissingerian rhetoric. Support for the invasion of East Timor and subsequent atrocities was reflexive, though a broader analysis should attend to the fact that the collapse of the Portuguese empire had many of the same consequences in Africa, where South Africa was the agent of Western-backed terror. Throughout, Cold War pretexts were routinely invoked, serving as a convenient disguise for ugly motives and actions, particularly so in Southeast Asia.

The Routine Response

According to reports in Fall 1999, the UN mission in East Timor has been able to account for just over 150,000 people out of an estimated population of 850,000.[22] It reports that 260,000 "are now languishing in squalid refugee camps in West Timor under the effective control of the militias after either fleeing or being forcibly removed from their homes," and that another 100,000 have been relocated to other parts of Indonesia. The rest are presumed to be hiding in the mountains. The Australian commander expressed the natural concern that displaced people lack food and medical supplies. Touring camps in East and West Timor, US Assistant Secretary of State Harold Koh reported that the refugees are "starving and terrorized," and that disappearances "without explanation" are a daily occurrence.

To appreciate the scale of this disaster, one has to bear in mind the virtual demolition of the physical basis for survival by the departing Indonesian army and its paramilitary associates ("militias"), and the reign of terror to which the territory has been subjected for a quarter-century.

For much of 1999, Western intellectuals have been engaged in one of history's most audacious displays of self-adulation over their magnificent performance in Kosovo. Among the many facets of this grand achievement dispatched to the proper place was the fact that the huge flow of brutalized refugees expelled after the bombing could receive little care, thanks to Washington's defunding of the responsible UN agency. Its staff was reduced 15 percent in 1998, and another 20 percent in January 1999; it now endures the denunciations of Tony Blair for its "problematic performance" in the wake of the atrocities that were the anticipated consequence of US/UK bombing. While the mutual admiration society was performing as required, atrocities mounted in East Timor.

As of October 1999, the US had provided no funds for the Australian-led UN intervention force (in contrast, Japan, long a fervent supporter of Indonesia, offered $100 million). But that is perhaps not surprising, in the light of its refusal to pay any of the costs of the UN civilian operations even in Kosovo. Washington has also asked the UN to reduce the scale of subsequent operations, because it might be called upon to pay some of the costs. Hundreds of thousands of missing people may be starving in the mountains, but no call has been heard for even elementary humanitarian measures. Hundreds of thousands more are facing a grim fate within Indonesia. A word from Washington would suffice to end their torment, but there is no word, and no comment.

In Kosovo, preparation for war crimes trials began in May 1999, expedited at US-UK initiative, including unprecedented access to intelligence information. In East Timor, investigations of crimes, with Indonesian participation, are "an absolute joke, a complete whitewash," according to UN officials quoted in the British press. A spokesperson for Amnesty International added that the inquiry as planned "will cause East Timorese even more trauma than they have suffered already. It would be really insulting at this stage." Indonesian generals "do not seem to be quaking in their boots," the Australian press reports. One reason is that "some of the most damning evidence is likely to be ... material plucked from the air waves by sophisticated US and Australian electronic intercept equipment," and the generals feel confident that their old friends will not let them down — if only because the chain of responsibility might be hard to snap at just the right point.

There is also little effort to unearth evidence of atrocities in East Timor. In striking contrast, Kosovo has been swarming with police and medical forensic teams from the US and other countries in the hope of discovering large-scale atrocities that can be transmuted into justification for the NATO bombing of which they were the anticipated consequence — as Milosevic had planned all along, it is now claimed, though NATO Commander General Wesley Clark reported a month after the bombing that the alleged plans "have never been shared with me" and that the NATO operation "was not designed [by the political leadership] as a means of blocking Serb ethnic cleansing.... There was never any intent to do that. That was not the idea."

Commenting on Washington's refusal to lift a finger to help the victims of its crimes, the veteran Australian diplomat Richard Butler observed that "it has been made very clear to me by senior American analysts that the facts of the alliance essentially are that: the US will respond proportionally, defined largely in terms of its own interests and threat assessment." The remarks were not offered in criticism of Washington; rather, of his fellow Australians, who do not comprehend the facts of life: that others are to shoulder the burdens, and face the costs — which for Australia, may not be slight. It will hardly come as a great shock if a few years hence US corporations are cheerfully picking up the pieces in an Indonesia that resents Australian actions, but has few complaints about the overlord.

The chorus of self-adulation has subsided a bit, though not much. Far more important than these shameful performances is the failure to act — at once, and decisively — to cast aside mythology and face the causes and consequences of our actions, and to save the remnants of one of the most terrible tragedies of this awful century.

5

"Plan Colombia"

In 1999, Colombia became the leading recipient of US military and police assistance, replacing Turkey (Israel and Egypt are in a separate category). Colombia receives more US military aid than the rest of Latin
America and the Caribbean combined. The total for 1999 reached about
$300 million, along with $60 million in arms sales, approximately a
threefold increase from 1998. The figure is scheduled to increase still
more sharply with the anticipated passage of some version of Clinton's
Colombia Plan, submitted to Congress in April 2000, which called for a
$1.6 billion "emergency aid" package for two years. Through the 1990s,
Colombia has been by far the leading recipient of US military aid in Latin
America, and has also compiled by far the worst human rights record, in
conformity with a well-established and long-standing correlation.[1]

In theory, "Plan Colombia" is a two-year Colombian government
program of $7.5 billion, with the US providing the military muscle and
token funds for other purposes, and some $6 billion from the Colombian
government, Europe, the IMF, and the World Bank for social and economic programs that Colombia is to prepare. According to non-US diplomats, the draft of "Plan Colombia" was written in English, not Spanish.
The military program (arms, training, intelligence infrastructure) was in
place in late 1999, but "the Colombian government has yet to present a
coherent social investment program" as of mid-2000, and few governments are "willing to climb aboard what is widely perceived as an American project to clean up its backyard," by means that are familiar to those
who do not choose what has been called "intentional ignorance."[2]

We can often learn from systematic patterns, so let us tarry for a moment on the previous champion, Turkey. As a major US military ally and

strategic outpost, Turkey has received substantial military aid from the origins of the Cold War. But arms deliveries began to increase sharply in 1984. Evidently, there was no Cold War connection at all. Rather, that was the year when Turkey initiated a large-scale counterinsurgency campaign in the Kurdish southeast, which also is the site of major US air bases and the locus of regional surveillance, so that everything that happens there is well known in Washington. Arms deliveries peaked in 1997. In that year alone, they exceeded the total from the entire period 1950–83. US arms amounted to about 80 percent of Turkish military equipment, including heavy armaments (jet planes, tanks, etc.), often evading congressional restrictions.[3]

By 1999, Turkey had largely suppressed Kurdish resistance by extreme terror and ethnic cleansing, leaving some 2 to 3 million refugees, 3,500 villages destroyed (seven times as high as in Kosovo under NATO bombs), and tens of thousands killed, primarily during the Clinton years. A huge flow of US arms was no longer needed to accomplish these objectives. Turkey can therefore be singled out for praise for its "positive experiences" in showing how "tough counterterrorism measures plus political dialogue with non-terrorist opposition groups" can overcome the plague of violence and atrocities, so we learn from the lead article in the *New York Times* on the State Department's "latest annual report describing the administration's efforts to combat terrorism."[4] More evidence, if such is needed, that cynicism is utterly without limits.

A few days later more was reported about Turkey's "positive experiences" with "tough counterterrorism measures." Turkey's parliamentary human rights commission described "widespread resort to torture" by the police and "an array of torture equipment," and a spokesperson informed the press that visits to the eastern region had "confirmed grim tales of torture" in police prison cells, specifically those of anti-terrorism units. The commission then released a six-volume report based on a two-year investigation, with photographs and other details, confirming extensive evidence that the abuses are systematic, and continue without significant change. These revelations received little notice, ignoring Washington's involvement, but the press did feature impassioned rhetoric on the need to maintain very harsh sanctions against Cuba because its human rights violations so offend our humanitarian sensibilities. The parliamentary inquiry into the ongoing atrocities supported lavishly by

Washington perhaps received oblique acknowledgment in a report by
New York Times bureau chief Stephen Kinzer on Turkey's current progress, shown by the military's willingness to permit films that "portray
the torture that was widespread in military prisons" in the early 1980s.[5]

Nevertheless, despite the great success achieved by some of the
most violent state terror of the 1990s, military operations continue,
while Kurds are still deprived of elementary rights.[6] On April 1, 2000,
10,000 Turkish troops began new ground sweeps in the regions that had
been most devastated by the US-Turkish terror campaigns of the preceding years, also launching another offensive into northern Iraq to attack
Kurdish guerrilla forces (PKK) — in a no-fly zone where Kurds are protected by the US air force from the (temporarily) wrong oppressor.
Asked about the renewed operations in Iraq, State Department spokesperson James Rubin said that US "policy remains the same. We support
the right of Turkey to defend itself against PKK attacks, so long as its in-
cursions are limited in scope and duration and fully respect the rights of
the civilian inhabitants of the region"; he declined to answer the question whether Turkey had been "attacked," stating only that the US had
no "independent confirmation" of Turkish military operations in this region of intense surveillance and regular US bombardment.[7]

As the renewed Turkish campaigns were beginning, Secretary of
Defense William Cohen addressed the American-Turkish Council, a
festive occasion with much laughter and applause, according to the government report.[8] He praised Turkey for taking part in the humanitarian
bombing of Yugoslavia, apparently without embarrassment, and announced that Turkey had been invited to join in co-production of the
new Joint Strike Aircraft, just as it has been co-producing the F-16s that
it used to such good effect in approved varieties of ethnic cleansing and
atrocities within its own territory, as a loyal member of NATO.

In Colombia, however, the military armed and trained by the United
States has not crushed domestic resistance, though it continues to produce its regular annual toll of atrocities. Each year, some 300,000 new
refugees are driven from their homes, with a death toll of about 3,000
and many horrible massacres. The great majority of atrocities are attributed to paramilitary forces. These are closely linked to the military, as
documented in considerable and shocking detail once again in February
2000 by Human Rights Watch, and in April 2000 by a UN study which

reported that the Colombian security forces that are to be greatly strengthened by the Colombia Plan maintain an intimate relationship with death squads, organize paramilitary forces, and either participate in their massacres directly or, by failing to take action, have "undoubtedly enabled the paramilitary groups to achieve their exterminating objectives." In more muted terms, the State Department confirms the general picture in its annual human rights reports, again in the report covering 1999, which concludes that "security forces actively collaborated with members of paramilitary groups" while "government forces continued to commit numerous, serious abuses, including extrajudicial killings, at a level that was roughly similar to that of 1998," when the report attributed about 80 percent of attributable atrocities to the military and paramilitaries. The picture is confirmed as well by the Colombian Office of UN Human Rights Commissioner Mary Robinson. Its director, a respected Swedish diplomat, assigns the responsibility for "the magnitude and complexity of the paramilitary phenomenon" to the Colombian government, hence indirectly to its US sponsor.[9]

Resort to paramilitary forces for atrocities is well-established practice, for understandable reasons, including in recent years Serbia in Kosovo and Indonesia in East Timor (though in the latter case, the facts were suppressed in favor of "militia violence" and "rogue elements" as long as possible). There is a long history in the practice of terrorist states and imperial powers.

The Colombian Commission of Jurists reported in September 1999 that the rate of killings had increased by almost 20 percent over the preceding year, and that the proportion attributable to the paramilitaries had risen from 46 percent in 1995 to almost 80 percent in 1998, continuing through 1999. The Colombian government's Human Rights Ombudsman's Office (*Defensoria del Pueblo*) reported a 68 percent increase in massacres in the first half of 1999 as compared to the same period of 1998, reaching more than one a day, overwhelmingly attributed to paramilitaries. Daniel Bland, a human rights researcher who worked in Colombia through most of the 1990s, concludes that in the past three years alone, "more than a million people have been forced from their homes in the countryside, and between 5,000 and 7,000 unarmed peasants have been slaughtered by right-wing paramilitaries." Of nine people he interviewed for a documentary on human rights in 1997 —

professors, journalists, priests, human rights workers — "three have since been murdered by paramilitary gunmen; four have fled with their families after receiving death threats." UNICEF and the Colombian Human Rights Information Bureau CODHES estimate that in June-August 1999 alone, 200,000 more people were driven from their homes.[10]

It would be unfair to charge Washington with lack of concern over paramilitary terror. After the April 2000 release of its annual report "describing the administration's efforts to combat terrorism," praising Turkey for its "positive experiences" in this common pursuit, the State Department held a press conference on the report. Counterterrorism Coordinator Michael Sheehan was asked why the Colombian paramilitaries are not listed among terrorist groups, though the State Department has long recognized them to be responsible for the overwhelming majority of the atrocities, including the most atrocious of them, and they are surely the most violent and brutal terrorist organization in the Western hemisphere, ranking high in the world. They are, furthermore, agents of the more serious crime of state terrorism, in view of their close relation to the military establishment in Colombia, hence also the United States. Sheehan explained that the paramilitaries do not escape Washington's vigilant eye, but the Department cannot jump to conclusions. Terrorists are identified in the report only after scrupulous investigation: "it's a legal process, and one that was very meticulous." The paramilitaries are "under review right now" and "if we come up with a case, if we can make the case from our legal definition, they'll be designated" as terrorists.

In contrast, Cuba easily satisfies the requirements as one of the seven states engaged in terrorism, as demonstrated in the 85 words devoted to it in this 107-page document. The State Department would be "absolutely" ready to take its case against Cuba to Court, Sheehan stated: after all, Cuba "has links to several terrorist organizations that it needs to address," including the Colombian guerrilla organizations. These do satisfy the Department's meticulous criteria — by definition, a realistic commentator might add, since the US opposes them.[11]

We may recall that in the early months of 1999, while massacres were proceeding at over one a day in Colombia, there was also a large increase in atrocities (including many massacres) in East Timor, carried out by Indonesian commandoes armed and trained by the US. In one massacre alone, in a church in Liquica on April 6, 1999, Western investigators believe that 200 or more people were murdered. An American police officer on the scene comments that "officially we must stay with the number of bodies that we have actually lifted, but the total number of people killed in this district is much, much higher than that, perhaps even astronomical." The full story will never be known, because the plea of the UN mission for forensic experts was rejected by the US and its allies — unlike Kosovo, teeming with investigators at once in an effort to find atrocities that could provide retrospective justification for the NATO bombing that precipitated them, by intriguing logic.[12]

In both Colombia and East Timor, the conclusion drawn was exactly as in Turkey: support the killers. There was also one reported massacre in Kosovo, at Racak on January 15, 1999 (45 killed). That event allegedly inspired such horror among Western humanitarians that it was necessary to bomb Yugoslavia 10 weeks later with the expectation, quickly fulfilled, that the consequence would be a sharp escalation of atrocities. The accompanying torrent of self-adulation, which has few, if any, counterparts, heralded a "new era" in human affairs in which the "enlightened states" will selflessly dedicate themselves to the defense of human rights, guided by "principles and values" for the first time in history.[13] Putting aside the actual facts about Kosovo, the performance was greatly facilitated by silence or deceit about the active participation of the same powers in comparable or worse atrocities at the very same time.

Returning to Colombia, prominent human rights activists continue to flee abroad under death threats, including the courageous head of the Church-based human rights group Justice and Peace, Father Javier Giraldo, who has played an outstanding role in defending human rights. The AFL-CIO reports that several trade unionists are murdered every week, mostly by paramilitaries supported by the government security forces. Forced displacement in 1998 was 20 percent above 1997, and increased again in 1999 in some regions, according to Human Rights Watch. Colombia now has the largest displaced population in the world, after Sudan and Angola.[14]

Hailed as a leading democracy by Clinton and other US leaders and political commentators, Colombia did at last permit an independent party (UP, Patriotic Union) to challenge the long-standing elite system of power-sharing. The UP party, founded by the guerrillas (primarily the FARC, Revolutionary Armed Forces of Colombia) and drawing in part from their constituencies, faced certain difficulties, however, including the rapid assassination of about 3,000 activists, including presidential candidates, mayors, and legislators. The results taught lessons to the guerrillas about the prospects for entering the political system.[15] Washington also drew lessons from these and related events of the same period. The Clinton administration was particularly impressed with the performance of President César Gaviria, who presided over the escalation of state terror — so impressed that it induced (some say compelled) the Organization of American States to accept him as Secretary-General on grounds that "he has been very forward looking in building democratic institutions in a country where it was sometimes dangerous to do so" — which is surely true, in large measure because of the actions of his government. A more significant reason, perhaps, is that he was also "forward-looking ... on economic reform in Colombia and on economic integration in the hemisphere," code words that are readily interpreted.[16]

Meanwhile, deplorable socioeconomic conditions persist, leaving much of the population in misery in a rich country with concentration of wealth and land-ownership that is high even by the shameful standards of Latin America generally. The situation became worse in the 1990s as a result of the "neoliberal reforms" formalized in the 1991 constitution, which reduced still further "the effective participation of civil society" in policy formation by "reforms intended to enhance executive power and reduce the autonomy of the judicial and legislative branches, and by concentrating macroeconomic planning in the hands of a smaller circle of technocrats" — in effect, adjuncts of Washington. The "neoliberal reforms have also given rise to alarming levels of poverty and inequality; approximately 55 percent of Colombia's population lives below the poverty level" and "this situation has been aggravated by an acute crisis in agriculture, itself a result of the neoliberal program," as in Latin America generally.[17]

The respected president of the Colombian Permanent Committee for Human Rights, former Minister of Foreign Affairs Alfredo Vázquez Carrizosa, writes that it is "poverty and insufficient land reform" that "have made Colombia one of the most tragic countries of Latin America," though as elsewhere, "violence has been exacerbated by external factors," primarily the initiatives of the Kennedy administration, which "took great pains to transform our regular armies into counterinsurgency brigades." These initiatives ushered in "what is known in Latin America as the National Security Doctrine," which is not concerned with "defense against an external enemy" but rather "the internal enemy." The new "strategy of the death squads" accords the military "the right to fight and to exterminate social workers, trade unionists, men and women who are not supportive of the establishment, and who are assumed to be communist extremists." The general goal, as explained by the foremost US academic specialist on human rights in Latin America, was "to destroy permanently a perceived threat to the existing structure of socio-economic privilege by eliminating the political participation of the numerical majority," the "popular classes."[18]

As part of its strategy of converting the Latin American military from "hemispheric defense" to "internal security" — meaning war against the domestic population — Kennedy dispatched a military mission to Colombia in 1962 headed by Special Forces General William Yarborough. He proposed "reforms" to enable the security forces to "as necessary execute paramilitary, sabotage, and/or terrorist activities against known Communist proponents" — the "communist extremists" to whom Vázquez Carrizosa alludes.[19]

Again the broader patterns are worth noting. Shortly after, Lyndon Johnson escalated Kennedy's war against South Vietnam — what is called here "the defense of South Vietnam," just as Russia called its war against Afghanistan "the defense of Afghanistan." In January 1965, US special forces in South Vietnam were issued standing orders "to conduct operations to dislodge VC-controlled officials, to include assassination," and more generally to use such "pacification" techniques as "ambushing, raiding, sabotaging, and committing acts of terrorism against known VC personnel," the counterparts of the "known Communist proponents" in Colombia.[20]

A Colombian governmental commission concluded that "the criminalization of social protest" is one of the "principal factors which permit and encourage violations of human rights" by the military and police authorities and their paramilitary collaborators. Ten years ago, as US-backed state terror was increasing sharply, the Minister of Defense called for "total war in the political, economic, and social arenas," while another high military official explained that guerrillas were of secondary importance: "the real danger" is "what the insurgents have called the political and psychological war," the war "to control the popular elements" and "to manipulate the masses." The "subversives" hope to influence unions, universities, media, and so on. "Every individual who in one or another manner supports the goals of the enemy must be considered a traitor and treated in that manner," a 1963 military manual prescribed, as the Kennedy initiatives were moving into high gear. Since the official goals of the guerrillas are social democratic, the circle of treachery targeted for terror operations is wide.[21]

In the years that followed, the Kennedy-Yarborough strategy was developed and applied broadly in "our little region over here," as the Western hemisphere was described by FDR's Secretary of War Henry Stimson when he was explaining why the US was entitled to control its own regional system while all others were to be dismantled. Violent repression spread throughout Latin America, beginning in the southern cone and reaching its awesome peak in Central America in the 1980s as the stern disciplinarian of the North responded with extreme violence to efforts by the Church and other "subversives" to confront a terrible legacy of misery and repression. Colombia's advance to first rank among the criminal states in "our little region" is in part the result of the decline in US-managed state terror in Central America, which achieved its primary aims as in Turkey 10 years later, leaving in its wake a "culture of terror" that "domesticat[es] the expectations of the majority" and undermines aspirations towards "alternatives different to those of the powerful," in the words of Salvadoran Jesuits, who learned the lessons from bitter experience; those who survived the US assault, that is. In Colombia, however, the problem of establishing approved forms of democracy and stability remains, and is even becoming more severe. One approach would be to address the needs and concerns of the poor majority. Another is to provide arms and military training to keep things as they are.

Quite predictably, the announcement of the Colombia Plan led to countermeasures by the guerrillas, in particular, a demand that everyone with assets of more than $1 million pay a "revolutionary tax" or face the threat of kidnapping (as the FARC puts it, the threat of jailing for non-payment of taxes). The motivation is explained by the London *Financial Times:* "In the Farc's eyes, financing is required to fight fire with fire. The government is seeking $1.3 [billion] in military aid from the US, ostensibly for counter-drugs operations: the Farc believe the

new weapons will be trained on them. They appear ready to arm themselves for battle," which will lead to military escalation and undermining
of the fragile but ongoing peace negotiations.[22]

According to *New York Times* reporter Larry Rohter, "ordinary Colombians" are "angered" by the government's peace negotiations, which
ceded control to the FARC of a large region that they already controlled,
and the "embittered residents" of that region also oppose the guerrillas.
No evidence is cited. The leading Colombian military analyst Alfredo
Rangel sees matters differently. He "makes a point of reminding inter-
viewers that the FARC has significant support in the regions where it op-
erates," Alma Guillermoprieto reports. Rangel cites "FARC's ability to
launch surprise attacks" in different parts of the country, a fact that is
"politically significant" because "in each case, a single warning by the
civilian population would be enough to alert the army, and it doesn't
happen."[23]

The situation is not unfamiliar. An example that should be well
known is the startling success of the Tet offensive throughout South
Vietnam in January 1968, in cities and towns as well as rural areas.
Though the territory was occupied by over half a million US troops, with
a huge client army and police apparatus, the uprising of South Vietnamese guerrillas came as an almost complete surprise, with no advance
warning, revealing how deeply the guerrillas were embedded in the general population (North Vietnamese forces were largely confined to border regions, according to US intelligence). Though more convenient
tales have been constructed in the course of reshaping of history, the
facts were clear enough to convince US elites that the effort to crush resistance in South Vietnam was too costly to pursue.

On the same day that Rohter reported "the anger of ordinary Colombians," the London *Financial Times* reported an "innovative forum" in
the FARC-controlled region, one of many held there to allow "members
of the public to participate in the current peace talks." They come from
all parts of Colombia, speaking before TV cameras and meeting with senior FARC leaders. Included are union and business leaders, farmers,
and others. A trade union leader from Colombia's second-largest city,
Cali, "gave heart to those who believe that talking will end the country's
long-running conflict," addressing both the government and FARC
leaders. He directed his remarks specifically to "Señor Marulanda," the

long-time FARC peasant leader "who minutes earlier had entered to a rousing ovation," telling him that "unemployment is not a problem caused by the violence," but "by the national government and the businessmen of this country." Business leaders also spoke, but "were heckled by the large body of trade union representatives who had also come to speak." Against a background of "union cheers," a FARC spokesperson "put forward one of the clearest visions yet of his organization's economic program," calling for freezing of privatization, subsidizing energy and agriculture as is done in the rich countries, and stimulation of the economy by protecting local enterprises. The government representative, who "emphasized export-led growth and private participation," nevertheless described the FARC statement as "raw material for the negotiations," though FARC, "bolstered by evident popular discontent with 'neoliberal' government policies," argued that those who "have monopolized power" must yield in the negotiations.[24]

The potential scale of the Colombia Plan is suggested by regional US military projects. The Salvadoran press reports a US-Salvadoran agreement, still to be ratified by the Salvadoran legislature, to allow the US Navy to use a Salvadoran airport as a "Forward Operating Location" (FOL), in addition to US Air Force FOLs in the Ecuadoran port city of Manta and the Dutch colonies of Aruba and Curaçao. The intergovernmental agreements reportedly allow the US total discretion over aircraft and weaponry, with no local inspection or control permitted. Ecuadoran military experts express concern that the Manta military base is perhaps being prepared for "eventual Kosovo-style aerial bombardments, ... an air war waged from bases used by the United States in the region, and from sea, in which planes and missiles would play a major role."[25]

The Colombia Plan is officially justified in terms of the "drug war,"[26] a claim taken seriously by few competent analysts. The US Drug Enforcement Administration (DEA) reports that "all branches of government" in Colombia are involved in "drug-related corruption." In November 1998, US Customs and DEA inspectors found 415 kg of cocaine and 6 kg of heroin in a Colombian Air Force plane that had landed in Florida, leading to the arrest of several Air Force officers and enlisted personnel.[27] Other observers too have reported the heavy involvement of the military in narcotrafficking, and the US military has also been drawn in. The wife of Colonel James Hiett pleaded guilty to conspiracy to smuggle heroin from Colombia to New York, and shortly after, it was reported that Colonel Hiett himself, who is in charge of US troops that trained Colombian security forces in "counternarcotics operations," was "expected to plead guilty" to charges of complicity.[28]

The paramilitaries openly proclaim their reliance on the drug business. "The leader of the paramilitaries [Carlos Castaño] acknowledged last week in a television interview that the drug trade provided 70 percent of the group's funding," correspondent John Donnelly reported in March 2000. This was the first appearance on Colombian TV of Castaño, who heads the largest and most brutal of the paramilitary organizations. He claimed to command a force of 11,200 men "financed by extortion and income from 30,000 hectares of coca fields in Norte de Santander."[29] But "the US-financed attack stays clear of the areas controlled by paramilitary forces," Donnelly observes, as have many others. The targets of the Colombia Plan are guerrilla forces based on the peasantry and calling for internal social change, which would interfere with integration of Colombia into the global system on the terms that the US demands: dominated by elites linked to US power interests that are accorded privileged access to Colombia's valuable resources, including oil — quite possibly a significant factor behind the Colombia Plan.

In standard US terminology, the FARC forces are "narcoguerrillas," a useful concept as a cover for counterinsurgency, but one that has been disputed by knowledgeable observers. It is agreed — and FARC leaders say — that they rely for funding on coca production, which they tax, as they tax other businesses. But " 'the guerrillas are something different from the traffickers,' says Klaus Nyholm, who runs the UN Drug Control Program," which has agents throughout the drug-producing regions. He believes the local FARC fronts to be "quite autonomous."[30] In some areas "they are not involved at all" in coca production, and in others "they actively tell the farmers not to grow [coca]." Andean drug specialist Ricardo Vargas describes the role of the guerrillas as "primarily focused on taxation of illicit crops." They have called for "a development plan for the peasants" that would "allow eradication of coca on the basis of alternative crops." "That's all we want," their leader Marulanda has publicly announced, as have other spokespersons.[31]

But let us put these matters aside and consider a few other questions.

Why do peasants in Colombia grow coca, not other crops? The reasons are understood. "Peasants grow coca and poppies," Vargas observes, "because of the crisis in the agricultural sector of Latin American countries, escalated by the general economic crisis in the region." Peasants began colonizing the Colombian Amazon in the 1950s, he writes, "following the violent displacement of peasants by large landholders," and they found that coca was "the only product that was both profitable and easy to market." Pressures on the peasantry substantially increased as "ranchers, investors, and legal commercial farmers have created and strengthened private armies" — the paramilitaries — that "serve as a means to violently expropriate land from indigenous people, peasants, and settlers," with the result that "traffickers now control much of Colombia's valuable land." The counterinsurgency battalions armed and trained by the US do not attack traffickers, Vargas reports, but "have as their target the weakest and most socially fragile link of the drug chain: the production by peasants, settlers, and indigenous people." The same is true of the chemical and biological weapons that Washington employs, used experimentally in violation of manufacturers' specifications, and over the objections of the Colombian government and agricultural associations. These measures multiply the "dangers to the civilian population, the environment, and legal agriculture." They destroy "legal food crops like yucca and bananas, water sources, pastures, livestock, and all the crops included in crop substitution programs," including those of well-established Church-run development projects that have sought to develop alternatives to coca production. There are also uncertain but potentially severe effects "on the fragile tropical rainforest environment."[32]

Traditional US programs, and the current Colombia Plan as well, primarily support the social forces that control the government and the military/paramilitary system, and that have largely created the problems by their rapacity and violence. The targets are the usual victims.

There are other factors that operate to increase coca production. Colombia was once a major wheat producer. That was undermined in the 1950s by "Food for Peace" aid, a program that provided taxpayer subsidies to US agribusiness and induced other countries to "become dependent on us for food" (Senator Hubert Humphrey, representing Midwest agricultural exporters), with counterpart funds for US client states, which they commonly used for military spending and counterinsurgency. A year before President Bush announced the "drug war" with great fanfare (once again), the international coffee agreement was suspended under US pressure, on grounds of "fair trade violations." The result was a fall of prices of more than 40 percent within two months for Colombia's leading legal export.[33]

Related factors are discussed by political economist Susan Strange.[34] In the 1960s, the G77 governments (now 133, accounting for 80 percent of the world's population) initiated a call for a "new international economic order" in which the needs of the large majority of people of the world would be a prominent concern. Specific proposals were formulated by the UN Conference on Trade and Development (UNCTAD), which was established in 1964 "to create an international trading system consistent with the promotion of economic and social development." The UNCTAD proposals were summarily dismissed by the great powers, along with the call for a "new international order" generally; the US, in particular, insists that "development is not a right," and that it is "preposterous" and a "dangerous incitement" to hold otherwise in accord with the socioeconomic provisions of the Universal Declaration of Human Rights, which the US rejects.[35] The world did move — or more accurately, was moved — towards a new international economic order, but along a different course, catering to the needs of a different sector, namely its designers — hardly a surprise, any more than one should be surprised that in standard doctrine the instituted form of "globalization" should be depicted as an inexorable process to which "there is no alternative" (TINA), as Margaret Thatcher thoughtfully declared.

One early UNCTAD proposal was a program for stabilizing commodity prices, routine practice within the industrial countries by means of public subsidy, though it was threatened briefly in the US when Congress was taken over in 1994 by right-wing elements that seemed to believe their own rhetoric, much to the consternation of business leaders who understand that market discipline is for the defenseless, not for them. The upstart free-market ideologues were soon taught better manners or dispatched back home, but not before Congress passed the 1996 "Freedom to Farm Act" to liberate American agriculture from the "East German socialist programs of the New Deal," as Newt Gingrich put it, ending market-distorting subsidies — which quickly tripled, reaching a

record $23 billion in 1999, and are scheduled to increase. The market
has worked its magic, however: the taxpayer subsidies go disproportionately to large agribusiness and the "corporate oligopolies" that dominate
the input and output side, Nicholas Kristof observed. Those with market
power in the food chain (from energy corporations to retailers) are enjoying great profits while the agricultural crisis, which is real, is concentrated in the middle of the chain, among smaller farmers, who produce
the food.[36]

One of the leading principles of modern economic history is that the
devices used by the rich and powerful to ensure that they are protected
by the nanny state are not to be available to the poor. Accordingly, the
UNCTAD initiative to stabilize commodity prices was quickly shot
down; the organization itself has been largely marginalized and tamed,
along with others that reflect, to some extent at least, the interests of the
global majority.[27] Reviewing these events, Strange observes that farmers were therefore compelled to turn to crops for which there is a stable
market. Large-scale agribusiness can tolerate fluctuation of commodity
prices, compensating for temporary losses elsewhere. Poor peasants
cannot tell their children: "don't worry, maybe you'll have something to
eat next year." The result, Strange continues, was that drug entrepre-
neurs could easily "find farmers eager to grow coca, cannabis, or
opium," for which there is always a ready market in the rich societies.

Other programs of the US and the global institutions it dominates
magnify these effects. The current Clinton plan for Colombia includes
only token funding for alternative crops, and none at all for areas under
guerrilla control, though FARC leaders have repeatedly expressed their
hope that alternatives will be provided so that peasants will not be compelled to grow coca to survive. "By the end of 1999, the United States
had spent a grand total of $750,000 on alternative development pro-
grams," the Center for International Policy reports, "all of it in heroin
poppy-growing areas far from the southern plains" that are targeted in
the Colombia Plan, which does, however, call for "assistance to civilians
to be displaced by the push into southern Colombia," a section of the plan
that the Center finds "especially disturbing." The Clinton administration
also insists — over the objections of the Colombian government — that
any peace agreement must permit crop destruction measures.[38] Constructive approaches are not barred, but they are someone else's business.

The US will concentrate on military operations — which, incidentally, happen to benefit the high-tech industries that produce military equipment and are engaged in "extensive lobbying" for the Colombia Plan, along with Occidental Petroleum, which has large investments in Colombia, and other corporations.[39]

Furthermore, IMF–World Bank programs demand that countries open their borders to a flood of (heavily subsidized) agricultural products from the rich countries, with the obvious effect of undermining local production. Those displaced are either driven to urban slums (thus lowering wage rates for foreign investors) or instructed to become "rational peasants," producing for the export market and seeking the highest prices — which translates as "coca, cannibis, opium." Having learned their lessons properly, they are rewarded by attack by military gunships while their fields are destroyed by chemical and biological warfare, courtesy of Washington.

Much the same is true throughout the Andean region. The issues broke through briefly to the public eye just as the Colombia Plan was being debated in Washington. On April 8, 2000, the government of Bolivia declared a state of emergency after widespread protests closed down the city of Cochabamba, Bolivia's third largest. The protests were over the privatization of the public water system and the sharp increase in water rates to a level beyond the reach of much of the population. In the background is an economic crisis attributed in part to the neoliberal policies that culminate in the drug war, which has destroyed more than half of the country's coca-leaf production, leaving the "rational peasants" destitute. A week later, farmers blockaded a highway near the capital city of La Paz to protest the eradication of coca leaf, the only mode of survival left to them under the "reforms," as actually implemented.

Reporting on the protests over water prices and the eradication programs, the *Financial Times* observes that "the World Bank and the IMF saw Bolivia as something of a model," one of the great success stories of the "Washington consensus," but the April protests reveal that "the success of eradication programs in Peru and Bolivia has carried a high social cost." The journal quotes a European diplomat in Bolivia who says that "until a couple of weeks ago, Bolivia was regarded as a success story" — by those who "regard" a country while disregarding its people. But now, he continues, "the international community has to recognize that the economic reforms have not really done anything to solve the growing problems of poverty"; they may well have deepened it. The secretary of the Bolivian bishops' conference, which mediated an agreement to end the crisis, described the protest movement as "the result of dire poverty. The demands of the rural population must be listened to if we want lasting peace."[40]

The Cochabamba protests were aimed at the World Bank and the San Francisco/London-based Bechtel corporation, the main financial power behind the transnational conglomerate that bought the public water system amidst serious charges of corruption and give-away, then doubled rates for many poor customers. Under Bank pressure, Bolivia has sold major assets to private (almost always foreign) corporations. The sale of the public water system and rate increases set off months of protest culminating in the demonstration that paralyzed the city. Government policies adhered to World Bank recommendations that "no subsidies should be given to ameliorate the increase in water tariffs in Cochabamba"; all users, including the very poor, must pay full costs. Using the internet, activists in Bolivia called for international protests, which had a significant impact, presumably amplified by the Washington protests over World Bank–IMF policies then underway. Bechtel backed off, and the government rescinded the sale.[41] But a long and difficult struggle lies ahead.

As martial law was declared in Bolivia, a report from southern Colombia described the spreading fears that fumigation planes were coming to "drop their poison on the coca fields, which would also kill the farmers' subsistence crops, cause massive social disruption, and stir up the ever-present threat of violence." The pervasive fear and anger reflect "the level of dread and confusion in this part of Colombia."[42]

Another question lurks not too far in the background. Just what right does the US have to carry out military operations and chemical-biological warfare in other countries to destroy a crop it doesn't like? We can put aside the cynical response that the governments requested this "assistance"; or else. We therefore must ask whether others have the same extraterritorial right to violence and destruction that the US demands.

The number of Colombians who die from US-produced lethal drugs exceeds the number of North Americans who die from cocaine, and is far greater relative to population. In East and Southeast Asia, US-produced lethal drugs contribute to millions of deaths. These countries are compelled not only to accept the products but also advertising for them, under threat of trade sanctions. The effects of "aggressive marketing and advertising by American firms is, in a good measure, responsible for ... a sizeable increase in smoking rates for women and youth in Asian countries where doors were forced open by threat of severe US trade sanctions," public health researchers conclude.[43] The Colombian cartels, in contrast, are not permitted to run huge advertising campaigns in which a Joe Camel counterpart extols the wonders of cocaine.

Thanks to the US passion for "free trade" and "freedom of speech" for advertisers of murderous substances, global cigarette exports have expanded sharply, with a fivefold increase from 1975 to 1996,[44] a dramatic illustration of some of the welfare outcomes of the fanatic political theology that elevates "trade" to the highest rank among human values — "trade" in quotes, because of the highly ideological construction of the concept.

We are therefore entitled, indeed, morally obligated, to ask whether Colombia, Thailand, China, and other targets of US trade policies and aggressive promotion of lethal exports have the right to conduct military, chemical, and biological warfare in North Carolina. And if not, why not?

We might also ask why there are no Delta Force raids on US banks and chemical corporations, though it is no secret that they too are engaged in the narcotrafficking business. We might ask further why the Pentagon is not gearing up to attack Canada, now displacing Colombia and Mexico as a supplier of marijuana; high-potency varieties have become British Columbia's most valuable agricultural product and one of the most important sectors of the economy (in Quebec and Manitoba as well), with a tenfold increase in the past two years. Or to attack the United States, a major producer of marijuana with production rapidly expanding, including hydroponic groweries, and long the center of manufacture of high-tech illicit drugs (ATS, amphetamine-type stimulants), the fastest-growing sector of drug abuse, with 30 million users worldwide, probably surpassing heroin and cocaine.[45]

There is no need to review in detail the lethal effects of US drugs. The Supreme Court recently concluded that it has been "amply demonstrated" that tobacco use is "perhaps the single most significant threat to public health in the United States," responsible for more than 400,000 deaths a year, more than AIDS, car accidents, alcohol, homicides, illegal drugs, suicides, and fires combined; the Court virtually called on Congress to legislate controls. As use of this lethal substance has declined in the US, and producers have been compelled to pay substantial indemnities to victims, they have shifted to markets abroad, another standard practice. The death toll is incalculable. Oxford University epidemiologist Richard Peto estimated that in China alone, among children under 20 today, 50 million will die of cigarette-related diseases, a substantial number because of highly selective US "free trade" doctrine.[46]

In comparison to the 400,000 deaths caused by tobacco every year in the United States, drug-related deaths reached a record 16,000 in 1997. Furthermore, only 4 out of 10 addicts who needed treatment received it, according to a White House report.[47] These facts raise further questions about the motives for the drug war. The seriousness of concern over use of drugs was illustrated again when a House Committee was considering the Clinton Colombia Plan. It rejected an amendment proposed by California Democrat Nancy Pelosi calling for funding of drug demand-reduction services. It is well known that treatment and prevention are far more effective than forceful measures. A widely cited Rand Corporation study sponsored by the US Army and Office of National Drug Control Policy found that funds spent on domestic drug treatment were 23 times as effective as "source country control" (Clinton's Colombia Plan), 11 times as effective as interdiction, and 7 times as effective as domestic law enforcement.[48]

But the inexpensive and effective path will not be followed. Rather, the "drug war" is crafted to target poor peasants abroad and poor people at home; by the use of force, not constructive measures to alleviate the problems that allegedly motivate it, at a fraction of the cost.

While Clinton's Colombia Plan was being formulated, senior administration officials discussed a proposal by the Office of Management and Budget to take $100 million from the $1.3 billion then planned for Colombia, to be used for treatment for US addicts. There was near-unanimous opposition, particularly from "drug czar" General Barry McCaffrey, and the proposal was dropped. In contrast, when Richard Nixon — in many respects the last liberal president — declared a drug war in 1971, two-thirds of the funding went to treatment, which reached record numbers of addicts; there was a sharp drop in drug-related arrests and the number of federal prison inmates. Since 1980, however, "the war on drugs has shifted to punishing offenders, border surveillance, and fighting production at the source countries."[49] One consequence is an enormous increase in drug-related (often victimless) crimes and an explosion in the prison population, reaching levels far beyond that in any industrial country and possibly a world record, with no detectable effect on availability or price of drugs.

Such observations, hardly obscure, raise the question of what the drug war is all about. It is recognized widely that it fails to achieve its stated ends, and the failed methods are then pursued more vigorously, while effective ways to reach the stated goals are rejected. It is therefore only reasonable to conclude that the "drug war," cast in the harshly puni-tive form implemented in the past 20 years, is *achieving* its goals, not failing. What are these goals? A plausible answer is implicit in a com-ment by Senator Daniel Patrick Moynihan, one of the few senators to pay close attention to social statistics, as the latest phase of the "drug war" was declared. By adopting these measures, he observed, "we are choosing to have an intense crime problem concentrated among minori-ties." Criminologist Michael Tonry concludes that "the war's planners knew exactly what they were doing." What they were doing is, first, get-ting rid of the "superfluous population," the "disposable people" — *"desechables,"* as they are called in Colombia, where they are elimi-nated by "social cleansing"; and second, frightening everyone else, not an unimportant task in a period when a domestic form of "structural ad-justment" is being imposed, with significant costs for the majority of the population.[50]

"While the War on Drugs only occasionally serves and more often degrades public health and safety," a well-informed and insightful review concludes, "it regularly serves the interests of private wealth: interests re-vealed by the pattern of winners and losers, targets and non-targets, well-funded and underfunded," in accord with "the main interests of US foreign and domestic policy generally" and the private sector that "has overriding influence on policy."[51]

One may debate the motivations, but the consequences in the US and abroad seem reasonably clear.

6

Cuba and the US Government
David vs. Goliath

Cuba and the United States have quite a curious — in fact, unique — status in international relations. There is no similar case of such a sustained assault by one power against another — in this case the greatest superpower against a poor, Third World country — for 40 years of terror and economic warfare.

In fact, the fanaticism of this attack goes back a long, long time. From the first days of the American Revolution the eyes of the founding fathers were on Cuba. They were quite open about it. It was John Quincy Adams, when he was secretary of state, who said our taking Cuba is "of transcendent importance" to the political and commercial future of the United States. Others said that the future of the world depended on our taking Cuba. It was a matter "of transcendent importance" from the beginning of US history, and it remains so. The need to possess Cuba is the oldest issue in US foreign policy.

The US sanctions against Cuba are the harshest in the world, much harsher than the sanctions against Iraq, for example. There was a small item in the *New York Times* recently that said that Congress is passing legislation to allow US exporters to send food and medicine to Cuba. It explained that this was at the urging of US farmers. "Farmers" is a euphemism that means "US agribusiness" — it sounds better when you call them "farmers." And it's true that US agribusiness wants to get back into this market. The article didn't point out that the restriction against the sale and export of food and medicines is in gross violation of international humanitarian law. It's been condemned by almost every relevant body. Even the normally quite compliant Organization of American

States, which rarely stands up against the boss, did condemn this as illegal and unacceptable (see Chapter 12).

US policy towards Cuba is unique in a variety of respects, first of all because of the sustained attacks, and secondly because the US is totally isolated in the world — in fact, 100 percent isolated, because the one state that reflexively has to vote with the United States at the UN, Israel, also openly violates the embargo, contrary to its vote.

The United States government is also isolated from its own population. According to the most recent poll I've seen, about two-thirds of the population in the United States is opposed to the embargo. They don't take polls in the business world, but there's pretty strong evidence that major sectors of the business world, major corporations, are strongly opposed to the embargo. So the isolation of the US government is another unusual element. The US government is isolated from its own population, from the major decisionmakers in this society, which largely control the government, and from international opinion, but is still fanatically committed to this policy, which goes right back to the roots of the American republic.

Cuba has brought out real hysteria among planners. This was particularly striking during the Kennedy years. The internal records from the Kennedy administration, many of which are available now, describe an atmosphere of what was called "savagery" and "fanaticism" over the failure of the US to reconquer Cuba. Kennedy's own public statements were wild enough. He said publicly that the United States would be swept away in the debris of history unless it reincorporated Cuba under its control.

In 1997 at the World Trade Organization (WTO) when the European Union brought charges against the United States for blatant, flagrant violation of WTO rules in the embargo, the US rejected its jurisdiction, which is not surprising, because it rejects the jurisdiction of international bodies generally. But the reasons were interesting. It rejected its jurisdiction on the grounds of a national security reservation. The national security of the United States was threatened by the existence of Cuba, and therefore the US had to reject WTO jurisdiction. Actually, the US did not make that position official, because it would have subjected itself to international ridicule, but that was the position, and it was publicly stated, repeatedly. It's a national security issue; we therefore cannot consider WTO jurisdiction.

You'll be pleased to know that the Pentagon recently downgraded the threat of Cuban conquest of the United States. It's still there, but it's not as serious as it was. The reason, they explained, is the deterioration of the awesome Cuban military forces after the end of the Cold War, when the Soviet Union stopped supplying them. So we can rest a little bit easier; we don't have to hide under tables the way we were taught to do in first grade. This elicited no ridicule when it was publicly announced, at least here. I'm sure it did elsewhere; you might recall the response of the Mexican ambassador when John F. Kennedy was trying to organize collective security in defense against Cuba back in the early '60s in Mexico: the ambassador said he would regretfully have to decline because if he were to tell Mexicans that Cuba was a threat to their national security, 40 million Mexicans would die laughing.

This hysteria and fanaticism is indeed unusual and interesting, and it deserves inquiry and thought. Where does it come from? The historical depth partly explains it, but there's more to it than that in the current world. A good framework within which to think of it is what has now become the leading thesis in intellectual discourse, in serious journals especially. It's what's called the "new humanism," which was proclaimed by Clinton and Blair and various acolytes with great awe and solemnity. According to this thesis, which you read over and over, we're entering a glorious new era, a new millennium. It actually began 10 years ago when the two enlightened countries, as they call themselves, were freed from the shackles of the Cold War and were therefore able to rededicate themselves with full vigor to their historic mission of bringing justice and freedom to the suffering people of the world and protecting human rights everywhere, by force if necessary — something they were prevented from doing during the Cold War interruption.

That renewal of the saintly mission is quite explicit; it's not left to the imagination. Clinton gave a major speech at the Norfolk Air Station on April 1, 1999, explaining why we have to bomb everybody in sight in the Balkans. He was introduced by the secretary of defense, William Cohen, who opened his remarks by reminding the audience of some of the dramatic words that had opened the last century. He cited Theodore Roosevelt, later to be president, who said that "unless you're willing to fight for great ideals, those ideals will vanish." And just as Theodore Roosevelt opened the century with those stirring words, William Clinton, his successor, was closing the century with the same stand.

That was an interesting introduction for anyone who had taken a course in American history, that is, a real course. Theodore Roosevelt, as they would have learned, was one of the most extraordinary racist, raving lunatics of contemporary history. He was greatly admired by Hitler, and for good reason. His writings are shocking to read. He won his fame through participation in the US invasion of Cuba. By 1898 Cuba had essentially liberated itself from Spain after a long struggle, but the US wasn't having any of that, so it invaded to prevent the independence struggle from succeeding. Cuba was quickly turned into what two Harvard professors, the editors of the recent *Kennedy Tapes,* call "a virtual colony" of the United States, as it remained up until 1959. It's an accurate description. Cuba was turned into a "virtual colony" after the invasion, which was described as a humanitarian intervention, incidentally.

At that time, too, the United States was quite isolated. The United States government was isolated, of course, from the Cuban people, but it was also isolated from the American population, who were foolish enough to believe the propaganda and were overwhelmingly in favor of *Cuba libre*, not understanding that that was the last thing in the minds of their leaders — or, from another point of view, the first thing in their minds, because they had to prevent it.

The noble ideals that Roosevelt was fighting for were in fact those, in part: to prevent independence through humanitarian intervention. However, at the time he actually spoke, in 1901 or so, the values that we had to uphold by force were being demonstrated far more dramatically elsewhere than in Cuba, namely in the conquest of the Philippines. That was one of the most murderous colonial wars in history, in which hundreds of thousands of Filipinos were slaughtered. The press recognized that it was a massive slaughter, but advised that we must continue to kill "the natives in English fashion," until they come to "respect our arms" and ultimately to respect our good intentions. This was also a so-called humanitarian intervention.

Fruits of Conquest

There were a couple of problems. President McKinley did say that we can't claim at this point to have the consent of the Filipinos, but that's unimportant because we have the consent of our consciences in performing this great act of humanity, and after all, that's what counts. A small number of people opposed the war pretty strongly — Mark Twain for example, who was silenced for 90 years, and whose anti-imperialist essays just came out in 1992. But McKinley pointed out that "it is not a good time for the liberator to submit important questions concerning liberty and government to the liberated while they are engaged in shooting down their rescuers." So we'll wait until they stop shooting down their rescuers, and then we'll explain to them the issues of liberty. Those were the values that were being upheld, with hundreds of thousands of corpses and tremendous destruction, in the early part of the century, and those are the values we are now told we have to fight for and uphold, as the current inheritor of Theodore Roosevelt's values proclaims.

It takes a good deal of faith in the US doctrinal system to pronounce those words and expect people not to be outraged, and apparently that faith is merited. No outrage was recorded, to my knowledge, except in the usual marginal circles. That period was a turning point in modern history, certainly in US history, hence in world history. Up until that time, since the Revolution, the United States had been engaged in its primary task, namely, as one leading diplomatic historian put it in 1969, the task of "felling trees and Indians and of rounding out their natural boundaries." One of the salutary effects of the activism of the 1960s is that not only a leading historian but even a jingoist lunatic could not pronounce those words today. Nobody would write that now. They might think it, but they would know not to say it.

So, after "felling trees and Indians and rounding out [our] natural boundaries," it was necessary to turn to new worlds to conquer. In 1888 Secretary of State James Blaine announced the next conquests. He said, there are three places of value enough to be taken quickly: Hawaii, Cuba, and Puerto Rico. A few years later, the US minister in Hawaii informed Washington that "the Hawaiian pear is now fully ripe," ready to be plucked, and the US plucked it, taking Hawaii away from its people by a combination of overwhelming force and guile. That was one. The minister was in fact repeating the words of John Quincy Adams 70 years earlier, who had described Cuba as not yet a "ripe fruit," but had said it will become a ripe fruit, and when it does become a ripe fruit it will fall into our hands "by the laws of political gravitation." That was around 1820.

The problem throughout the 19th century was the British deterrent. In the 1960s and '70s and '80s it was the Russian deterrent. But the great enemy in the 19th century, the enemy that had to be brought to its feet, as was pointed out over and over, was Britain. That's why Canada and Cuba are still a different color on the map. And that deterrent set limits on the liberating zeal of the revolutionaries and their inheritors. But Adams pointed out quite correctly, as did Thomas Jefferson and others, that over time the balance of forces would change, the British deterrent would not be that effective, and the US would be able to take over Cuba, as it must do because of its transcendent importance to the United States, by the laws of political gravitation, meaning, by force. That happened in 1898. The United States invaded Cuba to prevent the ultimate threat, namely its liberation from Spain. Puerto Rico was taken over in the same year, and the Philippines came along as an extra bonus. It hadn't been contemplated, but it turned out to be a ripe fruit, too, fertilized by plenty of corpses.

These events were all related in planning. Actually the biggest fruit of all by a huge order was China. For 2,000 years China had been one of the most important countries in the world, a leading commercial and industrial power, but by the 19th century that had changed. By the end of the century the European powers and Japan were busy carving China up, and the United States wanted to get into the act as a rising power. The China trade was a great myth from the early days of New England: the New England merchants were going to make money from the China trade. In order to exploit the China trade and take our proper role in carving up China, it was necessary to turn the Caribbean and the Pacific into "American lakes," as planners put it. That meant taking Cuba, controlling the Caribbean, stealing what was called Panama from Colombia (another one of Theodore Roosevelt's achievements), building the canal, taking over Hawaii, taking over the Philippines as another base for trade with China, and in fact effectively turning those two seas, the Caribbean and the Pacific, into American lakes, as they remain today.

Every one of these 1898 actions and what followed was connected in some fashion or another, usually quite explicitly, to this long-term objective. This includes the so-called Theodore Roosevelt Corollary to the Monroe Doctrine, which formally established the US right to rule the Caribbean. The repeated invasions of Nicaragua, Woodrow Wilson's very bloody invasions of the Dominican Republic and Haiti — particularly ugly in Haiti because it was also suffused by extreme racism (Haiti will never recover from that and in fact may not be habitable in a couple of decades) — and many other actions in that region were all part of the new humanism, which we're now reviving.

Probably the major achievement was in Venezuela, where in 1920 Woodrow Wilson succeeded in kicking out the British enemy, at that time weakened by the First World War. Venezuela was extremely important. The world was shifting to an oil-based economy at the time. North America, mainly the US, was by far the major producer of oil, and remained so until about 1970, but Venezuela was an important oil resource, one of the biggest in the world — in fact, the biggest single exporter until 1970, and still the biggest exporter to the United States. So kicking the British out of there was very important. Venezuela also had other resources, such as iron, and US corporations enriched themselves in Venezuela for decades — and still do — while the US supported a series of murderous dictators to keep the people in line.

The "Kennedy tapes," the secret tapes of the Cuban missile crisis, are not all that revealing since almost everything in there had already come out in one way or another, but they do reveal a few new things. One of the new things is an explanation of one of the reasons the Kennedy brothers, Robert and John F., were concerned about missiles in Cuba. They were concerned that they might be a deterrent to a US invasion of Venezuela, which they thought might be necessary because the situation there was getting out of hand. Missiles in Cuba might deter an invasion. Noting that, John F. Kennedy said that the Bay of Pigs was right. We're going to have to make sure we win; we can't face any such deterrent to our benevolence in the region. After the missile crisis, contrary to what's often said, the US made no pledge not to invade Cuba. It stepped up the terrorism, and of course the embargo was already in place and imposed more harshly, and so matters have essentially remained.

The Castro Threat

As I mentioned, Cuba was a virtual colony of the United States until January 1959; it didn't take long before the wheels started turning again. By mid-1959 — we now have a lot of declassified records from that period, so the picture's pretty complete — the Eisenhower administration had determined informally to reconquer Cuba. By October 1959 planes based in Florida were already bombing Cuba. The US claimed not to be able to do anything about it, and has remained "helpless" throughout the most recent acts of terrorism, which are traceable to CIA-trained operatives, as usual.

In March 1960 the Eisenhower administration secretly made a formal decision to conquer Cuba, but with a proviso: it had to be done in such a way that the US hand would not be evident. The reason for that was because they knew it would blow up Latin America if it were obvious that the US had retaken Cuba. Furthermore, they had polls indicating that in Cuba itself there was a high level of optimism and strong support for the revolution; there would obviously be plenty of resistance. They had to overthrow the government, but in such a way that the US hand would not be evident.

Shortly after that, the Kennedy administration came in. They were very much oriented towards Latin America; just before taking office Kennedy had established a Latin American mission to review the affairs of the continent. It was headed by historian Arthur Schlesinger. His report is now declassified. He informed President Kennedy of the results of the mission with regard to Cuba. The problem in Cuba, he said, is "the spread of the Castro idea of taking matters into one's own hands." He said, that is an idea that has a great deal of appeal throughout Latin America, where "the distribution of land and other forms of national wealth greatly favors the propertied classes ... [and] the poor and under-privileged, stimulated by the example of the Cuban revolution, are now demanding opportunities for a decent living."[1] That's the threat of Castro. That's correct. In fact, if you read through the record of internal planning over the years, that has always been the threat. The Cold War is a public pretext. Take a look at the record; in case after case, it's exactly this. Cuba is what was called a "virus" that might infect others who might be stimulated by "the Castro idea of taking matters into [their] own hands" and believing that they too might have a decent living.

It's not that Russia wasn't mentioned. Russia is mentioned in the Schlesinger report. He says, in the background, Russia is offering itself as "the model for achieving modernization in a single generation," and is offering aid and development loans. So there was a Russian threat. We are instructed vigorously that when we inspect the new humanism, we're not supposed to look at those musty old stories about the Cold War, when we were blocked by the Russians from doing wonderful things. It's very important not to look, because the institutions have remained unchanged, the planning remains unchanged, the decisions are unchanged, and the policies are unchanged. It's far better to ensure that people don't know about them.

The Kennedy administration took over, and so matters continued up until the end of the Cold War. It's not that nothing changed at the end of the Cold War; it did. The main thing that changed was that there no longer was a Soviet deterrent. That meant that the US was much more free than before, along with its loyal attack dog, the UK. So the US and UK are now much more free to use force than they were when there was a deterrent. That was recognized right away. But new pretexts are needed. You can no longer say that everything we do is against the Russians.

The Berlin Wall fell in November 1989. That ended the Cold War as far as any sane person was concerned. In October 1989, a month before, the Bush administration had released a secret national security directive, now public, in which it called for support for our great friend Saddam Hussein and other comparable figures in the Middle East in defense against the Russians. That was October 1989. In March 1990 — that's four months after the fall of the Berlin Wall — the White House had to make its annual presentation to Congress calling for a huge military budget, which was the same as in all earlier years, except for the pretexts. Now it wasn't because the Russians are coming, because obviously the Russians aren't coming, it was because of what they called the "technological sophistication" of Third World powers. With regard to the Middle East, instructions had been changed from October — then, it was: "the Russians are coming." In March, it was: our intervention forces have to be aimed at the Middle East as before, where the threat to our interests "could not be laid at the Kremlin's door," contrary to the lies of the

last 40 years. Case by case, the pretext changed, the policies remained —
but were now without restraints.

That was immediately obvious in Latin America. A month after the
fall of the Berlin Wall the US invaded Panama, killing a couple of hundred or maybe a couple of thousand people, destroying poor neighbor-
hoods, reinstating a regime of bankers and narcotraffickers — drug
peddling and money laundering shot way up, as congressional research
bureaus soon advised — and so on. That's normal, a footnote to history,
but there were two differences: one difference is that the pretexts were
different. This was the first intervention since the beginning of the Cold
War that was not undertaken to defend ourselves from the Russians.
This time, it was to defend ourselves from Hispanic narcotraffickers.
Secondly, the US recognized right away that it was much freer to invade
without any concern that somebody, the Russians, might react somewhere in the world, as former Undersecretary of State Abrams happily
pointed out.

The same was true with regard to the Third World generally. The
Third World could now be disregarded. There's no more room for
non-alignment. So forget about the Third World and their interests; you
don't have to make a pretense of concern for them. That's been very evident in policy since.

With regard to Cuba, it's about the same. Right after the fall of the
Soviet Union, the embargo against Cuba became far harsher, under a liberal initiative, incidentally: it was a Torricelli-Clinton initiative. And the
pretexts were now different. Before, it was that the Cubans were a tenta-
cle of the Soviet beast about to strangle us; now it was suddenly our love
of democracy that made us oppose Cuba.

The US does support a certain kind of democracy. The kind of democracy it supports was described rather frankly by a leading scholar
who dealt with the democratic initiatives of the Reagan administration in
the 1980s and who writes from an insider's point of view because he was
in the State Department working on "democracy enhancement" projects:
Thomas Carothers. He points out that though the Reagan administration,
which he thinks was very sincere, undermined democracy everywhere,
it nevertheless was interested in a certain kind of democracy — what he
calls "top-down" forms of democracy that leave "traditional structures

of power" in place, namely those with which the US has long had good relations. As long as democracy has that form, it's no problem.

The real problem of Cuba remains what it has always been. It remains the threat of "the Castro idea of taking matters into [your] own hands," which continues to be a stimulus to poor and underprivileged people who can't get it driven into their heads that they have no right to seek opportunities for a decent living. And Cuba, unfortunately, keeps making that clear, for example, by sending doctors all over the world at a rate way beyond any other country despite its current straits, which are severe, and by maintaining, unimaginably, a health system that is a deep embarrassment to the United States. Because of concerns such as these, and because of the fanaticism that goes way back in American history, the US government, for the moment, at least, is continuing the hysterical attack, and will do so until it is deterred.

And though foreign deterrents, which weren't that effective, don't exist anymore, the ultimate deterrent is where it always was, right at home. Two-thirds of the population oppose the embargo even without any discussion. Imagine what would happen if the issues were discussed in a serious and honest way — that leaves enormous opportunities for that deterrent to be exercised.

7

Putting on the Pressure
Latin America

At the end of the Second World War the US was creating an international order in which there were to be no regional systems that the US couldn't penetrate and control, except for one, which was going to be separated from the world system, strengthened, and centralized under our control — namely, the western hemisphere, or, "our little region over here," as it was called by Secretary of War Henry Stimson.

So, what about "our little region over here"? It's been on the front pages recently, with the release of the report by the UN commission on war crimes and atrocities in Guatemala. The report attributed virtually all of the atrocities — and they are monstrous, up to genocide — to the government. This is the ruling government system that was installed by the United States by a military coup in 1954; it has been maintained very strongly by the United States ever since, right through the worst atrocities, with increasing enthusiasm. In fact, the support has been bipartisan.

Exercising Pressure

Guatemala's experiment with democracy, its first and only experiment, which went on for 10 years, was overthrown by the Eisenhower administration in 1954, opening a period of brutal repression and tortures supported strongly by the Kennedy administration, which essentially constructed the national security doctrine, not just for Guatemala but for the whole hemisphere. That led to a plague of repression over the hemisphere, with direct US involvement strongly supported by Johnson as atrocities mounted in the late '60s, and so it continued. The atrocities peaked in the early 1980s under the Reagan administration, which pub-

93

licly and openly — and, in fact, rather passionately — supported the killers now identified by the UN commission. This was known at the time
perfectly well. Congress compelled the administration to state repeatedly that the human rights condition was improving not only in Guatemala but in El Salvador and Honduras so that the US could continue to
support the regimes. Congress knew they were hearing lies; that is now
recognized. The UN commission gives a grim report on Guatemala;
there is an equally grim one to be given on El Salvador.

There's more. In presenting the report, the chair of the commission
emphasized that the US government and private companies "exercised
pressure to maintain the country's archaic and unjust socioeconomic
structure."[1] The chair of the commission emphasized that because it's at
the core of the issue wherever there are atrocities and terror. These reflect the socioeconomic structure, which is one of brutal repression for a
large majority of the population. When people try to gain and protect
some rights, an iron fist comes down, with the hemispheric superpower
backing it. That's the story of "our little region over here."

Washington protested that this part of the report was unfair. It was,
in a sense — it was far too polite and kind. It was not a mandate of the
commission to look into this issue, so they just stressed it, but left it
unanalyzed.

On the same day as the report was announced, there was another announcement. The Phillips-Van Heusen Corporation closed its factory in
Guatemala — not a random factory; it closed the only unionized factory
among 200 export-oriented apparel factories in Guatemala.[2] This union
victory was finally won after a six-year struggle with plenty of support
here from solidarity groups and boycotts. They finally got a union, so the
factory was closed. The president of the US Union of Needletrades, Industrial, and Textile Employees said accurately that Philips-Van Heusen
is sending a message to workers in Guatemala: "if you fight for justice, if you
fight for a union, we will not honor your contract. We will walk away."

That's a message to workers in Guatemala and, in fact, everywhere.
It is a message that reinforces the archaic and unjust socioeconomic
structure that is at the core of the generations of terror and violence, as
the UN commission reported on the same day. So the US government
and private companies continue to exercise pressure to maintain that archaic and unjust socioeconomic structure, which, incidentally, is in vio-

lation of the Universal Declaration of Human Rights. Article 23 guarantees the right to form unions in principle, but not in fact. "Exercise pressure" is an understatement. The term "exercise pressure" refers to years and years of massacres and slaughters and torture and mutilation and, in fact, genocidal attacks; it's describing 45 years of state terror. Again, it was not within the mandate of the commission to investigate how the maintenance of the archaic socioeconomic structure leads to terror.

One thing that ought to have been discussed — and that would have been discussed by any journalists or commentators who wanted to meet minimal standards of honesty — is why it all happened. Why did the United States overthrow the one democratic capitalist government in Guatemala, and why has it maintained support for state terror ever since? It's not enough to just say it was a mistake due to Cold War excesses. There were reasons, and it's not hard to find them.

There's a rich documentary record of internal US planning documents. In the early 1950s there was a lot of talk about the Russians and communism. Here's what was said internally. In 1952 US intelligence warned of "Communist influence ... based on militant advocacy of social reforms and nationalistic policies identified with the Guatemalan revolution of 1944," which initiated the 10-year democratic interlude that was terminated by the US coup. "The radical and nationalist policies" of this democratic capitalist government, including the "persecution of foreign economic interests, especially the United Fruit Company," had gained "the support or acquiescence of almost all Guatemalans." The government was creating "mass support for the present regime" by labor organization and agrarian reform, and proceeding "to mobilize the hitherto politically inert peasantry" while undermining the power of large landholders. Furthermore, "Guatemalan official propaganda, with its emphasis on conflict between democracy and dictatorship and between national independence and 'economic imperialism,' is a disturbing factor in the Caribbean area."[3] The background is US support for dictatorships and its natural fear of independent democratic tendencies.

Also disturbing was Guatemalan support for the democratic elements of other Caribbean countries and their struggles against dictatorships. They had in mind the democratic revolution that was taking place in Costa Rica at the time, which was getting support, the US alleged, from the terrible government in Guatemala. US intelligence reported further that the 1944 democratic revolution had aroused "a strong national movement to free Guatemala from the military dictatorship, social backwardness, and 'economic colonialism,' which had been the pattern of the past," and it "inspired the loyalty and conformed to the self-interest of most politically conscious Guatemalans." Social and economic programs of the elected government met the aspirations of labor and the peasantry; hence "neither the landholders nor the [United] Fruit Company can expect any sympathy in Guatemalan public opinion."[4] That's the background for the military coup in 1954.

Guatemala was becoming what's called a "virus" which might infect others. It was threatening what's called "stability." "Stability" was defined by the US embassy as follows: Guatemala has become an increasing threat to the stability of Honduras and El Salvador. Its

> agrarian reform is a powerful propaganda weapon; its broad social program of aiding the workers and peasants in a victorious struggle against the upper classes and large foreign enterprises has a strong appeal to the populations of Central American neighbors where similar conditions prevail.[5]

And that's unacceptable. That's undermining stability. The US coup restored "stability," restored the traditional social order, by violence. It's been maintained by extreme violence. The coup was undertaken and the terrorist regimes have been maintained for exactly the reasons just stated very clearly: to contain the threat of democracy and to roll back the social programs that were undermining stability because of their strong appeal to the population, not only in Guatemala, but in other countries of the region.

If you read the newspapers where the UN Commission study is reported, there's an explanation. It says, yes, we made a mistake. Cold War excesses, you know. We won't make that mistake again. There are several problems with that. The "mistake" was not a mistake. It was planned. It was planned and explained and justified on rational grounds, namely those I've just excerpted. Furthermore, since the grounds were rational, the same so-called mistake was made consistently in different places in different times with the same internal justifications. Furthermore, the Cold War had virtually nothing to do with it, as this account illustrates.

It's pretty obvious just by looking at the relations of power in "our little region over here" that the Cold War was scarcely relevant. There was a Cold War connection, however. As the US was preparing to kill the virus of independent capitalist democracy, the US cut off military aid to Guatemala, and it threatened to attack. The purpose was to compel Guatemala to turn to other sources for support, for military aid to protect it from the impending US attack. Other countries were perfectly willing to give aid, but the US prevented European countries from giving any, so Guatemala was compelled to turn to the Soviet bloc, exactly as the US wanted.

At that point the US embassy in Guatemala advised that the US could now take steps to bar the "movement of arms and agents to Guatemala," stopping ships in international waters — which is, of course, illegal — "to such an extent that it would disrupt Guatemala's economy." That was the next step, and its purpose was to "encourage the Army or some other non-Communist element to seize power" — that is, to encourage a military coup that would overthrow and destroy the democratic virus. Or, alternatively, "the Communists will exploit the situation to extend their control," which would "justify the American community — or if they won't go along, the US [alone] — to take strong measures."[6]

So, the logic was, we compel Guatemala to defend itself from our threatened attack, thereby creating a threat to our security, which we exploit by destroying the Guatemalan economy so as to provoke a military coup or an actual communist takeover, which will then justify our violent response in self-defense. That's the real meaning of self-defense and of the Cold War, spelled out with brutal clarity, a lesson taught over and over again.

The Tombstone of Debt

Let's move on to other examples of maintaining socioeconomic supremacy in "our little region over here." Recently in Tegucigalpa, the capital of Honduras, there was a meeting of 17 Latin American countries on the debt. The archbishop of Tegucigalpa, president of the Latin American Conference of Bishops, speaking of the debt, said that it "is not one more problem for us to face — it is *the* problem. The foreign debt is like a tombstone."[7] *Latinamerica Press,* which comes from Peruvian liberation theology circles, reported what I'm now quoting, but it ought to be on the front pages here. It's a problem that we're creating and we're maintaining. But the conference was not even reported.

Then come the data. These are World Bank figures. The data roughly are the following: in the 1970s the Latin American debt was about $60 billion. By 1980 it had reached $200 billion. That's the result of very explicit World Bank and International Monetary Fund (IMF) policies that were urging banks to make huge loans and urging countries to accept those loans. Their economic theories ensured everyone that that was going to work great.

Those recommendations continued virtually right up to the day on which Mexico defaulted and the Latin American system collapsed. Up till then there was strong advice from the World Bank and the IMF to continue pouring in the loans. By 1990 the debt had gone from $200 billion to about $433 billion; by the end of 1999 it was expected to be about $700 billion. Meanwhile, from 1982 to 1996, about $740 billion has been sent back to the Northern banks and the international financial institutions in debt payment. In 1999, debt service alone amounted to about $120 billion. Just take a look at these numbers. It's clear that the debt will never be paid. It's impossible to pay. It's getting bigger and bigger, it's more and more of a capital drain from the poor to the rich, and that will continue and escalate without any change.[8]

I'll give a final example, from the *Wall Street Journal,* a very enlightening front-page article.[9] It's about Mexico since the North American Free Trade Agreement (NAFTA). NAFTA came along, and then the 1994 debacle occurred, when the Mexican economy went into a tailspin. The article starts out conventionally, reporting that since NAFTA, Mexico has been an economic miracle. It "enjoys a stellar reputation." It's a model that should be followed by other countries. The reason is that Mexico is following all the rules, doing just what the IMF tells it — meaning just what the US tells it, because the US decides what the IMF tells it. It's following all the rules, the macroeconomic statistics look great, foreign investors and wealthy Mexicans are prospering, everything is just perfect.

But. To the credit of the *Wall Street Journal,* it points out that there's a "but." Mexico has "a stellar reputation," and it's an economic miracle, but the population is being devastated. There's been a 40 percent drop in purchasing power since 1994. The poverty rate is going up and is in fact rising fast. The economic miracle wiped out, they say, a generation of progress; most Mexicans are poorer than their parents. Other sources reveal that agriculture is being wiped out by US-subsidized agricultural imports, manufacturing jobs have actually declined, manufacturing wages have declined about 20 percent, general wages even more.[10] In fact, NAFTA is a remarkable success: it's the first trade agreement in history that's succeeded in harming the populations of all three countries involved. That's quite an achievement.

Furthermore, this was predictable — and predicted. For example, it was predicted by the Office of Technology Assessment, Congress's own research bureau, which did an analysis of NAFTA and predicted that if it went through by the White House plan, it would in fact harm the people of all three countries. They suggested alternatives that might not have had that effect. The US labor movement said exactly the same thing. None of this appeared in discussions in the United States because it was blacked out of the free press. Congressional analysis — its own research bureau — and the position of the labor movement were not permitted expression. Now, the results are there, and you can see them, but we're not supposed to connect these things up in our heads. Unless, of course, we choose to.

The economic miracle devastated the population, and, to their credit, the *Wall Street Journal* points this out. They then make the following interesting and enlightening comment: they say Brazil now faces the same problems that Mexico did back in 1994, but Mexico enjoyed one "benefit" that Brazil lacks. That benefit is that Mexico is a dictatorship. Therefore, it can force the poor to accept the costs of economic rectitude. But Brazil lacks that "benefit." The leadership in Brazil may be incapable of transferring the pain and costs of following the rules to the poor while the rich and foreign investors benefit. That is correct. The problem is that Brazil may be too democratic, or maybe just too chaotic and uncontrolled, to be able to force the transfer of costs to the poor population while the rich in Mexico and foreign investors get their rights, and are rewarded properly.

That's an old problem, one that appears over and over again: namely, the institution of the socioeconomic structures from which terror and repression result. The problem was faced in a Latin American strategy workshop at the Pentagon in 1990, which was concerned with US relations with Mexico. This was a high-level meeting, part of the pre-NAFTA planning, and they concluded at the workshop that relations between the US and the Mexican dictatorship were just fine, but there was one potential problem: "a 'democracy opening' in Mexico could test the special relationship by bringing into office a government more interested in challenging the US on economic and nationalist grounds."[11] Something like Guatemala in 1950. There might be a democracy opening, and that's a problem, so we have to do something about it. NAFTA is what they did about it. The point of NAFTA was to lock in the so-called reforms by treaty, so that even if there is a democracy opening — that hated danger — they won't be able to do much about it, because they're locked into these arrangements. The problem now is to see whether Brazil, which lacks the benefit of dictatorship, will be able to follow the same programs.

8

Jubilee 2000

The Jubilee 2000 call for debt cancellation is welcome and merits support, but is open to some qualifications. The debt does not go away. Someone pays, and the historical record generally confirms what a rational look at the structure of power would suggest: risks tend to be socialized, just as costs commonly are, in the system mislabelled "free market capitalism."

A complementary approach might invoke the old-fashioned capitalist idea that those who borrow are responsible for repayment, and those who lend take the risk. The money was not borrowed by campesinos, assembly plant workers, or slum-dwellers. The mass of the population gained little from the borrowing, indeed often suffered grievously from its effects. But according to prevailing ideology, they are to bear the burdens of repayment, while risks are transferred to taxpayers in the West by IMF bailouts (of lenders and investors, not the countries) and other devices; recent "IMF bailout loans" keep to the norm as "private-sector creditors walked away with the IMF money, while debtor countries effectively nationalized the private-sector debts."[1] The operative principles protect the banks that made bad loans and the economic and military elites who enriched themselves while transferring wealth abroad and taking over the resources of their own countries. The debt may be a "crisis" for the poor, who are subjected to harsh structural adjustment programs to facilitate debt repayment, at enormous human cost, and a lesser crisis for Northern taxpayers to whom high-yield and hence risky loans are shifted if they go unpaid. But to wealth and privilege, the arrangements are quite congenial.

The Latin American debt that reached crisis levels from 1982 would have been sharply reduced — in some cases, overcome — by return of

flight capital, though all figures are dubious for these secret and often illegal operations. According to Karin Lissakers, currently US executive
director of the IMF, "bankers contend that there would be no [debt] crisis if flight capital — the money the citizens of the borrowing countries
sent abroad for investment and safekeeping — were available for debt
payments," although "these same bankers are active promoters of flight
capital." The World Bank estimated that Venezuela's flight capital exceeded its foreign debt by some 40 percent by 1987. In 1980–82, capital
flight reached 70 percent of borrowing for eight leading debtors, *Business Week* estimated.[2] That is a regular pre-collapse phenomenon, as
again in Mexico in 1994. The 1998 IMF "rescue package" for Indonesia
approximated the estimated wealth of the Suharto family. One Indonesian economist estimates that 95 percent of the foreign debt of some $80
billion is owed by 50 individuals, not the 200 million who suffer the
costs in the "Stalinist state set on top of Dodge City," as Asia scholar
Richard Robison describes Indonesia.[3]

The debt of the 41 highly indebted poor countries is on the order of
the bailout of the US Savings & Loan institutions in the past few years,
one of many cases of socialization of risk and cost that was accelerated
by Reaganite "conservatives" along with increase of debt and government spending (relative to GDP). Foreign-held wealth of Latin Americans is perhaps 25 percent higher than the S&L bailout, close to $250
billion by 1990.[4]

The picture generalizes, and breaks little new ground. A study of
the global economy points out that "defaults on foreign bonds by US
railroads in the 1890s were on the same scale as current developing
country debt problems."[5] Britain, France, and Italy defaulted on US
debts in the 1930s. After World War II, there was reported to be heavy
flow of capital from Europe to the United States. Cooperative controls
could have kept the funds at home for post-war reconstruction, but,
some analysts allege, policymakers preferred to have wealthy Europeans send their capital to New York banks, with the costs of reconstruction transferred to US taxpayers. The Marshall Plan approximately
covered the "mass movements of nervous flight capital" that leading
economists had predicted.[6]

There are other relevant precedents. When the US took over Cuba
100 years ago it cancelled Cuba's debt to Spain on the grounds that the

burden was "imposed upon the people of Cuba without their consent and by force of arms." Such debts were later called "odious debt" by legal scholarship, "not an obligation for the nation," but the "debt of the power that has incurred it," while the creditors who "have committed a hostile act with regard to the people" can expect no payment from the victims. Rejecting a British challenge to Costa Rican debt cancellation, the arbitrator — US Supreme Court Chief Justice William Howard Taft — concluded that the bank lent the money for no "legitimate use," so its claim for payment "must fail." The logic extends readily to much of today's debt: "odious debt" with no legal or moral standing, imposed upon people without their consent, often serving to repress them and enrich their masters. The principle of odious debt, "if applied today would wipe out a substantial portion of the Third World's indebtedness," Lissakers comments.

In some cases, there are solutions to the debt crisis that are even simpler and more conservative than the unthinkable capitalist idea or the US government's principle of odious debt. Central America is suffering severely from the debt crisis. The highest per capita debt in the region is Nicaragua's, currently $6.4 billion and clearly unpayable. The human costs of the IMF programs designed to ensure that lenders are compensated many times over are incalculable. About $1.5 billion is from the Somoza years, hence clearly "odious debt," of no standing. Another $3 billion is from the post-1990 period when the US regained control over Nicaragua; also odious debt. The remainder is the direct responsibility of the United States, which was conducting brutal economic warfare and a murderous terrorist war against Nicaragua, for which it was condemned by the World Court, which ordered the US to pay reparations, variously estimated in the range of $17 billion. Accordingly, the highly conservative principle of adhering to international law, as determined by the highest international judicial body, would suffice to eliminate Nicaragua's debt, with a good deal left over. Were elementary moral principles even to be imaginable in elite Western culture, similar conclusions would at once be drawn far more broadly throughout Europe and the US, even without World Court judgments. But that day remains very distant.[7]

Bank lending more than doubled from 1971 to 1973, then "levelled off for the next two years, despite the enormous increase in oil bills" from late 1973, the OECD reported, adding that "the most decisive and

dramatic increase in bank lending was associated with the major commodity price boom of 1972–73 — before the oil shock." One example
was the tripling in price of US wheat exports.[8] Lending later increased as
banks sought to recycle petrodollars. The (temporary) rise in oil prices
led to sober calls that Middle East oil "could be internationalized, not on
behalf of a few oil companies, but for the benefit of the rest of mankind."[9] There were no similar proposals for internationalization of US
agriculture, highly productive as a result of natural advantages and
public-sector research and development for many years, not to speak of
the measures that made the land available, hardly through the miracle of
the market.

The banks were eager to lend, and upbeat about the prospects. On
the eve of the 1982 disaster, Citibank director Walter Wriston, known
in the financial world as "the greatest recycler of them all," described
Latin American lending as so risk-free that commercial banks could
safely treble Third World loans (as a proportion of assets). After disaster
struck, Citibank declared that "we don't feel unduly exposed" in Brazil,
which had doubled bank debt in the preceding four years, with Citibank
exposure in Brazil alone greater than 100 percent of capital. In 1986,
after the collapse of the international lending boom in which he was a
prime mover, Wriston wrote that "events of the past dozen years would
seem to suggest that we [bankers] have been doing our job [of risk as-
sessment] reasonably well"; true enough, if we factor in the ensuing socialization of risk through government intervention, welcomed by
Wriston and others famous for their contempt of government and adulation of the free market.[10]

The international financial institutions also played their part in the
catastrophe (for the poor). In the 1970s, the World Bank actively promoted borrowing: "there is no general problem of developing countries
being able to service debt," the Bank announced authoritatively in 1978.
Several weeks before Mexico defaulted in 1982, setting off the crisis, a
joint publication of the IMF and World Bank declared that "there is still
considerable scope for sustained additional borrowing to increase
productive capacity" — for example, for the useless Sicartsa steel plant
in Mexico, funded by British taxpayers in one of the exercises of
Thatcherite mercantilism.[11]

The record continues to the present. Mexico was hailed as a free market triumph and a model for others until its economy collapsed in December 1994, with tragic consequences for most Mexicans, even beyond what they had suffered during the "triumph." The cheers now resound once again, while wages have fallen more than 25 percent since 1994 (the first year of NAFTA), after a very severe decline from the early 1980s, when the liberal reforms were initiated; real minimum wages dropped more than 80 percent from 1981 to 1998.[12] Just as the Asian financial crisis erupted, the World Bank and IMF published studies praising the "sound macroeconomic policies" and "enviable fiscal record" of Thailand and South Korea, singling out the "particularly intense" progress of "the most dynamic emerging [capital] markets," namely "Korea, Malaysia, and Thailand, with Indonesia and the Philippines not far behind." These models of free market success under IMF–World Bank guidance "stand out for the depth and liquidity" they have achieved, and other virtues. As the fairy tales collapsed, the OECD also came out with a report in 1997 hailing the marvels of liberalization, which, though it had been accompanied by a sharp deterioration in growth of GDP and other macroeconomic indicators over 20 years, was soon to reveal its promise, thanks to the dynamism of the "emerging non-OECD economies" led by the "Big Five of Brazil, China, India, Indonesia, and Russia."[13]

Failure of prediction is no sin; fundamental elements of the international economy "are only dimly understood" (Jeffrey Sachs). It is, however, hard to overlook the observation that "bad ideas flourish because they are in the interest of powerful groups" (Paul Krugman). Confidence in what is serviceable is also fortified by blind faith in the "religion" that markets know best (Joseph Stiglitz).[14] The religion is, furthermore, as hypocritical as it is fanatic. Over the centuries, "free market theory" has been double-edged: market discipline is just fine for the poor and defenseless, but the rich and powerful take shelter under the wings of the nanny state.

Another factor in the debt crisis was the liberalization of financial flows from the early 1970s. The post-war Bretton Woods system was designed by the US and UK to liberalize trade while exchange rates were stabilized and capital movements were subject to regulation and control. The decisions were based on the belief that liberalization of finance may interfere with trade and economic growth, and on the clear understanding that it would undermine government decisionmaking, hence also the welfare state, which had enormous popular support. Not only the social contract that had been won by long and hard struggle, but even substantive democracy, would be damaged by loss of control on capital movements.

The Bretton Woods system remained in place through the "golden age" of economic growth and significant welfare benefits. It was dismantled by the Nixon administration, with the support of Britain and others. This was a major factor in the enormous explosion of capital flows in the years that followed. Their composition also changed radically. In 1970, 90 percent of transactions were related to the real economy (trade and long-term investment). By 1995 it was estimated that 95 percent was speculative, most of it very short term (80 percent with a return time of a week or less), with the aggregate effect of drawing more "resources into finance while deterring real capital formation."[15]

The outcome generally confirms the expectations of Bretton Woods. There has been a serious attack on the social contract and an increase in protectionism and other market interventions, led by the Reaganites. Markets have become more volatile, with more frequent crises. The IMF virtually reversed its function: from helping to constrain financial mobility, to enhancing it while serving as "the credit community's enforcer," in Lissakers's words.

It was predicted at once that financial liberalization would lead to a low-growth, low-wage economy in the rich societies. That happened, too. For the past 25 years, growth and productivity rates have declined significantly. In the US, wages and income have stagnated or declined for the majority while the top few percent have gained enormously. By now the US has the worst record among the industrial countries by standard social indicators. England follows closely, and similar though less extreme effects can be found throughout the OECD.

The effects have been far more grim in the Third World. Comparison of the East Asia growth areas with Latin America is illuminating. Latin America has the world's worst record for inequality; East Asia ranks among the best. The same holds for education, health, and social welfare generally. Imports to Latin America have been heavily skewed towards consumption for the rich; to East Asia, towards productive investment. Unlike Latin America, East Asia controlled capital flight. In Latin America, the wealthy "refuse to pay taxes" and are exempt from social obligations generally.[16] East Asia differed sharply.

The Latin American country considered the leading exception to the generally dismal record, Chile, is an instructive case. The free market experiment of the Pinochet dictatorship had utterly collapsed by the early 1980s. Since then, the economy has recovered with a mixture of state intervention (including the nationalized copper firm, a major income producer), controls on short-term capital inflow, and increased social spending.

Financial liberalization had spread to Asia by the 1990s. That is widely regarded as a significant element in the subsequent financial crisis, along with serious market failures, corruption, and structural problems.

The debt is a social and ideological construct, not a simple economic fact. Furthermore, as understood long ago, liberalization of capital flow serves as a powerful weapon against social justice and democracy. Recent policy decisions are choices by the powerful, based on perceived self-interest, not mysterious "economic laws" that leave "no alternative," in Thatcher's cruel phrase. Technical devices to alleviate their worst effects were proposed years ago, but have been dismissed by powerful interests that benefit. And the institutions that design the national and global systems are no more exempt from the need to demonstrate their legitimacy than predecessors that have thankfully been dismantled.

9

"Recovering Rights"
A Crooked Path

The Confucian *Analects* describe the exemplary person — the master himself — as "the one who keeps trying although he knows that it is in vain." The thought is not easy to suppress at the 50th anniversary of the signing of the Universal Declaration of Human Rights (UD).

Regular human rights reports provide sufficient testimony to the dismal story, which continues to the present, as always including the major powers. To mention only one current example, the "collateral damage" of the latest US-UK bombardment of Iraq merits little notice,[1] taking its place alongside the wanton destruction of a major African pharmaceutical plant a few months earlier, and other trivia.

And trivia they are, viewed against the background of other exploits: in Washington's "backyard," for example, the liberal press was giving "Reagan & Co. good marks" for their support for state terror in El Salvador as it peaked in the early 1980s, urging that more military aid be sent to "Latin-style fascists ... regardless of how many are murdered" because "there are higher American priorities than Salvadoran human rights," and that Nicaragua be restored to the "Central American mode" of El Salvador and Guatemala under a "regional arrangement that would be enforced by Nicaragua's neighbors," the terror states then busy slaughtering their populations with US aid.[2] The comments are from left-liberal sectors; the rest take a harsher line.

Interpretations are different a step removed. A Jesuit-organized conference in San Salvador considered the state terrorist project that peaked in the 1980s and its continuation since then by the socioeconomic policies imposed by the victors. Its report noted the effect of the residual "culture of terror" on "domesticating the expectations of the majority vis-à-vis alternatives different to those of the powerful."[3] The great achievement of the terror operations has been to destroy the hopes that had been raised in the 1970s, inspired by popular organizing throughout the region, the overthrow of the Somoza dictatorship, and the "preferential option for the poor" adopted by the Church, which was severely punished for this deviation from good behavior.

The Jesuit report generalizes to much of the Third World; and also to growing numbers at home, as the Third World model of sharply two-tiered societies is internationalized. The real world was captured in remarks by the secretary-general of UNCTAD, which was established "to create an international trading system consistent with the promotion of economic and social development." Representing the UN at the 50th anniversary of the world trade system (GATT, WTO, etc.), he observed that "no one should be fooled by the festive atmosphere of these celebrations. Outside there is anguish and fear, insecurity about jobs, and what Thoreau described as 'a life of quiet desperation.' "[4] The event received ample coverage, but the media preferred the festive atmosphere within.

The devastating consequences of Hurricane Mitch in October 1998 were graphically reported, but not their roots in the "economic miracle" instituted by "Latin-style fascists" guided by US experts — a development model geared towards a "high level of poverty and [of] favoritism towards the minority while the majority has just the minimum to survive," a conservative Honduran bishop observed, condemning new programs that will perpetuate the disaster. He was quoted in a rare discussion of its causes by a veteran Central America journalist who observes that hopes for change were terminated by the US-trained armies that "caused the disappearance of the most vocal proponents of sharing the land," along with hundreds of thousands of others.[5]

A fuller picture is far more grim, and instructive, but I will put it aside.

The direct impact of the hurricane is reviewed in the research journal of the Jesuit University in Managua. The analysts ask: "Did Mitch have a class bias?" The hurricane had a devastating effect on poor farmers, who "have been pushed into the most ecologically fragile zones, those least appropriate for agriculture": Posoltega, for example, the site of the murderous mudslide that horrified the world. A few miles away, the San Antonio refinery, "one of Nicaragua's most emblematic economic emporiums," made out well, as did agro-export industries generally, benefitting from the rains on the fertile soil they monopolize. Basic crop production (corn and beans) was ruined, a disaster for the farmers and the general population. Reconstruction is directed to magnifying the same distinctions in a "New Nicaragua," highly regarded for its impressive economic growth, while the population sinks to Haitian levels. That includes funds from abroad as well as the domestic institutions, redesigned to satisfy the requirements of the international financial institutions. Credit, research, and policy generally are being directed even more than before to provide "services exclusively to those who can pay for them," undermining what is left of agrarian reform. "The class bias" of the hurricane and the aftermath is not "divine will or [a] mythical curse against the poor," but "the result of very concrete social, economic, and environmental factors."[6] The story again generalizes to much of the world.

A side effect of the hurricane was to scatter tens of thousands of land mines that are a relic of the Nicaraguan component of Washington's terrorist wars of the 1980s. Fortunately, a team of de-mining experts was sent to help — from France. The facts were reported in the pacifist press.[7] The lack of concern in a more obvious place is not surprising in view of the reaction to far more extreme human rights violations of a similar sort, proceeding as we meet. Perhaps the most striking example is the human toll of the anti-personnel weapons littering the Plain of Jars in Laos, the scene of the heaviest bombing of civilian targets in history, it appears, and arguably the most cruel: this furious assault on a poor peasant society had little to do with Washington's wars in the region.

New Rights?

Let us move on to the general setting in which the rights that have been sought gain their life and substance.

The UD broke new ground in significant respects. It enriched the realm of enunciated rights, and extended them to all persons. In a major law review essay on the 50th anniversary, Harvard law professor Mary Ann Glendon observes that the Declaration "is not just a 'universalization' of the traditional 18th-century 'rights of man,' but part of a new 'moment' in the history of human rights ... belong[ing] to the family of post–World War II rights instruments that attempted to graft social justice onto the trunk of the tree of liberty," specifically Articles 22–27, a "pillar" of the Declaration "which elevates to fundamental rights status several 'new' economic, social, and cultural rights." It is fair to regard the UD as another step towards "recovering rights" that had been lost to "conquest and tyranny," promising "a new era to the human race," to recall the hopes of Thomas Paine two centuries ago.[8]

Glendon stresses further that the UD is a closely integrated document: there is no place for the "relativist" demand that certain rights be relegated to secondary status in light of "Asian values" or some other pretext.

The same conclusions are emphasized in the review of the human rights order issued by the United Nations on the 50th anniversary of the Charter, and in its contribution to the first World Conference on Human Rights at Vienna in June 1993. In his statement opening the conference, the secretary-general "stressed the importance of the question of interdependence of all human rights." Introducing the 50th-anniversary volume, he reports that the Vienna conference "emphasized that action for the promotion and protection of economic and social and cultural rights is as important as action for civil and political rights."[9]

The Vatican took a similar stand in commemorating the 50th anniversary of the UD. In his 1999 New Year's Day message, Pope John Paul II denounced Marxism, Nazism, fascism, and, "no less pernicious," the ideology of "materialist consumption" in which "the negative aspects on others are considered completely irrelevant" and "nations and peoples" lose "the right to share in the decisions which often profoundly modify their way of life." Their hopes are "cruelly dashed" under market arrangements in which "political and financial power is concentrated," while financial markets fluctuate erratically and "elections can be manipulated." Guarantees for "the global common good and the exercise of economic and social rights" and "sustainable development of society" must be the core element of "a new vision of global progress in solidarity."[10]

A tepid version of the Vatican's "post-liberation theology," as it is called, is admissible into the free market of ideas, unlike the liberation theology it replaces. The latter heresy "is almost, if not quite, extinct,"[11] commentators inform us. The modalities of extinction have been consigned to their proper place in history, along with the archbishop whose assassination opened the grim decade of Washington's war against the Church and other miscreants, and the leading Jesuit intellectuals whose assassination by the same US-backed "Latin-style fascists" marked its close. The two theologies differ in one particularly critical respect. The "preferential option for the poor" that somehow became extinct encouraged the poor to participate in shaping their own social world, while the tolerable version of the replacement asks them only to plead with the rich and powerful to share some crumbs. In the tolerable version, the Church is to "rattle the conscience" of the rich and powerful, instructing them in "Catholic values of generosity and self-sacrifice" instead of organizing Christian base communities that might offer people a way to exercise the "right to share in the decisions which often profoundly modify their way of life" that has been transmuted to a plea for more benevolent rule as it passed through the doctrinal filters.

Glendon observes that recent discussion is mistaken in supposing that socioeconomic and cultural rights were included in the UD "as a concession to the Soviets": on the contrary, support was "very broad-based." We may recall that such ideals were deeply entrenched in anti-fascist popular forces in Europe and in the colonial world, and among the population of the United States as well. These facts were profoundly disturbing to US political and economic elites, who had a different vision of the world they intended to create. They expressed their concerns about "the hazard facing industrialists" at home in "the newly realized political power of the masses," and about the "new aspirations" among populations abroad who were "convinced that the first beneficiaries of the development of a country's resources should be the people of that country" rather than US investors. The steps taken to overcome these hazards constitute major themes of post-war history, matters that I have to put aside here, despite their evident relevance.

There were some, of course, who dismissed the UD with contempt as just a "collection of pious phrases," the oft-quoted remark of Soviet delegate Andrei Vyshinsky, whose own record need not detain us; or as "a letter to Santa Claus.... Neither nature, experience, nor probability informs these lists of 'entitlements,' which are subject to no constraints except those of the mind and appetite of their authors" — in this case, Reagan's UN ambassador, Jeane Kirkpatrick, deriding the socioeconomic and cultural provisions of the UD. A few years later, Ambassador

Morris Abram described such ideas as "little more than an empty vessel into which vague hopes and inchoate expectations can be poured," a "dangerous incitement," and even "preposterous." Abram was speaking at the UN Commission on Human Rights, explaining Washington's rejection of the right to development, which sought to guarantee "the right of individuals, groups, and peoples to participate in, contribute to, and enjoy continuous economic, social, cultural and political development, in which all human rights and fundamental freedoms can be fully realized." The US alone vetoed the Declaration, thus implicitly vetoing the Articles of the UD that it closely paraphrased.[12]

Despite the relativist onslaught, the UD is surely worth defending. But without illusions: the world's most powerful state has been a leader of the relativist camp, and even within the subcategory of human rights it professes to uphold, "there is a persistent and widespread pattern" of abuses, Amnesty International concludes in a recent review.[13]

The Economic Order and Human Rights

The human rights regime was one of three related pillars of the New World Order established by the victors in the aftermath of World War II. A second was the political order articulated in the UN Charter; the third the economic order formulated at Bretton Woods. Let us take a brief look at these components of the projected international system, focusing on the human rights dimension.

The Bretton Woods system functioned into the early 1970s, a period sometimes called the "Golden Age" of post-war industrial capitalism, marked by high growth of the economy and progress in realizing the socioeconomic rights of the UD. These rights were a prominent concern of the framers of Bretton Woods, and their extension during the Golden Age was a contribution to translating the UD from "pious phrases" and a "letter to Santa Claus" to at least a partial reality.

One basic principle of the Bretton Woods system was regulation of finance, motivated in large part by the understanding that liberalization could serve as a powerful weapon against democracy and the welfare state, allowing financial capital to become a "virtual Senate" that can impose its own social policies and punish those who deviate by capital flight. The system was dismantled by the Nixon administration with the

cooperation of Britain and other financial centers. The results would not
have surprised its designers.

For the major industrial powers, the period since has been marked
by slower growth and the dismantling of the social contract, notably in the
US and Britain. In the US, the recovery of the '90s was one of the weakest
since World War II and unique in American history in that the majority
of the population has barely recovered even the level of the last business
cycle peak in 1989, let alone that of a decade earlier. The typical family
puts in 15 weeks of work a year beyond the level of 20 years ago, while
income and wealth have stagnated or declined. The top 1 percent has
gained enormously, and the top 10 percent have registered gains, while
for the second decile, net worth — assets minus debt — declined during
the recovery of the 1990s. Inequality, which steadily reduced during the
Golden Age, is returning to pre–New Deal levels. Inequality correlates
with hours of work. In 1970, the US was similar to Europe in both categories, but it now leads the industrial world in both, mostly by wide
margins. It is alone in lacking legally mandated paid vacation. Open
government complicity in corporate crime during the Reagan years,
sometimes accurately reported in the business press, and continuing
since, has severely undermined labor rights. All this proceeds in direct
conflict with the UD — that is, with the parts that are denied status under
the prevailing relativism.[14]

The press regularly reports "an age of almost unparalleled prosperity" in the US that Europe should aspire to emulate, and a "remarkably
successful US economy."[15] The reports are based primarily on "the return on capital achieved by American companies" — which has indeed
been "spectacular," as the business press has been exulting through the
Clinton years — and the vast increase in stock prices, which has con-
ferred remarkable prosperity upon the 1 percent of families who own almost half the stock and the top 10 percent who hold most of the rest, and
who jointly are the beneficiaries of 85 percent of the gains of asset values in the "fairy tale economy." Good deeds do not pass unnoticed. President Clinton was "likened to Martin Luther King, Jr. and generally
celebrated at a Wall Street conference" in mid-January 1999, the press
reported, citing the president of the New York Stock Exchange, who
"told Mr. Clinton that Dr. King was surely smiling down on the gather-
ing" at the annual King memorial, recognizing how Clinton had bene-

fited "my little corner of southern Manhattan."[16]

Other little corners fared somewhat differently.

The fairy tale was attributed in part to "greater worker insecurity" by Federal Reserve Chair Alan Greenspan, citing a near-doubling of the proportion of workers fearing layoffs in large industries from 1991 to 1996. Other studies reveal that 90 percent of workers are concerned about job security. In a 1994 survey of working people, 79 percent of respondents said efforts to seek union representation are likely to lead to firing, and 41 percent of non-union workers said they think they might lose their own jobs if they tried to organize. Decline in unionization is generally taken by labor economists to be a significant factor in the stagnation or decline of wages and the deterioration of working conditions.[17]

Polls also report "consumer confidence"; it is tempered, however, by the observation that "expectations have diminished." The director of the University of Michigan's Survey Research Center comments that "it is a little like people are saying, 'I am not earning enough to get by, but it is not as bad as it could be,' while in the '60s they thought, 'How good can it get?' "[18]

For the "developing world," the post–Bretton Woods era has been largely a disaster, though some escaped, temporarily at least, by rejecting the "religion" that markets know best, to borrow the words of the chief economist of the World Bank. He points out that the "East Asian miracle," which is "historically unprecedented," was achieved by a significant departure from the prescribed formulas, though its rising star, South Korea, was badly damaged after agreeing to liberalization of finance in the early '90s, a significant factor in its current crisis, he and many other analysts believe, and a step towards "Latin Americanization." Latin American elites experience far greater inequality and a "weaker sense of community than found among nationalistic East Asian counterparts," and are "connected more with foreign high finance" — factors that enter into their "avid pursuit of European and US high-style consumption and high culture," international economist David Felix points out. "Mobile wealth has also enabled Latin America's wealthy to veto progressive taxes and limit outlays on basic and secondary education while extracting generous state bailouts when suffering financial stress," a typical feature of free market doctrine for centuries.[19]

In his highly regarded history of the international monetary system, Barry Eichengreen brings out a crucial difference between the current phase of "globalization" and the pre–World War I era that it partially resembles.[20] At that time, government policy had not yet been "politicized by universal male suffrage and the rise of trade unionism and parliamentary labor parties." Hence the severe costs of financial rectitude imposed by the "virtual Senate" could be transferred to the general population. But that luxury was no longer available in the more democratic Bretton Woods era, so that "limits on capital mobility substituted for limits on democracy as a source of insulation from market pressures." It is therefore natural that the dismantling of the post-war economic order should be accompanied by a sharp attack on substantive democracy and the principles of the UD, primarily by the US and Britain.

There is a great deal to say about these topics, but with regard to the human rights aspect, the facts seem reasonably clear and in conformity with the expectations of the founders of the Bretton Woods system.

The Political Order and Human Rights

The third pillar of post–World War II world order, standing alongside the Bretton Woods international economic system and the UD, is the UN Charter. Its fundamental principle is that the threat or use of force is barred, with two exceptions: when specifically authorized by the Security Council, or in self-defense against armed attack until the Security Council acts (according to Article 51). There is no enforcement mechanism apart from the great powers, decisively the US. But Washington flatly rejects the principles of the Charter, both in practice and official doctrine, as already discussed.

The framework of world order has long ceased to exist, even in words, as the rhetoric has become too inconvenient to sustain. The approved principle is the rule of force. The sophisticated understand that an appeal to legal obligations and moral principle is legitimate as a weapon against selected enemies, or "to gild our positions with an ethos derived from very general moral principles," in Dean Acheson's words. But nothing more than that. The level of support for this stand among educated sectors should not be taken lightly. The human rights implications require no comment.

In brief, of the three pillars of the post–World War II international order, two — the Bretton Woods system and the Charter — have largely collapsed. And the third, the UD, remains to a large extent "a letter to Santa Claus," as the leaders of the relativist crusade contend.

Rights for Whom?

As widely noted, a major innovation of the UD was the extension of rights to all persons, meaning persons of flesh and blood. The real world is crucially different. In the US, the term "person" is officially defined "to include any individual, branch, partnership, associated group, association, estate, trust, corporation or other organization (whether or not organized under the laws of any State), or any government entity."[21] That concept of "person" would have shocked James Madison, Adam Smith, or others with intellectual roots in the Enlightenment and classical liberalism. But it prevails, giving a cast to the UD that is far from the intent of those who formulated and defend it.

Through radical judicial activism, the rights of persons have been granted to "collectivist legal entities," as some legal historians call them; and more narrowly, to their boards of directors, "a new 'absolutism' " bestowed by the courts.[22] These newly created immortal persons, protected from scrutiny by the grant of personal rights, administer domestic and international markets through their internal operations, "strategic alliances" with alleged competitors, and other linkages. They demand and receive critical support from the powerful states over which they cast the "shadow" called "politics," to borrow John Dewey's aphorism, giving no little substance to the fears of James Madison 200 years ago that private powers might demolish the experiment in democratic government by becoming "at once its tools and its tyrants." While insisting on powerful states to serve as their tools, they naturally seek to restrict the public arena for others, the main tenet of "neoliberalism." The basic thesis was expressed well by David Rockefeller, commenting on the trend towards "lessen[ing] the role of government." This is "something business people tend to be in favor of," he remarked, "but the other side of that coin is that somebody has to take government's place, and business seems to me to be a logical entity to do it. I think that too many businesspeople simply haven't faced up to that, or they have said, 'It's somebody else's responsibility; it's not mine.' "[23]

Crucially, it is not the responsibility of the public. The great flaw of government is that it is to some degree accountable to the public, and offers some avenues for public participation. That defect is overcome when responsibility is transferred to the hands of immortal entities of enormous power, granted the rights of persons and able to plan and decide in insulation from the annoying public.

Current policy initiatives seek to extend the rights of "collectivist legal persons" far beyond those of persons of flesh and blood. These are central features of such trade treaties as NAFTA and the Multilateral Agreement on Investments (MAI), the latter temporarily derailed by public pressure, but sure to be reconstituted in some less visible form.[24] These agreements grant corporate tyrannies the rights of "national treatment" not enjoyed by persons in the traditional sense. General Motors can demand "national treatment" in Mexico, but Mexicans of flesh and blood will know better than to demand "national treatment" north of the border. Corporations can also (effectively) sue national states for "expropriation" — interpreted as failure to meet their demands for free access to resources and markets.

Even without such a formal grant of extraordinary rights in radical violation of classical liberal principles, something similar follows from the role of these collectivist entities as "tools and tyrants" of government and masters of doctrinal systems. One illustration is Article 17 of the UD, which states that "no one shall be arbitrarily deprived of his property." In the real world, the "persons" whose rights are most prominently secured are the collectivist entities, under a doctrine, formulated in the same years as the UD, which affirms the right to "adequate, effective, and prompt compensation" for expropriated property at "fair market value," as determined by those in a position to enforce their will. The formula, attributed to Roosevelt's secretary of state, Cordell Hull, has been termed the "international minimum standard of civilization" in respected treatises of international law.[25]

Criteria for application of the formula may appear inconsistent on the surface, but not when real-world factors are taken into account. The formula is the basis for US economic warfare against Cuba for 40 years, justified by the charge that Cuba has not met this "minimum standard of civilization." The formula does not, however, apply to US investors and the US government, who took the properties at the turn of the century when Cuba was under US military occupation. Nor does it apply to the US government and private powers who stole Spanish and British possessions in Cuba and the Philippines at the same time — for example, the Spanish-owned Manila Railway Company. After the bloody conquest of the Philippines, the US threw out the Spanish concession because it "had been inspired by Spanish imperialistic motives" — unlike the US possessions that Cuba nationalized when it was at last taken over by Cubans in 1959.

The formula also does not apply to the founding of the United States, which benefited from expropriation of British possessions and those of loyalists, who were probably as numerous as the rebels in the civil war with outside intervention known now as the American Revolution. New York State alone gained close to $4 million by taking loyalist property, a considerable sum in those days. In contrast, the formula does apply to Nicaragua. The US compelled Nicaragua to withdraw the claims for reparations awarded by the World Court, and, after Nicaragua capitulated on all fronts, the Senate voted 94 to 4 to ban any aid until Nicaragua meets the international minimum standard of civilization: returning or giving what Washington determines to be adequate compensation for properties of US citizens seized when Somoza fell, assets of participants in the crimes of the tyrant who had long been a US favorite, including wealthy Nicaraguan exiles who are retroactively US citizens.

Laws and other instruments are "spider webs," a popular 17th-century poet wrote: "Lesser flies are quickly ta'en / While the great break out again."[26] Some things change, others persist.

The Right to Information

The immortal collectivist persons are easily able to dominate information and doctrinal systems. Their wealth and power allow them to set the framework within which the political system functions, but these controls have become still more direct under recent Supreme Court rulings defining money as a form of speech. The 1998 election is an illustration. About 95 percent of winning candidates outspent their competitors. Business contributions exceeded those of labor by 12 to 1; individual contributions are sharply skewed.[27] By such means, a tiny fraction of the population effectively selects candidates. These developments are surely not unrelated to the increasing cynicism about government and unwillingness even to vote. It should be noted that these consequences are fostered and welcomed by the immortal persons, their media, and their other agents, who have dedicated enormous efforts to instill the belief that the government is an enemy to be hated and feared, not a potential instrument of popular sovereignty.

The realization of the UD depends crucially on the rights articulated in Articles 19 and 21: to "receive and impart information and ideas through any media" and to take part in "genuine elections" that ensure that "the will of the people shall be the basis of the authority of government." The importance of restricting the rights of free speech and democratic participation has been well understood by the powerful. There is a rich history, but the problems gained heightened significance in this century as "the masses promised to become king," a dangerous tendency that could be reversed, it was argued, by new methods of propaganda that enable the "intelligent minorities ... to mold the mind of the masses, ... regimenting the public mind every bit as much as an army regiments the bodies of its soldiers." I happen to be quoting a founder of the modern public relations industry, the respected New Deal liberal Edward Bernays, but the perception is standard, and clearly articulated by leading progressive public intellectuals and academics, along with business leaders.[28]

For such reasons, the media and educational systems are a constant terrain of struggle. It has long been recognized that state power is not the only form of interference with the fundamental right to "receive and impart information and ideas," and in the industrial democracies, it is far from the most important one — matters discussed by John Dewey and George Orwell, to mention two notable examples. In 1946, the prestigious Hutchins Commission on Freedom of the Press warned that "private agencies controlling the great mass media" constitute a fundamental threat to freedom of the press with their ability to impose "an environment of vested beliefs" and "bias as a commercial enterprise" under the influence of advertisers and owners. The European Commission of Human Rights has recognized "excessive concentration of the press" as an infringement of the rights guaranteed by Article 19, calling on states to prevent these abuses, a position recently endorsed by Human Rights Watch.[29]

For the same reasons, the business world has sought to ensure that private agencies *will* control the media and thus be able to restrict thought to "vested beliefs." They seek further to "nullify the customs of ages" by creating "new conceptions of individual attainment and community desire," business leaders explain, "civilizing" people to perceive their needs in terms of consumption of goods rather than quality of life and work, and to abandon any thought of a "share in the decisions which often profoundly modify their way of life," as called for by Vatican extremists. Control of media by a few megacorporations is a contribution to this end. Concentration has accelerated, thanks in part to recent deregulation that also eliminates even residual protection of public interest. In the latest edition of his standard review of the topic, Ben Bagdikian reports a decline in controlling firms from 50 in 1984 to 10 today — huge empires such as Disney and General Electric, though the spectrum has broadened with Rupert Murdoch's entry.[30]

Bagdikian also reviews the ever more blatant "manipulation of news to pursue the owners' other financial goals," along with those of advertisers, to ensure "the promotion of conservatism and corporate values," crucially including "materialist consumption" in which "the negative aspects on others are considered completely irrelevant." That process too has been accelerated by the merger/acquisition boom, which has "consolidated advertising dollars in the hands of a shrinking number of marketers," the *Wall Street Journal* reports in a lead story, describing how "Advertisers Flex Muscles" to assure that editors "get the message" about permissible content — but without "trying to impinge on their editorial integrity," the chief executive of a major ad agency assured the *Journal*.[31]

Young children are a particular focus of the massive onslaught, which extends to regimenting the minds and attitudes of the rest. The controls are to be extended worldwide, and must include the new media created in large measure within the huge state sector of the industrial economy. As a developing country, the US took "far-reaching precautions ... to insure that the telecommunications industry remained in US hands," a recent academic study points out; but having achieved global dominance thanks to crucial state intervention, the industry now demands that all others open themselves to "free competition," so that Article 19 will be effectively nullified worldwide.[32]

The dedication to this principle was revealed with unusual clarity when UNESCO considered proposals to democratize the international media system to permit some access on the part of the vast majority of the world. The US government, and the media, bitterly condemned UNESCO with a most impressive flood of deceit and lies — uncorrectable, and reiterated without change after refutation, which was rarely permitted expression. "The stunning irony of this achievement," an academic historian of US-UNESCO relations observes, "was that the United States, having proved that the free market in ideas did not exist, attacked UNESCO for planning to destroy it." A detailed review of media and government deceit was published by a university press, but was also ignored. That history provides a revealing measure of the attitudes towards the basic principles of freedom and democracy.[33]

Control of the Internet is currently the "hot issue." Developed primarily in the state sector for almost 30 years and commercialized against the will of two-thirds of the population, the Internet and the Web are regarded by the business world as "the primary platform for the essential business activities of computing, communications, and commerce," as "the world's largest, deepest, fastest, and most secure marketplace," not only for goods but also for "selling" ideas and attitudes. They are expected to provide enormous profits, as well as new means to carry forward the mission of civilizing attitudes and belief, if they can be brought under corporate control and commercial sponsorship — that is, if they can be taken from the public, the owner of the airwaves and cyberspace by law, and transferred to a handful of immortal and unaccountable collective "persons" with extraordinary global power. A primary goal, one trade journalist observes, is "to turn the once-eclectic Web into the ultimate 24-hour marketing machine."[34]

New software and technologies are being devised to direct this public creation to marketing, diversion, and other safe activities, undermining the "once-eclectic" character that has provided a way to escape doctrinal constraints and construct a public counterforce to concentrated power, sometimes to considerable effect. In Indonesia, a visiting Australian academic specialist writes, the Internet "proved a godsend" for communication and "mobilizing cultural and political activism," with results that are as unwelcome to domestic elites as to the foreign beneficiaries and supporters of the threatened regime, unusual in its corruption and brutality. Another notable recent example is the success of grassroots and public interest organizations in deflecting the state-corporate attempt to institute the MAI in secrecy, an achievement that elicited near-panic, and even the fear that it may become "harder to do deals behind closed doors and submit them for rubber-stamping by parliaments," as trade diplomats warned. Overcoming these hazards is a high priority for business leaders.[35]

It is only to be expected that private power and its "tools and tyrants" should seek to ensure that others can do no more than "keep trying although they know that it is in vain." But the Confucian judgment is surely too grim. The words are hard to utter after this terrible century, but there has been substantial improvement in many aspects of human life and consciousness, extending an earlier history of progress — agonizingly slow, often reversed, but nonetheless real. Particularly in the societies that are more privileged and that have won a significant measure of freedom, many choices are available, including fundamental institutional change if that is the right way to proceed. We need not quietly accept the suffering and injustice that are all around us, and the prospects, which are not slight, of severe catastrophes if human society continues on its present course.

10

The United States and the "Challenge of Relativity"

The adoption of the Universal Declaration of Human Rights (UD) on December 10, 1948, constituted a step forward in the slow progress towards protection of human rights. The overarching principle of the UD is universality. Its provisions have equal standing. There are no moral grounds for self-serving "relativism," which selects for convenience; still less for the particularly ugly form of relativism that converts the UD into a weapon to wield selectively against designated enemies.

The 50th anniversary of the UD provides a welcome occasion for reflection on such matters, and for steps to advance the principles that have been endorsed, at least rhetorically, by the nations of the world. The chasm that separates words from actions requires no comment; the annual reports of the major human rights organizations provide more than ample testimony. And there is no shortage of impressive rhetoric. One would have to search far to find a place where leadership and intellectuals do not issue ringing endorsements of the principles and bitter condemnation of those who violate them — notably excluding themselves and their associates and clients.

I will limit attention here to a single case: the world's most powerful state, which also has the most stable and long-standing democratic institutions and unparalleled advantages in every sphere, including the economy and security concerns. Its global influence has been unmatched during the half century when the UD has been in force (in theory). It has long been as good a model as one can find of a sociopolitical order in which basic rights are upheld. And it is commonly lauded, at home and abroad, as the leader in the struggle for human rights, democracy, freedom, and justice. There remains a range of disagreement over policy: at one extreme, "Wilsonian idealists" urge continued dedication to the traditional mission of upholding human rights and freedom worldwide, while "realists" counter that the United States may lack the means to conduct these crusades of "global meliorism" and should not neglect its own interests in the service of others. By "granting idealism a near exclusive hold on our foreign policy," we go too far, high government officials warn, with the agreement of many scholars and policy analysts.[1] Within this range lies the path to a better world.

To discover the true meaning of principles that are proclaimed, it is of course necessary to go beyond rhetorical flourishes and public pronouncements, and to investigate actual practice. Examples must be chosen carefully to give a fair picture. One useful approach is to take the examples chosen as the "strongest case" and see how well they withstand scrutiny. Another is to investigate the record where influence is greatest and interference least, so that we see the operative principles in their purest form. If we want to determine what the Kremlin meant by human rights and democracy, we pay little heed to *Pravda*'s denunciations of racism in the United States or state terror in its client regimes, even less to protestation of noble motives. Far more instructive is the state of affairs in the "people's democracies" of Eastern Europe. The point is elementary, and applies generally. For the US, the Western hemisphere is the obvious testing ground, particularly the Central America–Caribbean region, where Washington has faced few external challenges for almost a century. It is of some interest that the exercise is rarely undertaken and, when it is, castigated as extremist or worse.

Before examining the operative meaning of the UD, it might be useful to recall some observations of George Orwell's. In his preface to *Animal Farm,* Orwell turned his attention to societies that are relatively free from state controls, unlike the totalitarian monster he was satirizing. "The sinister fact about literary censorship in England," he wrote, "is that it is largely voluntary. Unpopular ideas can be silenced, and inconvenient facts kept dark, without any need for any official ban." He did not explore the reasons in any depth, merely noting the control of the press by "wealthy men who have every motive to be dishonest on certain important topics," reinforced by the "general tacit agreement," instilled by a good education, "that 'it wouldn't do' to mention that particular fact." As a result, "Anyone who challenges the prevailing orthodoxy finds himself silenced with surprising effectiveness."

As if to illustrate his words, the preface remained unpublished for 30 years.[2]

In the case under discussion here, the "prevailing orthodoxy" is well summarized by the distinguished Oxford-Yale historian Michael Howard: "For 200 years the United States has preserved almost unsullied the original ideals of the Enlightenment ..., and, above all, the universality of these values," though it "does not enjoy the place in the world that it should have earned through its achievements, its generosity, and its goodwill since World War II."[3] The record is unsullied by the treatment of "that hapless race of native Americans, which we are exterminating with such merciless and perfidious cruelty" (in the words of John Quincy Adams)[4]; by the fate of the slaves who provided cheap cotton to allow the industrial revolution to take off — not exactly through market forces; by the terrible atrocities the US was once again conducting in its "backyard" as the praises were being delivered; or by the fate of Filipinos, Haitians, Vietnamese, and a few others who might have somewhat different perceptions.

The favored illustration of "generosity and goodwill" is the Marshall Plan. That merits examination on the "strongest case" principle. The inquiry again quickly yields facts "that 'it wouldn't do' to mention." For example, the fact that "as the Marshall Plan went into full gear the amount of American dollars being pumped into France and the Netherlands was approximately equaled by the funds being siphoned from their treasuries to finance their expeditionary forces in Southeast Asia," to carry out terrible crimes.[5] And that under US influence Europe was reconstructed in a particular mode, not quite that sought by the anti-fascist resistance, though fascist and Nazi collaborators were generally satisfied.

Nor would it do to mention that the generosity was largely bestowed by US taxpayers upon the corporate sector, which was duly appreciative, recognizing years later that the Marshall Plan "set the stage for large amounts of private US direct investment in Europe,"[6] establishing the basis for the modern transnational corporations, which "prospered and expanded on overseas orders, ... fueled initially by the dollars of the Marshall Plan" and protected from "negative developments" by "the umbrella of American power."[7] Furthermore, "Marshall Plan aid was also crucial in offsetting capital flight from Europe to the United States," political economist Eric Helleiner alleges, a matter of which "American policymakers were in fact keenly aware," preferring that "wealthy Europeans" send their money to New York banks because "cooperative capital controls had proven unacceptable to the American banking community." "The enormity of Marshall Plan aid thus did not so much reflect the resources required to rebuild Europe, ... but rather the volume of funds that were needed to offset the 'mass movements of nervous flight capital' " predicted by leading economists, a flow that apparently *"exceeded"* the Marshall Plan aid provided by US taxpayers — effectively, to "wealthy Europeans" and New York banks.[8]

The "prevailing orthodoxy" has sometimes been subjected to explicit test, on the obvious terrain. Lars Schoultz, the leading academic specialist on human rights in Latin America, found that US aid "has tended to flow disproportionately to Latin American governments which torture their citizens, ... to the hemisphere's relatively egregious violators of fundamental human rights." That includes military aid, is independent of need, and runs through the Carter period.[9] More wide-ranging studies by economist Edward Herman found a similar correlation worldwide, also suggesting a plausible reason: aid is correlated with improvement in the investment climate, often achieved by murdering priests and union leaders, massacring peasants trying to organize, blowing up the independent press, and so on. The result is a secondary correlation between aid and egregious violation of human rights. It is not that US leaders prefer torture; rather, it has little weight in comparison with more important values. These studies precede the Reagan years, when the questions are not worth posing.[10]

By "general tacit agreement," such matters too are "kept dark," with memories purged of "inconvenient facts."

"Universal" Human Rights

The natural starting point for an inquiry into Washington's defense of "the universality of [Enlightenment] values" is the UD. It is accepted generally as a human rights standard. US courts have, furthermore, based judicial decisions on "customary international law, as evidenced and defined by the Universal Declaration of Human Rights."[11]

The UD became the focus of great attention in June 1993 at the World Conference on Human Rights in Vienna. A lead headline in the *New York Times* read: "At Vienna Talks, US Insists Rights Must be Universal." Washington warned "that it would oppose any attempt to use religious and cultural traditions to weaken the concept of universal human rights," Elaine Sciolino reported. The US delegation was headed by Secretary of State Warren Christopher, "who promoted human rights as Deputy Secretary of State in the Carter administration." A "key purpose" of his speech, "viewed as the Clinton administration's first major policy statement on human rights," was "to defend the universality of human rights," rejecting the claims of those who plead "cultural relativism." Christopher said that "the worst violators are the world's aggressors and those who encourage the spread of arms," stressing that "the universality of human rights set[s] a single standard of acceptable behavior around the world, a standard Washington would apply to all countries." In his own words, "The United States will never join those who would undermine the Universal Declaration" and will defend its universality against those who hold "that human rights should be interpreted differently in regions with non-Western cultures," notably the "dirty dozen" who reject elements of the UD that do not suit them.[12]

Washington's decisiveness prevailed. Western countries "were relieved that their worst fears were not realized — a retreat from the basic tenets of the 1948 Universal Declaration of Human Rights." The "Challenge of Relativity" was beaten back, and the conference declared that "The universal nature of these rights and freedoms is beyond question."[13]

A few questions remained unasked. Thus, if "the worst violators are the world's aggressors and those who encourage the spread of arms," what are we to conclude about the world's leading arms merchant, then boasting well over half the sales of arms to the Third World, mostly to brutal dictatorships — policies accelerated under Christopher's tenure at the State Department with vigorous efforts to enhance the publicly subsidized sales, opposed by 96 percent of the population but strongly supported by high-tech industry?[14] Or its colleagues Britain and France, who had distinguished themselves by supplying Indonesian and Rwandan mass murderers, among others?[15]

The subsidies are not only for "merchants of death." Revelling in the new prospects for arms sales with NATO expansion, a spokesman for the US Aerospace Industries Association observes that the new markets ($10 billion for fighter jets alone, he estimates) include electronics, communications systems, etc., amounting to "real money" for advanced industry generally. The exports are promoted by the US government with grants, discount loans, and other devices to facilitate the transfer of public funds to private profit in the US while diverting the "transition economies" of the former Soviet empire to increased military spending rather than the social spending that is favored by their populations (the US Information Agency reports). The situation is quite the same elsewhere.[16]

And if aggressors are "the worst violators" of human rights, what of the country that stands accused before the International Court of Justice for the "unlawful use of force" in its terrorist war against Nicaragua,[17] contemptuously vetoing a Security Council resolution calling on all states to observe international law and rejecting repeated General Assembly pleas to the same effect?[18] Do these stern judgments hold of the country that opened the post–Cold War era by invading Panama, where, four years later, the client government's Human Rights Commission declared that the right to self-determination and sovereignty was still being violated by the "state of occupation by a foreign army," condemning its continuing human rights abuses?[19] I omit more dramatic examples, such as the US attack against South Vietnam from 1961–62, when the Kennedy administration moved from support for a Latin American–style terror state to outright aggression, facts that it still "wouldn't do" to admit into history.[20]

Further questions are raised by Washington's (unreported) reservations concerning the Declaration of the Vienna Conference. The US was disturbed that the Declaration "implied that any foreign occupation is a human rights violation."[21] That principle the US rejects, just as, alone with its Israeli client, the US rejects the right of peoples "forcibly deprived of [self-determination, freedom, and independence] …, particularly peoples under colonial and racist regimes and foreign occupation or other forms of colonial domination,… to struggle to [gain these rights] and to seek and receive support [in accordance with the Charter and other principles of international law]" — facts that also remain unreported, though they might help clarify the sense in which human rights are advocated.[22]

Also unexamined was just how Christopher had "promoted human rights [under] the Carter administration." One case was in 1978, when the spokesman for the "dirty dozen" at Vienna, Indonesia, was running out of arms in its attack against East Timor, then approaching genocidal levels, so that the Carter administration had to rush even more military supplies to its bloodthirsty friend.[23] Another arose a year later, when the Carter administration sought desperately to keep Somoza's National Guard in power after it had slaughtered some 40,000 civilians, finally evacuating commanders in planes disguised with Red Cross markings (a war crime) to Honduras, where they were reconstituted as a terrorist force under the direction of Argentine neo-Nazis. The record elsewhere in the region was arguably even worse.[24]

Such matters too fall among the facts "that it 'wouldn't do' to mention."

The high-minded rhetoric at and about the Vienna conference was not besmirched by inquiry into the observance of the UD by its leading defenders.[25] These matters were, however, raised in Vienna in a Public Hearing organized by NGOs. The contributions by activists, scholars, lawyers, and others from many countries reviewed "alarming evidence of massive human rights violations in every part of the world as a result of the policies of the international financial institutions," the "Washington Consensus" among the leaders of the free world. This "neoliberal" consensus disguises what might be called "really existing free market doctrine": market discipline is of great benefit to the weak and defenseless, though the rich and powerful must shelter under the wings of the nanny state. They must also be allowed to persist in "the sustained assault on [free trade] principle" that is deplored in a scholarly review of the post-1970 ("neoliberal") period by GATT secretariat economist Patrick Low (now director of economic research for the World Trade Organization), who estimates the restrictive effects of Reaganite measures at about three times those of other leading industrial countries, as they "presided over the greatest swing toward protectionism since the 1930s," shifting the US from "being the world's champion of multilateral free trade to one of its leading challengers," the journal of the Council on Foreign Relations commented in a review of the decade.[26]

It should be added that such analyses omit the major forms of market interference for the benefit of the rich: the transfer of public funds to advanced industry that underlies virtually every dynamic sector of the US economy, often under the guise of "defense." These measures were escalated again by the Reaganites, who were second to none in extolling the glories of the free market — for the poor at home and abroad. The general practices were pioneered by the British in the 18th century and have been a dominant feature of economic history ever since, and are a good part of the reason for the contemporary gap between the First and the Third World (growing for many years along with the growing gap between rich and poor sectors of the population worldwide).[27]

The Public Hearing at Vienna received no mention in mainstream US journals, to my knowledge, but citizens of the free world could learn about the human rights concerns of the vast majority of the world's people from its report, published in an edition of 2,000 copies in Nepal.[28]

Civil and Political Rights

The provisions of the UD are not well known in the United States, but some are familiar. The most famous is Article 13 (2), which states that "Everyone has the right to leave any country, including his own." This principle was invoked with much passion every year on Human Rights Day, December 10, with demonstrations and indignant condemnations of the Soviet Union for its refusal to allow Jews to leave. To be exact, the words just quoted were invoked, but not the phrase that follows: "and to return to his country." The significance of the omitted words was spelled out on December 11, 1948, the day after the UD was ratified, when the General Assembly unanimously passed Resolution 194, which affirms the right of Palestinians to return to their homes or receive compensation if they choose not to return, and has been reaffirmed regularly since. But there was a "general tacit agreement" that it "wouldn't do" to mention the omitted words, let alone the glaringly obvious fact that those exhorting the Soviet tyrants to observe Article 13, to much acclaim, were its most dedicated opponents.

It is only fair to add that the cynicism has finally been overcome. At the December 1993 UN session, the Clinton administration changed US official policy, joining Israel in opposing UN 194, which was reaffirmed by a vote of 127 to 2. As is the norm, there was no report or comment. But at least the inconsistency is behind us: the first half of Article 13 (2) has lost its relevance, and Washington now officially rejects its second half.[29]

Let us move on to Article 14, which declares that "Everyone has the right to seek and to enjoy in other countries asylum from persecution" — Haitians, for example, including the 87 new victims captured by Clinton's blockade and returned to their charnel house, with scant notice, as the Vienna conference opened.[30] The official reason was that they were fleeing poverty, not the rampant terror of the military junta, as they claimed. The basis for this insight was not explained.

In her report on the Vienna conference a few days earlier, Sciolino had noted that "some human rights organizations have sharply criticized the administration for failing to fulfill Mr. Clinton's campaign promises on human rights," the "most dramatic case" being "Washington's decision to forcibly return Haitian boat people seeking political asylum." Looking at the matter differently, the events illustrate Washington's largely rhetorical commitment to "the universality of human rights," except as a weapon used selectively against others.

The US has upheld Article 14 in this manner since Carter (and Christopher) "promoted human rights" by shipping miserable boat people back to torment under the Duvalier dictatorship, a respected ally helping to convert Haiti to an export platform for US corporations seeking supercheap and brutalized labor — or, to adopt the terms preferred by USAID, to convert Haiti into the "Taiwan of the Caribbean." The violations of Article 14 were ratified formally in a Reagan-Duvalier agreement. When a military coup overthrew Haiti's first democratically elected president in September 1991, renewing the terror after a brief lapse, the Bush administration imposed a blockade to drive back the flood of refugees to their torture chamber.[31]

Bush's "reprehensible, ... illegal, and irresponsible refugee policy"[32] was bitterly condemned by candidate Bill Clinton, whose first act as president was to make the illegal blockade still harsher, along with other measures to sustain the junta, to which we return.

Again, fairness requires that we recognize that Washington did briefly depart from its rejection of Article 14 in the case of Haiti. During the few months of democracy (February-September 1991), the Bush administration gained a sudden and short-lived sensitivity to Article 14 as the flow of refugees declined to a trickle — in fact, reversed, as Haitians returned to their country in its moment of hope. Of the more than 24,000 Haitians intercepted by US forces from 1981 through 1990, Washington allowed 28 claims for asylum as victims of political persecution, granting 11 (in comparison with 75,000 out of 75,000 Cubans). During the seven-month democratic interlude under President Aristide, with violence and repression radically reduced, 20 claims were allowed from a refugee pool one-fiftieth the scale. Practice returned to normal after the military coup and the renewed terror.[33]

Concerned that protests might make it difficult to maintain the blockade, the Clinton administration pleaded with other countries to relieve the US of the burden of accommodating the refugees. Fear of a refugee flow was the major reason offered as the "national security" interest that might justify military intervention, eliciting much controversy. The debate overlooked the obvious candidate: Tanzania, which had been able to accommodate hundreds of thousands of Rwandans, and would surely have been able to come to the rescue of the beleaguered United States by accepting a few more black faces.

The contempt for Article 14 is by no means concealed. A front-page story in the Newspaper of Record on harsh new immigration laws casually records the fact and explains the reasons:

> Because the United States armed and financed the army whose brutality sent them into exile, few Salvadorans were able to obtain the refugee status granted to Cubans, Vietnamese, Kuwaitis, and other nationalities at various times. The new law regards many of them simply as targets for deportation [though they were fleeing] a conflict that lasted from 1979 until 1992, [when] more than 70,000 people were killed in El Salvador, most of them by the American-backed army and the death squads it in turn supported, [forcing] many people here to flee to the United States.[34]

The same reasoning extended to those who fled Washington's other terrorist wars in the region.

The interpretation of Article 14 is therefore quite principled: "worthy victims" fall under Article 14; "unworthy victims" do not. The categories are determined by the agency of terror and prevailing power interests. But the facts have no bearing on Washington's role as the crusader defending the universality of the UD from the relativist challenge.

The case is among the many that illustrate an omission in Orwell's analysis: the easy tolerance of inconsistency, when convenient.

Economic, Social, and Cultural Rights

Articles 13 and 14 fall under the category of Civil and Political Rights. The UD also recognizes a second category: Economic, Social, and Cultural Rights. These are largely dismissed in the West. UN Ambassador Jeane Kirkpatrick described these provisions of the UD as "a letter to Santa Claus .... Neither nature, experience, nor probability informs these lists of 'entitlements,' which are subject to no constraints except those of the mind and appetite of their authors." They were dismissed in more temperate tones by the US Representative to the UN Commission on Human Rights, Ambassador Morris Abram, who emphasized in 1990 that Civil and Political Rights must have "priority," contrary to the principle of universality of the UD.[35]

Abram elaborated while explaining Washington's rejection of the Report of the Global Consultations on the Right to Development, defined as "the right of individuals, groups, and peoples to participate in, contribute to, and enjoy continuous economic, social, cultural, and political development, in which all human rights and fundamental freedoms can be fully realized." "Development is not a right," Abram informed the Commission. Indeed, the proposals of the report yield conclusions that "seem preposterous," for example, that the World Bank might be obliged "to forgive a loan or to give money to build a tunnel, a railroad, or a school." Such ideas are "little more than an empty vessel into which vague hopes and inchoate expectations can be poured," Abram continued, and even a "dangerous incitement."[36]

Closely paraphrasing Abram's thesis, we may understand the fundamental error of the alleged "right to development" to be its tacit endorsement of the principle that

> everyone has the right to a standard of living adequate for the health and well-being of himself and his family, including food, clothing, housing, and medical care and necessary social services, and the right to security in the event of unemployment, sickness, disability, widowhood, old age, or other lack of livelihood in circumstances beyond his control.

If there is no right to development, as defined, then this statement too is an "empty vessel" and perhaps even "dangerous incitement." Accordingly, this principle too has no status: there are no such rights as those affirmed in Article 25 of the UD, just quoted.

The US alone vetoed the Declaration on the Right to Development, thus implicitly vetoing Article 25 of the UD as well.[37]

It is unnecessary to dwell on the status of Article 25 in the world's richest country, with a poverty level twice that of any other industrial society, particularly severe among children. Almost one in four children under six fell below the poverty line by 1995 after four years of economic recovery, far more than other industrial societies.[38] Britain, though, is gaining ground, with "one in three British babies born in poverty," the press reports, as "child poverty has increased as much as three-fold since Margaret Thatcher was elected," and "up to 2 million British children are suffering ill-health and stunted growth because of malnutrition." Thatcherite programs reversed the trend to improved child health and led to an upswing of childhood diseases that had been controlled, while public funds are used for such purposes as illegal projects in Turkey and Malaysia to foster arms sales by state-subsidized industry.[39] In accord with "really existing free market doctrine," public spending after 17 years of Thatcherite gospel is the same as when she took over.[40]

In the US, subjected to similar policies, 30 million people suffered from hunger by 1990, an increase of 50 percent from 1985, including 12 million children lacking sufficient food to maintain growth and development (before the 1991 recession). Forty percent of children in the world's richest city fell below the poverty line. In terms of such basic social indicators as child mortality, the US ranks well below any other industrial country, alongside of Cuba, which has less than 5 percent the GNP per capita of the United States and has undergone many years of terrorist attack and increasingly severe economic warfare at the hands of the hemispheric superpower.[41]

Given its extraordinary advantages, the US is in the leading ranks of relativists who reject the universality of the UD by virtue of Article 25 alone.

The same values guide the international financial institutions that the US largely controls. The World Bank and the IMF "have been extraordinarily human rights averse," the chairperson of the UN Committee on Economic, Social, and Cultural Rights, Philip Alston, observed with polite understatement in his submission to the Vienna countersession. "As we have heard so dramatically at this Public Hearing," Nouri Abdul Razzak of the Afro-Asian People's Solidarity Organization added, "the policies of the international financial institutions are contributing to the impoverishment of the world's people, the degradation of the global environment, and the violation of the most fundamental human rights."

In the face of such direct violations of the principles of the UD, it is perhaps superfluous to mention the refusal to take even small steps towards upholding them. UNICEF estimates that every hour, 1,000 children die from easily preventable disease, and almost twice that many women die or suffer serious disability in pregnancy or childbirth for lack of simple remedies and care. To ensure universal access to basic social services, UNICEF estimates, would require a quarter of the annual military expenditures of the "developing countries," about 10 percent of US military spending.[42] As noted, the US actively promotes military expenditures of the "developing countries"; its own remain at Cold War levels, increasing today while social spending is being severely cut. Also sharply declining in the 1990s is US foreign aid, already the most miserly among the developed countries, and virtually non-existent if we exclude the rich country that is the primary recipient (Washington's Israeli client).[43]

In his "Final Report" to the UN Commission on Human Rights, Special Rapporteur Leandro Despouy cites the World Health Organization's characterization of "extreme poverty" as "the world's most ruthless killer and the greatest cause of suffering on earth": "No other disaster compared to the devastation of hunger which had caused more deaths in the past two years than were killed in the two World Wars together." The right to a standard of living adequate for health and well-being is affirmed in Article 25 of the UD, he notes, and in the International Covenant on Economic, Social, and Cultural Rights, "which places emphasis more particularly on 'the fundamental right of everyone to be free from hunger.' "[44] But from the highly relativist perspective of the West, these principles of human rights agreements have no status, though they are officially endorsed.

There are other differences of interpretation concerning Article 25. The UN Commission on Human Rights was approached by Third World countries seeking means "to stem the huge flow of dangerous substances" to the poor countries, concerned that "dumping toxic products and wastes threatened the basic rights of life and good health" guaranteed by the UD. The UN investigator determined that the rich countries send "masses of toxic waste" to the Third World and, now, the former Soviet domains. "She said information she gathered shows 'serious violations of the right to life and health,' " the press reported, and "in some cases 'had led to sickness, disorders, physical or mental disability, and even death.' " Her information was limited, however, because she had "little cooperation from developed countries or corporations," and none at all from the US, which is moving to terminate her mission.[45]

Article 23 of the UD declares that "everyone has the right to work, to free choice of employment, to just and favorable conditions of work, and to protection against unemployment," along with "remuneration ensuring for himself and his family an existence worthy of human dignity, and supplemented, if necessary, by other means of social protection." We need not tarry on Washington's respect for this principle. Furthermore, "Everyone has the right to form and to join trade unions for the protection of his interests."

The latter right is technically upheld in the United States, though legal and administrative mechanisms ensure that it is increasingly observed in the breach. By the time the Reaganites had completed their work, the US was far enough off the spectrum so that the International Labor Organization, which rarely criticizes the powerful, issued a recommendation that the US conform to international standards, in response to an AFL-CIO complaint about strikebreaking by resort to "permanent replacement workers."[46] Apart from South Africa, no other industrial country tolerated these methods to ensure that Article 23 remains empty words; and with subsequent developments in South Africa, the US may stand in splendid isolation in this particular respect, though it has yet to achieve British standards, such as allowing employers to use selective pay increases to induce workers to reject union and collective bargaining rights.[47]

Reviewing some of the mechanisms used to render Article 23 inoperative, *Business Week* reported that from the early Reagan years, "US industry has conducted one of the most successful anti-union wars ever, illegally firing thousands of workers for exercising their rights to organize." "Unlawful firings occurred in one-third of all representation elections in the late '80s, vs. 8 percent in the late '60s." Workers have no recourse, as the Reagan administration converted the powerful state they nurtured to an expansive welfare state for the rich, defying US law as well as the customary international law enshrined in the UD. Management's basic goal, the journal explains, has been to cancel the rights "guaranteed by the 1935 Wagner Act," which brought the US into the mainstream of the industrial world.[48] That has been a basic goal since the New Deal provisions were enacted, and although the project of reversing the victory for democracy and working people was put on hold during the war, it was taken up again when peace arrived, with great vigor and considerable success.[49] One index of the success is provided by the record of ratification of ILO conventions guaranteeing labor rights. The US has by far the worst record in the Western hemisphere and Europe, with the exception of El Salvador and Lithuania. It does not recognize even standard conventions on child labor and the right to organize.[50]

"The United States is in arrears to the ILO in the amount of $92.6 million," the Lawyers Committee for Human Rights notes. This withholding of funds "seriously jeopardizes the ILO's operations"; Washington's plans for larger cuts in ILO funding "would primarily affect the ILO's ability to deliver technical assistance in the field," thus undermining Article 23 still further, worldwide.[51] This is only part of the huge debt to international organizations that the US refuses to pay (in violation of treaty obligations). Unpaid back dues to the UN are estimated at $1.3 billion. "Our doors are kept open," Secretary-General Kofi Annan writes, "only because other countries in essence provide interest-free loans to cover largely American shortfalls — not only NATO allies ... but also developing countries like Pakistan and even Fiji."[52] A few weeks later, still refusing to pay, the Senate voted 90 to 10 that the UN "thank the United States for its contributions," lower its obligations, "and publicly report to all member nations how much the United States has spent supporting Security Council resolutions since January 1, 1990."[53]

The illegal attack on unions in violation of Article 23 has many effects. It contributes to undermining health and safety standards in the workplace, which the government chooses not to enforce, leading to a sharp rise in industrial accidents in the Reagan years.[54] It also helps to undermine functioning democracy, as people with limited resources lose some of the few methods by which they can enter the political arena. And it accelerates the privatization of aspirations, dissolving the sense of solidarity and sympathy, and other human values that were at the heart of classical liberal thought but are inconsistent with the reigning ideology of privilege and power. More narrowly, the US Labor Department estimates that weakening of unions accounts for a large part of the stagnation or decline in real wages under the Reaganites, "a welcome development of transcendent importance," as the *Wall Street Journal* described the fall in labor costs from the 1985 high to the lowest in the industrial world (UK aside).[55]

Testifying before the Senate Banking Committee in February 1997, Federal Reserve Board Chair Alan Greenspan was highly optimistic about "sustainable economic expansion" thanks to "atypical restraint on compensation increases [which] appears to be mainly the consequence of greater worker insecurity," plainly a desideratum for a good society and yet another reason for Western relativists to reject Article 25 of the UD, with its "right to security." The February 1997 *Economic Report of the President,* taking pride in the Clinton administration's achievements, refers more obliquely to "changes in labor market institutions and practices" as a factor in the "significant wage restraint" that bolsters the health of the economy.[56]

The "free trade agreements," as they are common mislabelled (they include significant protectionist features and are "agreements" only if we discount popular opinion), contribute to these benign changes. Some of the mechanisms are spelled out in a study commissioned by the Labor Secretariat of the North American Free Trade Agreement "on the effects of the sudden closing of the plant on the principle of freedom of association and the right of workers to organize in the three countries." The study was carried out under NAFTA rules in response to a complaint by telecommunications workers on illegal labor practices by Sprint. The complaint was upheld by the US National Labor Relations Board, which ordered trivial penalties after years of delay, the standard procedure. The NAFTA study, by Cornell University Labor economist Kate Bronfenbrenner, was authorized for release by Canada and Mexico, but delayed by the Clinton administration. It reveals a significant impact of NAFTA on strikebreaking. About half of union organizing efforts are disrupted by employer threats to transfer production abroad, for example, by placing signs reading "Mexico Transfer Job" in front of a plant where there is an organizing drive. The threats are not idle. When such organizing drives nevertheless succeed, employers close the plant in whole or in part at triple the pre-NAFTA rate (about 15 percent of the time). Plant-closing threats are almost twice as high in more mobile industries (e.g., manufacturing vs. construction).[57]

These and other practices reported in the NAFTA study are illegal, but that is a technicality, as the Reagan administration had made clear, outweighed by the contribution to undermining the right to organize that is formally guaranteed by Article 23 — or, in more polite words, bringing about "changes in labor market institutions and practices" that contribute to "significant wage restraint" thanks to "greater worker insecurity," within an economic model offered with great pride to a backward world, and greatly admired among privileged sectors.

A number of other devices have been employed to nullify the pledge "never [to] join those who would undermine the Universal Declaration" (Christopher) in the case of Article 23. The further dismantling of the welfare system, sharply reduced from the '70s, drives many poor women to the labor market, where they will work at or below minimum wage and with limited benefits, with an array of government subsidies to induce employers to prefer them to low-wage workers. The likely effect is to drive down wages at the lower end, with indirect effects elsewhere. A related device is the increasing use of prison labor in the vastly expanding system of social control. Thus Boeing, which monopolizes US civilian aircraft production (helped by massive state subsidy for 60 years), not only transfers production facilities to China, but also to prisons a few miles from its Seattle offices, one of many examples.[58] Prison labor offers many advantages. It is disciplined, publicly subsidized, deprived of benefits, and "flexible" — available when needed, left to government support when not.

Reliance on prison labor draws from a rich tradition. The rapid industrial development in the southeastern region a century ago was based heavily on (black) convict labor, leased to the highest bidder. These measures reconstituted much of the basic structure of the plantation system after the abolition of slavery, but now for industrial development. The practices continued until the 1920s, until World War II in Mississippi. Southern industrialists pointed out that convict labor is "more reliable and productive than free labor" and overcomes the problem of labor turnover and instability. It also "remove[s] all danger and cost of strikes," a serious problem at the time, resolved by state violence that virtually destroyed the labor movement. Convict labor also lowers wages for "free labor," much as in the case of "welfare reform." The US Bureau of Labor reported that "mine owners [in Alabama] say they could not work at a profit without the lowering effect in wages of convict-labor competition."[59]

The resurgence of these mechanisms is quite natural as the superfluous population is driven to prisons on an unprecedented scale.

The attack on Article 23 is not limited to the US. The International Confederation of Free Trade Unions reports that "unions are being repressed across the world in more countries than ever before," while "poverty and inequality have increased in the developing countries, which globalization has drawn into a downward spiral of ever-lower labor standards to attract investment and meet the demands of enterprises seeking a fast profit" as governments "bow to pressure from the financial markets rather than from their own electorates," in accord with the "Washington consensus."[60] These are not the consequences of "economic laws" or what "the free market has decided, in its infinite but mysterious wisdom,"[61] as commonly alleged. Rather, they are the results of deliberate policy choices under really existing free market doctrine, undertaken during a period of "capital's clear subjugation of labor," in the words of the business press.[62]

Contempt for the socioeconomic provisions of the UD is so deeply engrained that no departure from objectivity is sensed when a front-page story lauds Britain's incoming Labor government for shifting the tax burden from "large businesses" to working people and the "middle class," steps that "set Britain further apart from countries like Germany and France that are still struggling with pugnacious unions, restrictive investment climates, and expensive welfare benefits."[63] Industrial "countries" never struggle with starving children, huge profits, or rapid increases in CEO pay (under Thatcher, double that of second-place US);[64] a reasonable stand under the "general tacit agreement" that the "country" equals "large businesses," along with doctrinal conventions about the health of the economy — the latter a technical concept, only weakly correlated with the health of the population (economic, social, or even medical).

Washington's rejection of the Economic, Social, and Cultural Rights guaranteed by the UD does receive occasional mention,[65] but the issue is generally ignored in the torrent of self-praise, and if raised, elicits mostly incomprehension.

To take some typical examples, *New York Times* correspondent Barbara Crossette reports that "the world held a human rights conference in Vienna in 1993 and dared to enshrine universal concepts," but progress was blocked by "panicked nations of the Third World." US diplomats are "frustrated at the unwillingness of many countries to take tough public stands on human rights," even though "diplomats say it is now easier to deal objectively with human rights abusers, case by case," now that the Cold War is over and "developing nations, with support from the Soviet bloc," no longer "routinely pass resolutions condemning the United States, the West in general, or targets like Israel and apartheid South Africa." Nonetheless, progress is difficult, "with a lot of people paying lip service to the whole concept of human rights in the Charter, in the Universal Declaration, and all that," but no more, UN Ambassador Madeleine Albright (now Secretary of State) observed.[66] On Human Rights Day, *New York Times* editors condemned the Asian countries that reject the UD and call instead for "addressing the more basic needs for people for food and shelter, medical care and schooling"[67] — in conformity with the UD.

The reasoning is straightforward. The US rejects these principles of the UD, so they are inoperative. By supporting these principles, the Asian countries are therefore rejecting the UD.

Puzzling over the contention that " 'human rights' extend to food and shelter," Seth Faison reviews a "perennial sticking point in United States–China diplomacy, highlighting the contrast between the American emphasis on individual freedom and the Chinese insistence that the common good transcends personal rights." China calls for a right to "food, clothing, shelter, education, the right to work, rest, and reasonable payment," and criticizes the US for not upholding these rights — which are affirmed in the UD, and are "personal rights" that the US rejects.[68]

Again, the reasoning is straightforward enough, once the guiding principles are internalized.

Human Rights Conditions

Under the impact of the popular movements of the 1960s, Congress imposed human rights conditions on military aid and trade privileges, compelling the White House to find various modes of evasion. These became farcical during the Reagan years, with regular solemn pronouncements about the "improvements" in the behavior of client murderers and torturers, eliciting much derision from human rights organizations but no policy change. The most extreme examples, hardly worth discussing, involved US clients in Central America. There are less egregious cases, beginning with the top recipient of US aid and running down the list. The leading human rights organizations have regularly condemned Israel's "systematic torture and ill-treatment of Palestinians under interrogation,"[69] along with apparent extrajudicial execution; legalization of torture; imprisonment without charge for as long as nine years for some of those kidnapped in Lebanon, now declared "legal" by the High Court as a "card to play" for hostage exchange[70]; and other abuses. US aid to Israel is therefore patently illegal under US law, Human Rights Watch and Amnesty International (AI) have insistently pointed out (as is aid to Egypt, Turkey, Colombia, and other high-ranking recipients).[71] In its annual report on US military aid and human rights, AI observes — once again — that "throughout the world, on any given day, a man, woman, or child is likely to be displaced, tortured, killed, or 'disappeared,' at the hands of governments or armed political groups. More often than not, the United States shares the blame," a practice that "makes a mockery of [congressional legislation] linking the granting of US security assistance to a country's human rights record."[72]

Such contentions elicit no interest or response in view of the "general tacit agreement" that laws are binding only when power interests so dictate.

The US also resorts regularly to sanctions, allegedly to punish human rights violations and for "national security" reasons. Of 116 cases of sanctions used since World War II, 80 percent were initiated by the US alone, measures that have often received international condemnation, particularly those against Cuba since 1961, which are by far the harshest.[73] The popular and congressional human rights programs from the early 1970s also sometimes called for sanctions against severe human rights violators; South Africa was the primary target outside of the Soviet sphere. The pressures, which were worldwide, had an impact. In 1976, the UN General Assembly called on the IMF to "refrain forthwith from extending credits to South Africa." The next day, at US-UK initiative, South Africa was granted more IMF funding than all of the rest of black Africa, in fact more than any country in the world apart from Britain and Mexico. The incoming Carter administration attempted (in vain) to block congressional efforts to impose human rights conditions on IMF funding to South Africa (claiming that it opposed "noneconomic factors," which it introduced under fraudulent pretexts to block loans to Vietnam).[74] After much delay and evasion, sanctions were finally imposed in 1985 and (over Reagan's veto) in 1986, but the administration "created glaring loopholes" that permitted US exports to increase by 40 percent between 1985 and 1988 while US imports increased 14 percent in 1988 after an initial decline. "The major economic impact was reduced investment capital and fewer foreign firms."[75]

The role of sanctions is dramatically illustrated in the case of the voice of the "dirty dozen," Indonesia. After the failure of a large-scale CIA operation to foment a rebellion in 1958, the US turned to other methods of overthrowing the Sukarno government. Aid was cut off, apart from military aid and training. That is standard operating procedure for instigating a military coup, which took place in 1965, with mounting US assistance as the new Suharto regime slaughtered perhaps half a million or more people in a few months, mostly landless peasants. There was no condemnation on the floor of Congress, and no aid to the victims from any major US relief agency. On the contrary, the slaughter (which the CIA compared to those of Stalin, Hitler, and Mao) aroused undisguised euphoria in a very revealing episode, best forgotten.[76] The World Bank quickly made Indonesia its third-largest borrower. The US and other Western governments and corporations followed along.

There was no thought of sanctions as the new government proceeded to compile one of the worst human rights records in the world or in the course of its murderous aggression in East Timor. Congress did, however, ban US military training after the Dili massacre in 1991. The aftermath followed the familiar pattern. Delicately selecting the anniversary of the Indonesian invasion, Clinton's State Department announced that "Congress's action did not ban Indonesia's purchase of training with its own funds," so it could proceed despite the ban, with Washington perhaps paying from some other pocket. The announcement received scant notice.[77] Under the usual "veil of secrecy," Congress (the House Appropriations Committee) expressed its "outrage," reiterating that "it was and is the intent of Congress to prohibit US military training for Indonesia": "we don't want employees of the US government training Indonesians," a staff member reiterated forcefully, but without effect.[78] Rather than impose sanctions, or even limit military aid, the US, UK, and other powers have sought to enrich themselves by participating in Indonesia's crimes.

Indonesian terror and aggression continue unhampered, along with harsh repression of labor in a country with wages half those of China. With the support of Senate Democrats, Clinton was able to block labor and other human rights conditions on aid to Indonesia. Announcing the suspension of review of Indonesian labor practices, Trade Representative Mickey Kantor commended Indonesia for "bringing its labor law and practice into closer conformity with international standards," a witticism that is in particularly poor taste.[79]

Also instructive is the record of sanctions against Haiti after the military coup of September 1991 that overthrew its first democratically elected government after seven months in office. The US had reacted to President Aristide's election with alarm, having confidently expected the victory of its own candidate, World Bank official Marc Bazin, who received 14 percent of the vote. Washington's reaction was to shift aid to anti-Aristide elements and, as noted, to honor asylum claims for the first time, restoring the normal defiance of Article 14 of the UD after the military junta let loose a reign of terror, killing thousands. The Organization of American States (OAS) declared an embargo, which the Bush administration quickly undermined by exempting US firms — "fine tuning" the sanctions, the press explained, in its "latest move" to find "more effective ways to hasten the collapse of what the administration calls an illegal government in Haiti."[80] US trade with Haiti remained high in 1992, increasing by almost half as Clinton extended the violations of the embargo, including purchases by the US government, which maintained close connections with the ruling torturers and killers; just how close we do not know, since the Clinton administration refuses to turn over to Haiti 160,000 pages of documents seized by US military forces — "to avoid embarrassing revelations" about US government involvement with the terrorist regime, according to Human Rights Watch.[81] President Aristide was allowed to return after the popular organizations that had swept him to power were subjected to three years of terror, and after he pledged to adopt the extreme neoliberal program of Washington's defeated candidate.

Officials of the US Justice Department revealed that the Bush and Clinton administrations had rendered the embargo virtually meaningless by authorizing illegal shipments of oil to the military junta and its wealthy supporters, informing Texaco Oil Company that it would not be penalized for violating the presidential directive of October 1991 banning such shipments. The information, prominently released the day before US troops landed to "restore democracy" in 1994, has yet to reach the general public, and is an unlikely candidate for the historical record.[82] These were among the many devices adopted to ensure that the popular forces that brought democracy to Haiti would have little voice in any future "democracy." The Clinton administration advertises this as a grand exercise in "restoring democracy," the prize example of the Clinton Doctrine[83] — to general applause, apart from those who see us as sacrificing too much in the cause of "global meliorism." None of this should surprise people who have failed to immunize themselves from "inconvenient facts."

The operative significance of sanctions is articulated honestly by the *Wall Street Journal,* reporting the call for economic sanctions against Nigeria. "Most Agree, Nigeria Sanctions Won't Fly," the headline reads: "Unlike in South Africa, Embargo Could Hurt West."[84] In brief, the commitment to human rights is instrumental. Where some interest is served, they are important, even grand ideals; otherwise the pragmatic criterion prevails. That too should come as no surprise. States are not moral agents; people are, and they can impose moral standards on powerful institutions. If they do not, the fine words will remain weapons.

Furthermore, lethal weapons. US economic warfare against Cuba for 40 years is a striking illustration. The unilateral US embargo against Cuba since 1961, the longest in history, is also unique in barring food and medicine. When the collapse of the USSR removed the traditional security pretext and eliminated aid from the Soviet bloc, the US responded by making the embargo far harsher, under new pretexts that would have made Orwell wince: The 1992 Cuban Democracy Act (CDA), initiated by liberal Democrats and strongly backed by President Clinton while he was undermining the sanctions against the mass murderers in Haiti. A year-long investigation by the American Association of World Health found that this escalation of US economic warfare had taken a "tragic human toll," causing "serious nutritional deficits" and "a devastating outbreak of neuropathy numbering in the tens of thousands." It also brought about a sharp reduction in medicines, medical supplies, and medical information, leaving children to suffer "in excruciating pain" because of lack of medicines. The embargo reversed Cuba's progress in bringing water services to the population and undermined its advanced biotechnology industry, among other consequences. These effects became far worse after the imposition of the CDA, which cut back licensed sales and donations of food and medical supplies by 90 percent within a year. A "humanitarian catastrophe has been averted only because the Cuban government has maintained" a health system that "is uniformly considered the preeminent model in the Third World."[85]

These do not count as human rights violations; rather, the public version is that the goal of the sanctions is to overcome Cuba's human rights violations.

The embargo has repeatedly been condemned by the United Nations. The Inter-American Commission on Human Rights of the OAS condemned US restrictions on shipments of food and medicine to Cuba as a violation of international law. Recent extensions of the embargo (the Helms-Burton Act; technically, the Cuban Liberty and Democratic Solidarity Act) were unanimously condemned by the OAS. In August 1996, its judicial body ruled unanimously that the act violated international law.

The Clinton administration's response is that shipments of medicine are not literally barred, only prevented by conditions so onerous and threatening that even the largest corporations are unwilling to face the prospects (huge financial penalties and imprisonment for what Washington determines to be violations of "proper distribution," banning of ships and aircraft, mobilization of media campaigns, etc.). And while food shipments are indeed barred, the administration argues that there are "ample suppliers" elsewhere (at far higher cost), so that the direct violation of international law is not a violation. Supply of medicines to

Cuba would be "detrimental to US foreign policy interests," the administration declared. When the European Union complained to the WTO
that the Helms-Burton Act, with its wide-ranging punishment of third
parties, violates trade agreements, the Clinton administration rejected
WTO jurisdiction, as its predecessors had done when the World Court
addressed Nicaragua's complaint about US international terrorism and
illegal economic warfare (upheld by the Court, irrelevantly). In a reaction that surpasses cynicism, Clinton condemned Cuba for ingratitude
"in return for the Cuban Democracy Act," a forthcoming gesture to improve US-Cuba relations.[86]

The official stand of the Clinton administration is that Cuba is a national security threat to the US, so that the WTO is an improper forum:
"bipartisan policy since the early 1960s [is] based on the notion that we
have a hostile and unfriendly regime 90 miles from our border, and that
anything done to strengthen that regime will only encourage the regime
to not only continue its hostility but, through much of its tenure, to try to
destabilize large parts of Latin America."[87] That stand was criticized by
historian Arthur Schlesinger, writing "as one involved in the Kennedy
administration's Cuban policy." The Clinton administration, he maintained, had misunderstood the reasons for the sanctions. The Kennedy
administration's concern had been Cuba's "troublemaking in the hemisphere" and "the Soviet connection," but these are now behind us, so the
policies are an anachronism.[88]

In secret, Schlesinger had explained the meaning of the phrase
"troublemaking in the hemisphere" — in Clintonite terms, trying to
"destabilize" Latin America. Reporting to incoming president Kennedy
on the conclusions of a Latin American Mission in early 1961, he described the Cuban threat as "the spread of the Castro idea of taking matters into one's own hands," a serious problem, he added later, when "the
distribution of land and other forms of national wealth greatly favors the
propertied classes" throughout Latin America, and "the poor and under-
privileged, stimulated by the example of the Cuban revolution, are now
demanding opportunities for a decent living." Schlesinger also explained
the threat of the "Soviet connection": "Meanwhile, the Soviet Union
hovers in the wings, flourishing large development loans and presenting
itself as the model for achieving modernization in a single generation."[89]

The US officially recognizes that "deliberate impeding of the delivery of food and medical supplies" to civilian populations constitutes a "violation of international humanitarian law," and "reaffirms that those who commit or order the commission of such acts will be held individually responsible in respect of such acts."[90] The reference is to Bosnia-Herzegovina. The president of the United States is plainly "individually responsible" for such "violations of international humanitarian law." Or would be, were it not for the "general tacit agreements" about selective enforcement, which reign with such absolute power among Western relativists that the simple facts are virtually undetectable.

Unlike such crimes as these, the regular administration contortions on human rights in China are a topic of debate. It is worth noting, however, that many critical issues are scarcely even raised: crucially, the horrifying conditions of working people, with hundreds, mostly women, burned to death, locked into factories; over 18,000 deaths from industrial accidents in 1995, according to Chinese government figures; and other gross violations of international conventions.[91] China's labor practices have been condemned, but narrowly: the use of prison labor for exports to the US. At the peak of the US-China confrontation over human rights, front-page stories reported that Washington's human rights campaign had met with some success: China had "agreed to a demand to allow more visits by American customs inspectors to Chinese prison factories to make sure they are not producing goods for export to the United States," also accepting US demands for "liberalization" and laws that are "critical elements of a market economy," all welcome steps towards a "virtuous circle."[92]

The conditions of "free labor" do not arise in this context. They are, however, causing other problems: "Chinese officials and analysts" say that the doubling of industrial deaths in 1992 and "abysmal working conditions," "combined with long hours, inadequate pay, and even physical beatings, are stirring unprecedented labor unrest among China's booming foreign joint ventures." These "tensions reveal the great gap between competitive foreign capitalists lured by cheap Chinese labor and workers weaned on socialist job security and the safety net of cradle-to-grave benefits." Workers do not yet understand that as they enter the free world, they are to be "beaten for producing poor quality goods, fired for dozing on the job during long work hours" and other such misdeeds, and locked into their factories to be burned to death. But apparently the

West understands, so China is not called to account for violations of labor rights; only for exporting prison products to the United States.

The distinction is easy to explain. Prison factories are state-owned
industry, and exports to the US interfere with profits, unlike the beating
and murder of working people and other means to improve the balance
sheet. The operative principles are clarified by the fact that the rules allow the United States to export prison goods. As China was submitting
to US discipline on export of prison-made goods to the US, California
and Oregon were exporting prison-made clothing to Asia, including spe-
cialty jeans, shirts, and a line of shorts quaintly called "Prison Blues."
The prisoners earn far less than the minimum wage and work under
"slave labor" conditions, prison rights activists allege. But their production does not interfere with the rights that count (in fact, enhances them
in many ways, as noted). So objection would be out of place.[93]

As the most powerful state, the US makes its own laws, using force
and conducting economic warfare at will. It also threatens sanctions
against countries that do not abide by its conveniently flexible notions of
"free trade." Washington has employed such threats with great effectiveness (and GATT approval) to force open Asian markets for US tobacco exports and advertising, aimed primarily at the growing markets
of women and children. The US Agriculture Department has provided
grants to tobacco firms to promote smoking overseas. Asian countries
have attempted to conduct educational anti-smoking campaigns, but
they are overwhelmed by the miracles of the market, reinforced by US
state power through the sanctions threat. Philip Morris, with an advertising and promotion budget of close to $9 billion in 1992, became China's
largest advertiser. The effect of Reaganite sanction threats was to increase advertising and promotion of cigarette smoking (particularly US
brands) quite sharply in Japan, Taiwan, and South Korea, along with the
use of these lethal substances. In South Korea, for example, the rate of
growth in smoking more than tripled when markets for US lethal drugs
were forced open in 1988. The Bush administration extended the threats
to Thailand in 1989, at exactly the same moment that its "war on drugs"
was prominently declared; the media were kind enough to overlook the
coincidence, even ignoring the outraged denunciations by the very conservative Surgeon-General C. Everett Koop. Oxford University epidemiologist Richard Peto estimated that among Chinese children under 20

today, 50 million will die of cigarette-related diseases, an achievement that ranks high even by 20th-century standards.[94]

While state power energetically promotes substance abuse in the interests of agribusiness, it adopts highly selective measures in other cases. In the context of "the war against drugs," the US has played an active role in the vast atrocities conducted by the security forces and their paramilitary associates in Colombia, the leading human rights violator in Latin America and the leading recipient of US aid and training, increasing under Clinton, consistent with traditional practice noted earlier. The war against drugs is "a myth," Amnesty International reports, agreeing with other investigators. Security forces work closely with narco-traffickers and landlords while targeting the usual victims, including community leaders, human rights and health workers, union activists, students, and the political opposition, but primarily peasants, in a country where protest has been criminalized. AI reports that "almost every Colombian military unit that Amnesty implicated in murdering civilians two years ago was doing so with US-supplied weapons," which they continue to receive, along with training.[95]

Other International Covenants

The UD calls on all states to promote the rights and freedoms proclaimed and to act "to secure their universal and effective recognition and observance" by various means, including ratification of treaties and enabling legislation. There are several such International Covenants, respected in much the manner of the UD. The Convention on the Rights of the Child, adopted by the UN in December 1989, has been ratified by all countries other than the US and Somalia (which has no government). After long delay, the US did endorse the International Covenant on Civil and Political Rights (ICCPR), "the leading treaty for the protection" of the subcategory of rights that the West claims to uphold, Human Rights Watch (HRW) and the American Civil Liberties Union (ACLU) observe in their report on continued US non-compliance with its provisions. The Bush administration ensured that the treaty would be inoperative, first, "through a series of reservations, declarations, and understandings" to eliminate provisions that might expand rights, and second, by declaring the US in full compliance with the remaining provisions. The treaty is

"non-self-executing" and is accompanied by no enabling legislation, so
it cannot be invoked in US courts. Ratification was "an empty act for
Americans," the HRW/ACLU report concludes.[96]

The exceptions are crucial, because the US violates the treaty "in
important respects," the report continues.[97] To cite one example, the US
entered a specific reservation to Article 7 of the ICCPR, which states
that "no one shall be subjected to torture or to cruel, inhuman, or degrading treatment or punishment." The reason is that conditions in US prisons violate these conditions as generally understood, just as they
seriously violate the provisions of Article 10 on humane treatment of
prisoners and on the right to "reformation and social rehabilitation,"
which the US rejects. Another US reservation concerns the death pen-
alty, which is not only employed far more freely than the norm but also
is "applied in a manner that is racially discriminatory," the HRW/ACLU
report concludes, as have other studies. Furthermore, "more juvenile offenders sit on death row in the United States than in any other country in
the world," HRW reports.[98] A UN Human Rights inquiry found the US
to be in violation of the Covenant for execution of juveniles (who committed the crimes before they were 18); the US is joined in this practice
only by Iran, Pakistan, Saudi Arabia, and Yemen. Executions are rare in
the industrial democracies, declining around the world, and rising in the
US, even among juveniles, the mentally impaired, and women, the UN
report observes.[99]

The US accepted the UN Convention Against Torture and Other
Forms of Cruel, Inhuman, or Degrading Treatment or Punishment, but
the Senate imposed restrictions, in part to protect a Supreme Court ruling allowing corporal punishment in schools.[100]

HRW also regards "disproportionate" and "cruelly excessive" sentencing procedures as a violation of Article 5 of the UD, which proscribes
"cruel, inhuman, or degrading treatment or punishment." The specific
reference is to laws that treat "possession of an ounce of cocaine or a $20
'street sale' [as] a more dangerous or serious offense than the rape of a
10-year-old, the burning of a building occupied by people, or the killing
of another human being while intending to cause him serious injury"
(quoting a federal judge). From the onset of Reaganite "neoliberalism,"
the rate of incarceration, which had been fairly stable through the post-
war period, has skyrocketed, almost tripling during the Reagan years

and continuing the sharp rise since, long ago leaving other industrial societies far behind. Eighty-four percent of the increase of admissions is for nonviolent offenders, mostly drug-related (including possession). Drug offenders constituted 22 percent of admissions in federal prisons in 1980, 42 percent in 1990, and 58 percent in 1992. The US apparently leads the world in imprisoning its population (perhaps sharing the distinction with Russia or China, where data are uncertain). By the end of 1996, the prison population had reached a record 1.2 million, increasing 5 percent over the preceding year, with the federal prison system 25 percent over capacity and state prisons almost the same. Meanwhile crime rates continued to decline.[101]

By 1998, close to 1.7 million were in federal and state prisons, or local jails. Average sentences for murder and other violent crimes have decreased markedly, while those for drug offenses have shot up, targeting primarily African-Americans and creating what two criminologists call "the *new American apartheid*."[102]

US crime rates, while high, are not out of the range of industrial societies, apart from homicides with guns, a reflection of the US gun culture. Fear of crime, however, is very high and increasing, in large part a "product of a variety of factors that have little or nothing to do with crime itself," the National Criminal Justice Commission concludes (as do other studies). The factors include media practices and "the role of government and private industry in stoking citizen fear." The focus is very specific: for example, drug users in the ghetto but not criminals in executive suites, though the Justice Department estimates the cost of corporate crime as 7 to 25 times as high as street crime. Work-related deaths are 6 times has high as homicides, and pollution also takes a far higher toll than homicide.[103]

Expert studies have regularly concluded that "there is no direct relation between the level of crime and the number of imprisonments" (European Council Commission). Many criminologists have pointed out further that while "crime control" has limited relation to crime, it has a great deal to do with control of the "dangerous classes"; today, those cast aside by the socioeconomic model designed to globalize the sharply two-tiered structural model of Third World societies. As noted at once, the latest "war on drugs" was timed to target mostly black males; trend lines on substance use sufficed to demonstrate that. By adopting these measures, Senator Daniel Patrick Moynihan observed, "we are choosing to have an intense crime problem concentrated among minorities." "The war's planners knew exactly what they were doing," criminologist Michael Tonry comments, spelling out the details, including the racist procedures that run through the system from arrest to sentencing, in part attributable to the close race-class correlation, but not entirely.[104]

As widely recognized, the "war on drugs" has no significant effect on use of drugs or street price, and is far less effective than educational and remedial programs. But it does not follow that it serves no purpose. It is a counterpart to the "social cleansing" — the removal or elimination of "disposable people" — conducted by the state terrorist forces in Colombia and other terror states. It also frightens the rest of the population, a standard device to induce obedience. Such policies make good sense as part of a program that has radically concentrated wealth while, for the majority of the population, living conditions and incomes stagnate or decline. It is, correspondingly, natural for Congress to require that sentencing guidelines and policy reject as "inappropriate" any consideration of such factors as poverty and deprivation, social ties, etc. These requirements are precisely counter to European crime policy, criminologist Nils Christie observes, but sensible on the assumption that "under the rhetoric of equality," Congress "envisions the criminal process as a vast engine of social control" (quoting former Chief Judge Bazelon).[105]

The vast scale of the expanding "crime control industry" has attracted the attention of finance and industry, who welcome it as another form of state intervention in the economy, a Keynesian stimulus that may soon approach the Pentagon system in scale, some estimate. "Businesses Cash In," the *Wall Street Journal* reports, including the construction industry, law firms, the booming private prison complex, and "the loftiest names in finance" such as Goldman Sachs, Prudential, and others, "competing to underwrite prison construction with private, tax-exempt bonds." Also standing in line is the "defense establishment, ... scenting a new line of business" in high-tech surveillance and control systems of a sort that Big Brother would have admired. The industry also offers new opportunities for corporate use of prison labor, as discussed earlier.[106]

Other international covenants submitted to Congress have also been restricted as "non-self-executing," meaning that they are of largely symbolic significance. The fact that covenants, if even ratified, are declared non-enforceable in US courts has been a "major concern" of the UN Human Rights Committee, along with the Human Rights organizations. The Committee also expressed concern that "poverty and lack of access to education adversely affect persons belonging to these groups in their ability to enjoy rights under the [ICCPR] on the basis of equality," even for that subcategory of the UD the US professes to uphold. And while (rightly) praising the US commitment to freedom of speech, the Committee also questioned Washington's announced principle that "money is a form of speech," as the courts have upheld in recent years, with wide-ranging effects on the electoral system.[107]

The US is a world leader in defense of freedom of speech, perhaps uniquely so since the 1960s.[108] With regard to civil-political rights, the US record at home ranks high by comparative standards, though a serious evaluation would have to take into account the conditions required to enjoy those rights, and also the "accelerated erosion of basic due process and human rights protections in the United States" as "US authorities at federal and state levels undermined the rights of vulnerable groups, making the year [1996] a disturbing one for human rights," with the president not only failing to "preserve rights under attack" but sometimes taking "the lead in eliminating human rights protections."[109] The social and economic provisions of the UD and other conventions are operative only insofar as popular struggle over many years has given them substance. The earlier record within the national territory is shameful, and the human rights record abroad is a scandal. The charge of "relativism" levelled against others, while fully accurate, reeks of hypocrisy.

But the realities are for the most part "kept dark, without any need for any official ban."

11

The Legacy of War

The Sacralization of War

Eight hundred years ago, a Spanish pilgrim on his way to Mecca observed that "the warriors are engaged in their wars while people are at ease," continuing their lives while the warrior castes pursued their age-old rituals of mayhem and murder. The origins of these rituals are not very clear. Some anthropologists have argued that they trace back to the origins of agriculture, when the decline of hunting left men in need of some new status symbol and means "to maintain the old glory and companionship which formerly existed during hunting expeditions." The constraints on the warrior elite that are described by the Spanish pilgrim, within Europe at least, may be related to what is sometimes called "the sacralization of war," that is, the merger of militarism and the Church. Church records from about that time reveal efforts to create some kind of space for the Church itself and for non-combatants more generally. One edict of 1045 declares that "there should be no attacks on clerics, monks, nuns, women, pilgrims, merchants, peasants, visitors to councils, churches and their surrounding grounds, cemeteries, cloisters, the lands of the clergy, shepherds and their flocks, agricultural animals, wagons in the fields, and olive trees."

How well this edict of the Council of Narbonne was observed beyond the domains of the Church one can learn from Arab sources on the "Frankish invasions" — what the West calls the Crusades. Refugees fleeing to Baghdad after the conquest of Jerusalem in 1099, half a century later, reported that the invaders had sacked and destroyed all the towns and cities in their path, massacred peasants and townspeople, and, when they reached the Holy City — quoting from contemporary chroniclers — "the fair-haired and heavily armored warriors spilled through the streets, swords in hand, slaughtering men, women, and children, plundering houses, sacking mosques, leaving not a single Muslim alive within the city walls." When the killing stopped a few days later there were thousands lying in pools of blood on the doorsteps of their homes or alongside the mosques. There was a Jewish community in Jerusalem — their fate was the same. The community finally retreated into the main synagogue, which was burned to the ground by the Frankish invaders, while those who managed to escape were hunted down and killed, and the rest burned alive. And so the first crusade came to an end with the blood of the conquered running down the streets as the knights, in their own words, "sobbing for excess of joy," came to the Church of the Sepulcher "and put their blood-stained hands together in prayer" — a quote from contemporary Western history in this case. The Frankish chroniclers themselves did not conceal these facts at the time. They described then how the warriors of the church "boiled Pagan adults in cooking pots" and "impaled chickens on spits and devoured them grilled." One Frankish chronicler felt that they went a bit far. "Not only did our troops not shrink from eating dead Turks and Saracens, they also ate dogs." There should be some limits, after all.

Richard the Lionhearted later followed similar practices, roping together prisoners who were a burden — captured soldiers, along with women and children of their families — and delivering them to soldiers of the Cross, who "fell upon them viciously with their sabres, lances, and stones until all the wails had been stilled," an Arab chronicler reports. The atrocities and the destruction peaked with the conquest of Constantinople in 1204, which led to huge massacres, pillage, carnage, and destruction of much of the residue of Greek and Byzantine civilizations, with mass killings of civilians, priests, monks, and others. Shortly after, the Mongol invaders, led by Genghis Khan, followed very much the same course in the same regions.

This, from the Christian side, was all part of the "sacralization of war," what modern historians call the "clerical reformation of the fighting laymen," an attempt to add a spiritual dimension to the atrocities and the brutalities of the age of chivalry. To quote a modern British historian,

> The knight who joined the crusades could attain what the spiritual side of his nature ardently sought — perfect salvation and remission of

sins. He might butcher all day 'til he waded ankle-deep in blood, and
then at nightfall kneel sobbing for joy [actually, "sobbing for excess of
joy," as they themselves put it] at the altar of the sepulcher, for was he
not red from the winepress of the Lord?

"One can understand the popularity of the crusades," the same historian
goes on — not the first, and certainly not the last, effort to cast the mantle
of nobility on some hideous and shameful enterprise.

All of these are among matters that might be borne in mind when we
read impressive rhetoric today about the coming clash of civilizations,
the paradigm for the new era now coming into view — and of course
what I have mentioned is only a pea on a mountain.

Let's go back to the edict of the Council of Narbonne in 1045. Recall the exceptions that were listed: there should be no attacks on clerics,
monks, nuns, women, etc. That list of exceptions gives some indication
of the targets of war — in other words, those that had to be excepted —
and its legacy. What the Spanish pilgrim described was no doubt true,
but it was a very unusual moment. The feats of the Warriors of the Cross
and Genghis Khan are much more typical.

Probably the extremes of savagery — recorded savagery, at least —
are in the earliest histories, in the Bible. I suppose that in the entire literary canon there is nothing that exalts genocide with such fervor and dedication and enthusiasm as the commandments of the warrior God to his
chosen people — for example, his commandments delivered to King
Saul by the prophet Samuel, who was the most just of the judges, and
who conveyed the commandment to Saul to attack Amalek and spare
nothing, killing all men, women, infants, and sucklings, oxen and sheep,
camels and asses — the reason being that centuries earlier the
Amalekites had stood in the way of the Hebrews conquering their Holy
Land. Saul, as you may remember, spared one person, the king of
Amalek, and some of the cattle. Samuel, when he discovered this, was
enraged and cut down the captured prisoner before the Lord at Gilgal.
And so the story continues.

These lessons were taken to heart by the Frankish warriors, certainly, as we know from their own records. They were also taken to heart
by the very devout Englishmen who conquered this country, seeing
themselves as the inheritors of the Israelites taking their promised land
and ridding the country of "that hapless race of Native Americans,

which we are exterminating with such merciless and perfidious cruelty." That's the way John Quincy Adams later described the project, long after his own major and very significant contributions to it had passed, and in fact when it was entering a new phase farther west.

It has only been in very recent years that the original sin of our own history has begun to be acknowledged. That's one of the many very positive legacies of the ferment of the 1960s, which has had a significant and, I hope, lasting effect in raising the moral and cultural level of this society.

European Conquests

European history has been particularly savage, including its conquest of most of the world. These conquests were mostly small wars from the European point of view, leading military historians point out. That is, they were nothing like the wars the Europeans were fighting among themselves. Take the American Revolution as an example. The American Revolution was a kind of side show as far as the British were concerned. In exactly the same years, they were fighting a war of comparable scale in India, the Marathi War. The American Revolution was itself a peripheral part of the global wars that were going on among the major European powers. The revolution here succeeded largely because at that particular moment Britain happened to be standing against the rest of the major European powers and couldn't devote much attention to the small war going on here, at the same time that a small war was going on in India and a major war was going on with France and Spain and others. The major powers, mainly France and England, were fighting a war here, a long-standing war, and different parts of the domestic population were supporting one side or the other. Those we call loyalists were supporting the British; those we call patriots were supported by the French; and much of the fighting was done by the powerful forces — the French and the British — with local assistance. I think that would probably be a more accurate way of describing the Revolutionary War.

To turn to another part of the world, Robert Clive's forces were outnumbered by about 10 to 1 at the crucial battle of 1757 that opened the way to the takeover of Bengal by the East India Company, setting the stage for the British conquest of all of India. Bengal was the richest area — so extraordinarily rich, in fact, that the British merchant adventurers and conquerors were amazed by its wealth. India itself was the commercial and manufacturing center of the world in the 18th century. It was, for example, producing more iron than all of Europe. It's striking that over the centuries extraordinarily rich and productive areas have become the very symbols of hopelessness and despair — such as Bangladesh and Calcutta. That's a typical feature of European conquest, which says a lot about the legacy of, in this case, small wars, from the point of view of the conquerors.

Haiti is another example. It was perhaps the richest colony in the world, and the source of much of France's wealth. It's now facing possible disappearance in the next few decades. Another example is the East Indies, contemporary Indonesia, which provided about 20 percent of the national income of the very wealthy Netherlands until World War II, and as a small footnote, we might bear in mind that the Marshall Plan aid to France and Holland, two major imperial powers, just about covered the costs of their bloody efforts to maintain their Southeast Asian colonies.

Probably the main factors in the European conquest were, perhaps, a slight edge in military technology, but primarily, I think, a kind of culture of savagery — "the all-destructive fury of European warfare" that "appalled" the conquered populations from the East Indies to the New World, quoting British military historian Geoffrey Parker. "Warfare in India was still a sport, while in Europe it had become a science," a recent history of the East India Company points out. Actually, Adam Smith had drawn similar conclusions at the time, denouncing what he called the "savage injustice of the Europeans," thinking primarily of the English, properly his main concern. The English settlers who arrived here carried on the tradition of extreme savagery in the Indian wars and the expansion of the national territory. For example, Andrew Jackson's conquest of Spanish Florida, an important event in many ways, and the first executive war in American history.

That's a tradition that has become the dominant one. You really have to look hard in modern history to find a war that isn't an executive war and that conforms to constitutional principles, which require that Congress declare war. Jackson's executive war was fought against those who were called the Seminoles. They were called the "mingled hordes of lawless Indians and Negroes." Lawless Indians and runaway slaves — that's the way the invaders put it. Jackson's tactics taught the "salutary efficacy" of terror, Secretary of State John Quincy Adams observed in a famous paper that justified the massive atrocities and the invasion and aggression of the executive war, a state paper that was much admired by Jefferson and leading 20th-century scholars.

I should add that these particular wars of extermination do survive in the national consciousness. Recently there was a front-page story in the *Wall Street Journal* on changes in culinary practices in the United States over the years. It opened with a discussion of "Seminole soup" without a trace of embarrassment. The Seminoles are also the mascot of a college football team that regularly competes for the national championship. If the Nazis had won World War II, maybe the Jews and the Gypsies would serve as mascots for the University of Munich. In general, the winners and the losers regard the legacy of war quite differently.

These traditions were carried on after the conquest of the national territory. Early in this century, US troops were liberating the Philippines — liberating several hundred thousand souls from life's sorrows and travails. The press was very much impressed by this heroic and generous endeavor, and described it with some accuracy. The war was led by old Indian fighters who were killing more "niggers," as they put it, so it was all old hat. The press reported very positively that the American forces were "slaughtering the natives in English fashion," so that "the misguided creatures who resist us will at least respect our arms" and later come to recognize our good intentions. The misguided creatures, those who remained alive, were really consenting to their slaughter, a leading American sociologist explained. He was developing the thesis that he called "consent without consent." It's the way a child can be said to consent implicitly when the parent prevents him or her from running into a busy street. Later the child will come to see that it was all for the good — in other words, that he or she was really consenting. Same with the misguided creatures who are resisting us.

These themes persist without much change right to the present day, and so, in fact, do the echoes of the Indian wars. They were revived again during the wars of Indochina in the military and in the popular literature. During the US terror wars in Central America in the 1980s, the leading liberal intellectual journal explained that we must proceed "regardless of how many are murdered" because we have our mission, like the self-described saints who massacred the Indians of New England while carrying the Holy Book; their predecessors; and many others like them: the Mongol hordes of Genghis Khan, for example, or the forces of Attila the Hun or the Romans or the Assyrians or the Hebrews conquering the land of Canaan, to sample from a very long list.

The peculiar savagery of European warfare may reflect the bloody history of Europe itself. For hundreds of years, in the leading centers of Western civilization — France and Germany — the highest and most noble vocation and duty was to slaughter one another. That exalted mission came to an end in 1945, but only because the science of war that European civilization had crafted reached such a grotesque level that the next episode would be the last, leaving no legacy of war, at least for anyone to record in chronicles or art.

The 20th Century

The legacy of world conquest itself is clear enough. To mention just the most obvious illustration, the only parts of the world that have developed outside of Europe are the parts that escaped its clutches: the United States, which joined the enterprise itself after it was liberated from England, and Japan, with some of its colonies in tow. It's worth noting that Japan, though a very brutal imperial power, happened to treat its colonies differently from the rest. It did not rob and destroy them. They didn't end up being Bangladesh or Haiti. Rather, it developed them at about the same rate as the imperial power itself. After World War II and its aftermath, they then resumed this growth, becoming the center of the East Asian growth area.

In the 20th century, civilian populations once again became a prime target, as in biblical days, the Frankish wars, and other unusually bloody eras. The Nazis broke new ground with industrialized genocide — and recall that this was the world's most advanced industrial and technological power and the cultural center of the West as well. Military attacks specifically targeting civilians peaked with the allied bombings of Germany and Japan. The most horrifying of these before Hiroshima-Nagasaki was the fire-bombing of Tokyo in March 1945. That killed somewhere between 80,000 and 200,000 people. Nobody was paying much attention to numbers at that point, so estimates range widely. It left more than a million homeless in the undefended city. The point of the fire-bombing was that the city was made out of wood, so you could get a huge firestorm, and the whole thing could turn into a horrendous monstrosity, as it did. It also removed Tokyo from the list of atom bomb targets on the recognition that further destruction would be unimpressive — it would just pile rubble upon rubble and bodies upon bodies. After the war the US Strategic Bombing Survey concluded that "probably more people lost their lives by fire in Tokyo in a six-hour period than at any time in the history of man." The 50th anniversary of this atrocity was commemorated with a vivid and horrifying report in the *Far Eastern Economic Review* in Hong Kong — the leading business journal in Asia, which is very conservative. Here, in the United States, the anniversary passed virtually without notice. To the extent that there was a reaction, it was more or less captured in a comment quoted in the *Washington Post:* "If that's what it took to win, that's what should have been done."

All this was amid a flood of very harsh condemnation of Japan for failing to give adequate recognition of its own guilt for bombing a military base in an American colony that had been taken from its inhabitants by force and guile half a century earlier. The bombing of Pearl Harbor was a crime, but in the array of crimes it's hard to claim that it ranks very high. Quoting from the Japanese apology, Japan had officially expressed "sincere repentance for our past, including aggression and colonial rule that caused unbearable suffering and sorrow" for China and other countries of Asia. That Japanese official statement was bitterly denounced in the United States, alongside sober articles about the strange flaws in the Japanese character that prevent them from acknowledging guilt. The reason was that the apology was accompanied by a mention of the fact that there had been other imperial atrocities in Asia, implying that the records of Holland, England, France, and the United States might also not have been utterly pure. That's outrageous, and the conclusion was that the Japanese were just once again seeking to evade their guilt. If Asians saw the matter differently, actually even welcoming the Japanese at first, that again just shows that they were "misguided creatures."

In Europe, the bombing of Dresden was the nearest counterpart to the fire-bombing of Tokyo; it took place at about the same time. US and British air forces destroyed the city, killing tens of thousands of people and destroying lots of great achievements of Western civilization. The 50th anniversary occurred at the same time as the 50th anniversary of the fire-bombing of Tokyo. It aroused considerable soul-searching in England, but I couldn't find any reference to it here. Remember that Britain was at that time under serious attack, something that the United States has not experienced since the War of 1812. The British had direct experience with the legacy of war. The United States had none, apart from its own murderous Civil War, since 1812. A prolonged record of victorious conquest is not good for the character, in my opinion, and I think history tends to substantiate that judgment. To take a recent example, Hitler was perhaps the most popular leader in German history, pre-Stalingrad.

The specific targeting of civilians continued after World War II, but with care to ensure they would be defenseless and could not retaliate. The most extreme example is the war in Indochina. To remind you of the basic facts: with US aid — in fact US Marshall Plan aid — France did try to reconquer its former colony after the Second World War. That left about half a million Vietnamese dead. In 1954 France withdrew, and there was a diplomatic settlement calling for the unification of the country in two years with elections; temporary demilitarized separation of the military forces for two years; then unification under elections. We know the US reaction to that; the documents have been declassified. Actually, they were released in the Pentagon Papers by Daniel Ellsberg, but they've since been declassified. The US strongly opposed the Geneva political settlement. Internally, in the major national security report, it was called a "disaster," and the United States decided internally within a few days after Geneva that no matter what happened, the United States was not going to permit the diplomatic settlement to take place. It included an interesting phrase. It said that in the case of "local Communist subversion or rebellion not constituting armed attack" — a crucial phrase — the United States will react with a series of measures, which go all the way up to attacking China, if decided to be necessary.

The phraseology and plans are interesting. The wording was chosen in order to make it very clear and explicit that the United States was going to purposely violate the major principle of international law, the UN Charter, which states that use of force is always illegitimate except when under armed attack and in an instantaneous reaction before the Security Council reacts. But the statement was: in the event of "local Communist subversion [we'll decide what that is] or rebellion not constituting armed attack" we will take military measures, including rearmament of Japan, attacks on China, setting up Thailand as the "focal point" for US subversive activity throughout the region, and so on. This blatant and purposeful violation of the fundamental principles of international law was then repeated year after year, in the same wording. It was in the Pentagon Papers — actually one of the few interesting revelations in the Pentagon Papers. Most of what appeared was pretty obvious, but this was new. It has yet to enter even most scholarly records. Apparently it's considered a little "too hot to handle," although it's now been 25 years since it was released, and it is very important. Those are the origins of the expansion of the war after the US undermined the Geneva agreements.

US Expansion of War

The US did undermine the Geneva agreements — it set up a rather typical Latin American–style terror state in the South and killed about 70,000 South Vietnamese by 1960. But the harsh repression elicited resistance. The regime that the US had set up was so flimsy that as soon as there was any reaction to its repression it immediately began to collapse. John F. Kennedy was faced with a problem — the client state was collapsing. He had to either pull out or escalate. He escalated. In 1961 and 1962, the US attacked South Vietnam directly. The US Air Force was sent to bomb South Vietnam. US Air Force pilots in US Air Force planes were carrying out about one-third of the missions by 1962. It's true that the planes were disguised with South Vietnamese markings, but it was known, and in fact reported. In 1961 and 1962 the Kennedy administration also authorized crop destruction (in violation of the Geneva conventions). In 1963, two years later, the South Vietnamese client regime was once again facing collapse and, worse than that, it was trying to negotiate a peaceful settlement. Kennedy's ambassador, Henry Cabot Lodge, complained in secret that the client regime was "not a thoroughly strong police state ... because, unlike Hitler's Germany, it is not efficient," and it was unable to suppress the "large and well-organized underground opponent strongly and ever freshly motivated by vigorous hatred" for the client regime and the foreign invaders who had imposed it. Incidentally, as this terminology reveals and the rest of the documentary records show, despite a few pretenses, there was no serious doubt internally that the United States was at war with South Vietnam. Whatever you think about the legitimacy of North Vietnamese involvement in Vietnam, the fact is, there was no direct North Vietnamese involvement even suspected until years later — well after the United States had extended the war to the bombing of North Vietnam.

Because of these flaws — that is, the lack of Hitler-like efficiency in suppression, and the steps towards diplomatic settlement — the client regime was overthrown by a military coup backed strongly by the Kennedy administration. That was following the policy that Kennedy, in fact, demanded until the end — he was one of the real hawks in his administration — namely that military victory in South Vietnam had to be guaranteed before there was any consideration of either a diplomatic settlement or withdrawal of the invading army that he had sent. There's a lot of confusion about this in the United States, connected to various Kennedy assassination theories, but the record is very rich and unusually clear and consistent.

In February 1965, the United States escalated the war against South Vietnam radically, and also, on the side, began regular bombing of the North at a much lower level. That was a big public issue in the United States: Should we bomb North Vietnam? The bombing of the South was ignored. The same shows up in the internal planning, for which we now have an extremely rich record, not only from the Pentagon Papers, but from tons of declassified documents that have been released in the last couple of years. It turns out — again, one of the very few interesting revelations of the Pentagon Papers — that there was no planning for the escalated bombing of the South. There was very meticulous planning about the bombing of the North — carefully calibrated, when should we do it, and a lot of agonizing about it. The bombing of the South at triple the scale of the North is barely discussed. There are a few casual decisions here and there. The same shows up in McNamara's recent memoirs. He discusses at great length the bombing of the North. The bombing of the South he literally doesn't mention. He mentions what he did on January 21, 1965, a really important day: there was a big discussion about whether to bomb North Vietnam. He doesn't mention what we know from other documents, that on that same day, he authorized for the first time the use of jet planes to escalate the bombing of South Vietnam over and above the massive bombing that had been going on for years — that's not even mentioned.

I think the reason for that in public consciousness and in internal planning is unpleasantly obvious, but it may be worth paying attention to, if people are willing to look in the mirror. The reason is that the bombing of North Vietnam was costly to the United States. For one thing, it was costly in international opinion because it was a bombing of what was by then regarded as a state, which had embassies and so on. Besides, there was a danger that there could be a retaliation. The United States was bombing an internal Chinese railroad, which went from southwest to southeast China. It was built through the northern part of Vietnam because of the way the French built railroads. The US was bombing Russian ships; it was bombing Russian embassies. China and Russia might respond. So it was dangerous. There were potential costs to the bombing of North Vietnam. On the other hand, the bombing of South Vietnam on a vastly greater scale was costless. There was nothing the South Vietnamese could do about it. Accordingly, it was not an issue at the time. There were no protests about it. Virtually none. Protests were almost entirely about the bombing of the North, and it has essentially disappeared from history, so that it doesn't have to be mentioned in McNamara's memoirs or in other accounts, and, as I say, there wasn't even any planning for it. Just a casual decision: it doesn't cost us anything, why not just kill a lot of people? It's an interesting incident that tells you a lot about the thinking that runs from the earliest days right to the present. We're not talking about ancient history as when we talk about Amalek and the Frankish wars and Genghis Khan.

The war then, of course, expanded. The US expanded the war to Laos and Cambodia. As in Vietnam, and Laos and Cambodia, too, the targets were primarily civilian. The main target, however, was always South Vietnam. That included saturation bombing of the densely populated Mekong Delta and air raids south of Saigon that were specifically targeting villages and towns. They were deciding, "let's put a B-52 raid on this town." Huge terror operations like "Speedy Express" and "Bold Mariner" and others were aimed specifically at destroying the civilian base of the resistance.

You might say that the My Lai massacre was a tiny footnote to one of these operations, insignificant in context. The Quakers had a clinic

nearby, and they knew about it immediately because people were coming in wounded and telling stories. They didn't even bother reporting it
because it was just standard, it was going on all the time. Nothing special
about My Lai. It gained a lot of prominence later, after a lot of suppression, and I think the reason is clear: it could be blamed on half-crazed,
uneducated GIs in the field who didn't know who was going to shoot at
them next, and it deflected attention away from the commanders who
were directing the atrocities far from the scene — for example, the ones
plotting the B-52 raids on villages. And it also deflected attention away
from the apologists at home who were promoting and defending all of
this. All of them must receive immunity from criticism, but it's okay to
say a couple of half-crazed GIs did something awful. I was asked by the
New York Review of Books to write an article about My Lai when it was
exposed, and I did, but I scarcely mentioned it. I talked about the context, which I think is correct.

By the early 1970s, it was clear enough that the United States had
basically won that war. It had achieved its basic war aims, which, as revealed in the documentary record, were to ensure that successful, independent development in Vietnam would not be what's called "a virus"
infecting others beyond, leading them to try the same course, perhaps
leading ultimately even to a Japanese accommodation with an independent Asia, maybe as the industrial heart of a kind of new order in Asia out
of US control. The US had fought World War II in the Pacific largely to
prevent that outcome, and was not willing to accept it in the immediate
aftermath of the war. Years later, McGeorge Bundy, who was national
security advisor for Kennedy and Johnson, reflected that the United
States should have pulled out of Vietnam in 1966, after the slaughter in
Indonesia. It was very much like what just happened in Rwanda. The
army either killed or inspired the killing of about half a million to a million people within a few months, with direct US support and encouragement. Crucially, it destroyed the only mass-based political party in the
country. The slaughter was mostly of landless peasants. The slaughter
was described by the CIA as comparable to those of Stalin, Hitler, and
Mao. It was greeted with undisguised euphoria here, across the political
spectrum, and very much in public. It has to be read to be believed. It
will surely disappear from history. It's just much too embarrassing, although it's available in public. Bundy's point was that with Vietnam al-

ready largely destroyed by 1966, and the surrounding territory now inoculated Indonesia-style, there was no longer any serious danger the virus would infect anyone, and the war was basically pointless for the United States.

After War

Well, the war did go on. We left a horrifying legacy: perhaps 4 million killed in Indochina and many millions more orphaned, maimed, and made into refugees, three countries devastated — not just Vietnam. In Laos at this moment people are still dying from unexploded bomblets that are left from the most intense bombing of civilian areas in history, later exceeded by the US bombing of Cambodia.

In Vietnam, one part of the legacy of the war in the present is the continuing impact of the unprecedented campaign of chemical warfare that was initiated under the Kennedy administration. The chemical warfare has indeed received a good deal of coverage here. The reason is that US veterans were affected by it. So, you know about Agent Orange and dioxin and their effect on US soldiers; that did receive coverage. Of course, however much they were affected, that's not a fraction of the effect on Vietnamese, and that receives virtually no attention, though there is occasionally some. I have found very few articles on this. The *Wall Street Journal* did have a lead story on this in February 1997. It reported that half a million children may have been born with dioxin-related deformities as a result of the millions of tons of chemicals that drenched South Vietnam during the US efforts to destroy crops and ground cover, starting with Kennedy. It also reported that Japanese scientists working together with Vietnamese scientists have found rates of birth defects four times as high in southern villages as in the north, which was spared this particular horror. That's not to speak of the stacks of jars with aborted, still-born fetuses, sometimes destroyed by rare cancers, that fill rooms in South Vietnamese hospitals and that are occasionally reported in the foreign press or sometimes in the technical literature here, and reproductive disorders that are still very high in the south, though not the north. The *Wall Street Journal* report did recognize that the United States is responsible for the atrocities it recounts, which still continue to plague South Vietnam. It also reports that Vietnam has received some

European and Japanese aid to try to cope with the disaster, but "the United States, emotionally spent after losing the war, paid no heed." "Losing the war" means not achieving the maximal goal of total conquest, only the basic war aims of destroying the virus and inoculating the region. But the point is that we suffered so from destroying Indochina and are so emotionally spent by this that we cannot be expected to help overcome the legacy of our aggression, let alone express some contrition about it.[1]

The last article I saw about it before this was a few years earlier, in 1992, in the *New York Times* science section, by Southeast Asia correspondent Barbara Crossette.[2] She reported that there was a feeling among scientists that our failure to become involved in this particular aspect of the legacy of war isn't a good idea. Our refusal to study the effects of chemical warfare, she wrote, is a mistake, and the reason is that Vietnam "furnishes an extensive control group." The point is that only southerners were sprayed — many of them with substantial exposure — while northerners were not, and, you know, they have the same genes and so on, so it's a kind of controlled experiment, and if we would only accept the Vietnamese offers of cooperation, we might learn a lot about the effects of dioxin from this interesting experiment, and the results might be useful for us. So it's a shame not to explore the opportunity. But nothing is our fault, and no other thoughts come to mind; we're too emotionally spent to offer any help.

I should say that this level of moral cowardice may break some records, but the full story is still more astonishing. In what must be, I think, the most amazing propaganda achievement in history, the United States has succeeded in shifting the blame to the Vietnamese. It turns out that we were the innocent victims when we attacked and destroyed them, but furthermore, we are so saintly that we do not seek retribution for their crimes against us — we only ask that they concede guilt and apologize — that's George Bush in a speech that was featured prominently on the front page of the *New York Times*. And right next to it there was another column, another one of the many stories condemning the Japanese and wondering what profound cultural inadequacy, or maybe genetic defect, makes it impossible for them to concede the crimes that they have carried out.

The spectacle continues year after year, eliciting no comment. It goes on today, in fact, continually reaching new and almost imaginable heights. It turns out that recently the Vietnamese were finally agreeing to face their guilt a little bit, and to pay us reparations for their crimes against us. There's a front-page *New York Times* story reporting that Vietnam agreed to pay us the debts that were incurred by the client regime that we installed in South Vietnam as a cover for the US attack, so the *Times* says we can now "celebrate the end of a raw chapter in American history." At last the criminals have begun to face their guilt, and we will therefore magnanimously forgive them now that they are at least paying for what they did, as well as acknowledging it, although we can never forget what they did to us, as George Bush and others have sternly admonished them.[3]

Well, maybe someday a new government in Afghanistan will repay Russia the debts incurred by the Soviet puppet regime in Kabul as a cover for Russia's invasion in Afghanistan in 1979 so that Russia can celebrate the end of a raw chapter in its history, and maybe even overcome the fact that they are so emotionally exhausted; and maybe the Afghans will finally acknowledge their guilt for resisting Russian invasion that cost perhaps a million lives and left the country in ruins, becoming even worse as the US-backed terrorist forces now ravage what is left of the place. However, that is not going to happen. The reason is that Russia lost that war and, shortly afterwards, collapsed, in part as a result of that defeat. In October 1989, the Gorbachev government recognized officially that its attack on Afghanistan was illegal and immoral, and that the 13,000 Russian dead and the many who remained behind in Afghan prisons were engaged in violation of international norms of behavior and law. That acknowledgment in 1989 received front-page headlines in the United States — very self-righteous rhetoric about the evil and godless communists who are at last beginning to rejoin Western civilization, although plainly they have a long way to go.

That the United States might follow suit with regard to its far more outrageous conduct in Indochina is utterly unthinkable. How unthinkable it remains was underscored once again by the furor over McNamara's best-selling memoir. You will recall that he was denounced as a traitor, or else praised for his courage, in admitting that the United States had made mistakes that were costly to us. He was condemned or praised for his apology, one or the other, not for his apology to victims of Indochina —

no apology at all to them — but for the apology he made to Americans. He asked whether the "high costs" were justified, referring to the loss of American lives and to the damage to the US economy and the "political unity" of the United States. There were no apologies to the victims, and surely no thought of helping those who continue to suffer and die. On the contrary, it's their responsibility to pay us reparations and to confess their guilt. It's rather striking that among those who praise McNamara for taking this position were some of the moral leaders who strongly opposed the war in Vietnam. They praised McNamara for finally coming around to their position, which, if they're thinking — I suspect they're not — would mean that their position was that it's fine to attack and destroy another country as long as it doesn't cost us too much, no matter what the effects are, and then to make them accept the blame and indeed pay us reparations for the costs that we incurred by destroying them. I doubt if anybody would agree that that's their own position, but it is the position that they are tacitly articulating.

The general lessons of history are clear enough. The legacy of war is faced by the losers. We have thousands of years of pretty consistent records about this. The powerful are too emotionally exhausted, or too overcome with self-adulation, to have any role or responsibility, though for them to portray themselves as suffering victims is an unusual form of moral cowardice. It's a good step beyond the "sacralization of war" and the new forms that it has taken with the rise of the secular religions of the modern era, including our own.

Another lesson of history is that it's very easy to see the other fellow's crimes and to express heartfelt anguish and outrage about them, which may well be justified — it may even lead to help for the victims, which is all to the good, as, for example, when the Soviet tyranny assisted victims of American crimes, as indeed it did. But by the most elementary moral standards, that performance is not very impressive. The very minimum of moral decency would be a willingness to shine the spotlight on oneself with candor and truth. That's the minimum. Proceeding beyond this bare minimum, elementary decency would require action for the benefit of the victims, and for the future victims who doubtless lie ahead if the causes of the crimes are not honestly and effectively addressed. Among these causes are the institutional structures that remain unchanged and from which the policies flow, and also the cultural attitudes and the doctrinal systems that support them and that lead to things of the kind that I have been talking about. These are matters that I think should concern us very deeply, and should be at the core of an educational program in a free society from early childhood and on through adult life.

12

Millennium Greetings

Y ear 2000 opened with familiar refrains, amplified by the numerology: a chorus of self-adulation, somber ruminations about the incomprehensible evil of our enemies, and the usual recourse to selective amnesia to smooth the way. A few illustrations follow, which may suggest the kind of evaluation that might have appeared, were different values to prevail in the intellectual culture.

Let's begin with the familiar litany about the monsters we have confronted through the century and finally slain, a ritual that at least has the merit of roots in reality. Their awesome crimes are recorded in the newly translated *Black Book of Communism* by French scholar Stephane Courtois and others, the subject of shocked reviews as the new millennium opened. The most serious, at least of those I have seen, is by political philosopher Alan Ryan, a distinguished academic scholar and social democratic commentator, in the year's first issue of the *New York Times Book Review*.[1]

The *Black Book* at last breaks "the silence over the horrors of Communism," Ryan writes, "the silence of people who are simply baffled by the spectacle of so much absolutely futile, pointless, and inexplicable suffering." The revelations of the book will doubtless come as a surprise to those who have somehow managed to remain unaware of the stream of bitter denunciations and detailed revelations of the "horrors of Communism" that I have been reading since childhood, notably in the literature of the left for the past 80 years, not to speak of the steady flow in newspapers and journals, film, libraries overflowing with books that range from fiction to scholarship — all unable to lift the veil of silence. But put that aside.

The *Black Book,* Ryan writes, is in the style of a "recording angel." It is a relentless "criminal indictment" for the murder of 100 million people, "the body count of a colossal, wholly failed social, economic, political, and psychological experiment." The total evil, unredeemed by even a hint of achievement anywhere, makes a mockery of "the observation that you can't make an omelet without broken eggs."

The vision of our own fundamental (if admittedly sometimes flawed) goodness in contrast to the incomprehensible monstrosity of the enemy — the "monolithic and ruthless conspiracy" (John F. Kennedy) dedicated to "total obliteration" of any shred of decency in the world (Robert McNamara) — recapitulates in close detail the imagery of the past half century (actually, well beyond, though friends and enemies rapidly shift, to the present). Apart from a huge published literature and the commercial media, it is captured vividly in the internal document NSC 68 of 1950, widely recognized as the founding document of the Cold War but rarely quoted, perhaps out of embarrassment at the frenzied and hysterical rhetoric of the respected statesmen Dean Acheson and Paul Nitze.[2]

The picture has always been an extremely useful one. Renewed once again today, it allows us to erase the record of hideous atrocities compiled by "our side" in past years. After all, these errors count as nothing when compared with the ultimate evil of the enemy. However grand the crime, it was "necessary" to confront the forces of darkness, now finally recognized for what they were. With only the faintest of regrets, we can therefore continue on our historical course, or perhaps even rise to more lofty heights in pursuing what is called, without irony, "America's mission," though as *New York Times* correspondent Michael Wines reminded us in the afterglow of the humanitarian triumph in Kosovo, we must not overlook some "deeply sobering lessons": "the deep ideological divide between an idealistic New World bent on ending inhumanity and an Old World equally fatalistic about unending conflict."[3] The enemy was the incarnation of total evil, but even our friends have a long way to go before they ascend to our dizzying heights. Nonetheless, we can march forward, "clean of hands and pure of heart," as befits a nation under God. And crucially, we can dismiss with ridicule any foolish inquiry into the institutional roots of the crimes of the state-corporate system, mere trivia that in no way tarnish the image of Good versus Evil, and

that teach no lessons, "deeply sobering" or not, about what lies ahead —
a convenient posture, for reasons too obvious to elaborate.

"Criminal Indictment" and Self-Adulation

Like others, Ryan reasonably selects as Exhibit A of the criminal indictment the Chinese famines of 1958–61, with a death toll of 25 to 40 million,
he reports, a sizeable chunk of the 100 million corpses the "recording an-
gels" attribute to "Communism" (whatever that is, but let us use the conventional term). The same shocking crime is featured a few weeks later
in the same journal as the ultimate proof of the absolute evil of the enemy. The crime is incomprehensible to us, John Burns writes, if we view
Mao "through the prism of our own values"; we can then only be awed
and bewildered that Mao "brought about the deaths of more of his own
people than any other leader in history" by inducing the famine, and
other crimes — awful, but not approaching this unthinkable defiance of
the cherished values we uphold.[4]

The terrible atrocity fully merits the harsh condemnation it has received for many years, renewed here. It is, furthermore, proper to attribute the famine to Communism. That conclusion was established most
authoritatively in the work of economist Amartya Sen, whose comparison of the Chinese famine to the record of democratic India received
particular attention when he won the Nobel Prize a few years ago.[5]

Writing in the early 1980s, Sen observed that India had suffered
no such famine since liberating itself from British rule. He attributed the
India-China difference in the post–World War II period to India's "political system of adversarial journalism and opposition," while in contrast,
China's totalitarian regime suffered from "misinformation" that undercut a serious response to the famine, and there was "little political pressure" from opposition groups and an informed public.[6]

The example stands as a damning "criminal indictment" of totalitarian Communism, exactly as Ryan, Burns, and the authors of the *Black
Book* stress, along with innumerable others before them. But before
closing the book on the indictment, we might want to turn to the other
half of Sen's India-China comparison, which somehow never seems to
surface, despite its central role in Sen's core argument and the great emphasis he placed on it.

India and China had "similarities [that] were quite striking," including death rates, when development planning began 50 years ago, Sen and his associate Jean Drèze observe, "but there is little doubt that as far as morbidity, mortality, and longevity are concerned, China has a large and decisive lead over India," as in education and other social indicators. From 1949 to 1979, "China ... achieved a remarkable transition in health and nutrition," while "no comparable transformation has occurred in India." As a result, as of 1979, "the life of the average Chinese has tended to be much more secure than that of the average Indian."[7] If India had adopted China's social programs, "there would have been about 3.8 million fewer deaths a year around the middle 1980s." "That indicates that every eight years or so more people in addition die in India — in comparison with Chinese mortality rates — than the total number that died in the gigantic Chinese famine (even though it was the biggest famine in the world in this century)." "India seems to manage to fill its cupboard with more skeletons every eight years than China put there in its years of shame," 1958–61.[8]

In both cases, the outcomes have to do with the "ideological predispositions" of the political systems, Drèze and Sen observe: for China, relatively equitable distribution of medical resources, including rural health services, public distribution of food, and other programs oriented to the needs of the vast majority of the population, all lacking in India. "China's remarkable achievements in matters of life and death cannot in any way be ascribed to a strategy of 'growth-mediated' security"; growth rates were comparable to India. It is, rather, in "support-led security" — social programs — that "the Chinese efforts have been quite spectacular," with corresponding achievements. Recall that these are the programs of "a colossal, wholly failed social, economic, political, and psychological experiment," an experiment with no redeeming features when viewed "through the prism of our own values."

China's "remarkable achievements in raising life expectancy and quality of life to levels that are quite unusual for poor countries" came to an end in 1979, when "the downward trend in mortality [in China was] at least halted, and possibly reversed."[9] The reversal in 1979 is directly traceable to the market reforms instituted that year.[10] These led to a "general crisis in health services." The standard neoliberal formulas required "severe financial stringency," which undermined the "rural

medical and health care" that were components of the communal agriculture system. The effects of the destruction of this "pillar of support for
China's innovative and extensive rural medical services" were "particularly severe on women and female children." From 1979, there was "a
steady decline in the female-male ratio in the population" and a decline
of two years in female life expectancy, after steady growth in the
pre-reform period.[11]

Sen's conclusion is that "countries tend to reap as they sow in the
field of investment in health and quality of life."[12] Half of that well-
established conclusion passes through the filters of Western ideology —
the half that can be exploited to sustain the fairly typical stance of privileged sectors, intellectuals included, through the centuries: awe and
shock at the incomprehensible evil of official enemies, and admiration
for our own wonderful selves.

Overcoming amnesia, suppose we now apply the methodology of
the *Black Book* and its reviewers to the full story, not just the doctrinally
acceptable half. We therefore conclude that in India the democratic capitalist "experiment" since 1947 has caused more deaths than in the entire
history of the "colossal, wholly failed ... experiment" of Communism
everywhere since 1917: over 100 million deaths by 1979, and tens of
millions more since, in India alone.

The "criminal indictment" of the "democratic capitalist experiment"
becomes harsher still if we turn to its effects after the fall of Communism: the increase of "skeletons in the cupboard," particularly female
skeletons, in China, as a result of the neoliberal reforms; and millions of
corpses in Russia, as Russia followed the confident prescription of the
World Bank that "countries that liberalize rapidly and extensively turn
around more quickly [than those that do not],"[13] returning to something
like what it had been before World War I, a picture familiar throughout
the "Third World." But "you can't make an omelet without broken
eggs," as Stalin would have said, and as we are reminded by those who
survey selected outcomes with shock and dismay.[14]

The indictment becomes far harsher if we consider the vast areas
that remained under Western tutelage, yielding a truly "colossal" record
of skeletons and "absolutely futile, pointless, and inexplicable suffering."[15] It becomes harsher still if we consider the effects of the neoliberal
reforms imposed under the conditionalities of the "Washington consen-

sus," justified in the name of a "debt burden" — an ideological construction, not a simple economic fact.[16] To take one example, three Africa specialists point out that these reforms "helped to precipitate a catastrophe in which virtually all economic, social, educational, and public health gains made in the 1960s and 1970s have been wiped out,"[17] with a human cost that is incalculable — at least, not calculated.

The indictment takes on further force when we add to the account the devastation caused by the direct assaults of Western power and its clients during the same years. The record need not be reviewed here, though it seems to be as unknown to respectable opinion as were the crimes of Communism before the appearance of the *Black Book.*

The authors of the *Black Book,* Ryan observes, did not shrink from confronting the "great question": "the relative immorality of communism and Nazism." Although "the body count tips the scales against communism," Ryan concludes that Nazism nevertheless sinks to the lower depths of immorality. Unasked is another "great question" posed by "the body count" when ideologically serviceable amnesia is overcome.

To make myself clear, I am not expressing my judgments; rather those that follow, clearly and unequivocally, from the principles that are employed to establish preferred truths — or that would follow, if doctrinal filters could be removed.

On the self-adulation, a virtual tidal wave in the final year of the millennium,[18] perhaps it is enough to recall Mark Twain's remark about one of the great military heroes of the mass slaughter campaign in the Philippines that opened the glorious century behind us: he is "satire incarnated"; no satirical rendition can "reach perfection" because he "occupies that summit himself." The reference reminds us of another aspect of our magnificence, apart from efficiency in massacre and destruction and a capacity for self-glorification that would drive any satirist to despair: our willingness to face up honestly to our crimes, a tribute to the flourishing free market of ideas. The bitter anti-imperialist essays of one of America's leading writers were not suppressed, as in totalitarian states; they are freely available to the general public, with a delay of only some 90 years.

In fairness, it should be mentioned that the chorus of self-adulation that closed the millennium was disrupted by some discordant notes. Questions were raised about the consistency of our adherence to the

guiding principles: the "new doctrine" that "universal standards of human
rights were putting at least some limits on sovereignty," as illustrated by
Kosovo and East Timor — the latter an interesting example, since there
was no issue of sovereignty, except for those who accord Indonesia the
right of conquest authorized by the guardian of international morality.

These topics were brought forth in the major think-piece on the
topic in the *New York Times Week in Review,* a front-page article by
Craig Whitney.[19] He concluded that the "new doctrine" that the world
"thought was emerging" may be failing its "harshest test": the vicious
Russian assault on Grozny.[20]

Apparently Whitney was not convinced by the explanation offered
by President Clinton four days earlier: our hands are tied because "a
sanctions regime has to be imposed by the United Nations," where it
would be blocked by the Russian veto.[21] Clinton's dilemma was illustrated shortly before, when, by a vote of 155 to 2 (US and Israel), the UN
once again called for an end to Washington's sanctions against Cuba.[22]
The Cuba sanctions are not the only ones that somehow escape Clinton's
dilemma. More than half the people in the world are subject to unilateral
coercive sanctions imposed by the US, according to a recent UN
commission established in response to a 1997 resolution of the General
Assembly condemning "unilateral coercive economic measures against
developing countries that were not authorized by relevant organs of the
UN or were inconsistent with the principles of international law, ... and
that contravened the basic principles of the multilateral trading system."[23] The UN Commission on Human Rights also condemned such
measures in April 1999. The European Union as well condemned "unilateral coercive economic measures that violate international law." In
response, the US agreed that multilateral sanctions are preferable, but
reserved for itself the right "to act unilaterally if important national interests or core values are at issue," as in the punishment of the people of
Cuba for refusing to bend to Washington's will.[24]

The Cuba sanctions are the harshest in the world. They have been in
force since 1960, but became much more severe, with a heavy human
toll, when the "monolithic and ruthless conspiracy" finally faded away
and it was impossible any longer to appeal to the grave national security
threat posed by Cuba — far short of the threat posed by Denmark or
Luxembourg to the USSR. These unilateral coercive measures do not

count as a "sanctions regime," however. They are "strictly a matter of bi-lateral trade policy and not a matter appropriate for consideration by the UN General Assembly," so the US explained in response to the UN vote (Deputy US Representative to the UN Peter Burleigh, speaking to the General Assembly, reiterated by the State Department). Repeating al-most verbatim Washington's reaction to the seven previous years' votes, Philip Reeker, a State Department spokesman, said that "the trade em-bargo is US law which we will enforce." It makes no difference what the world might think or decide.[25]

So there is no contradiction between the stance on Chechnya and on Cuba, and no counterexample to Clinton's firm adherence to interna-tional law and practice with regard to the propriety of "a sanctions re-gime." And furthermore, the latest UN vote condemning the US, and Washington's reaction, was yet another non-event, at least for those who receive their information from the national press, which did not re-port them.

Let's defer the two convincing illustrations of the "new doctrine" and turn to other tests of our dedication to the high ideals proclaimed, more instructive ones than the Russian assault in Chechnya, which does not pose "the harshest test" for the "new doctrine" or much of a test at all — perhaps the reason why it is constantly adduced, in preference to significant and instructive tests. However outrageous the Russian crimes, it is understood that very little can be done about them, just as lit-tle could be done to deter the US terrorist wars in Central America in the 1980s or its destruction of South Vietnam, then all Indochina, in earlier years. When a military superpower goes on the rampage, the costs of in-terference are too high to contemplate: deterrence must largely come from within. Such efforts had some success in the case of Indochina and Central America, though only very limited success as the fate of the vic-tims clearly reveals — or would, if it were conceivable to look at the consequences honestly and draw the appropriate conclusions.

More Serious Tests

Let's turn, then, to more serious tests of the "new doctrine": the reaction to atrocities that are easily ended, not by intervention, but simply by withdrawing participation. Evidently, these cases provide the clearest and most informative tests of the "new doctrine," as of the old. The end of 1999 offered several such tests. One, which requires separate treatment, is the move to escalate US-backed terror in Colombia, with ominous prospects (see Chapter 5). Several others illustrate with much clarity the content of the "new doctrine," as interpreted in practice.

In December 1999, there were many articles on the death of Croatian president Franjo Tudjman, a Milosevic clone who enjoyed generally warm relations with the West, though his authoritarian style and corruption "drew scathing criticism from American and Western European officials." Nevertheless, he will be remembered as "the father of independent Croatia," whose "crowning achievement came in military operations in May and August 1995," when his armies succeeded in recapturing Croatian territory held by Serbs, "sparking a mass exodus of Croatian Serbs to Serbia."[26] The "crowning achievement" also received a few words in a lengthy *New York Times* story by David Binder, who has reported on the region with much distinction for many years: Tudjman reluctantly agreed to take part in the US-run Dayton negotiations in late 1995, after "he had all but accomplished his goal of driving ethnic Serbs from what he viewed as purely Croatian land [Krajina]."[27]

The August phase of the military campaign, Operation Storm, was the largest single ethnic cleansing operation of the Yugoslav wars of secession. The UN reports that "approximately 200,000 Serbs fled their homes in Croatia during and immediately after the fighting," while "the few that remained were subjected to violent abuse." A few weeks afterwards, Richard Holbrooke, who directed Clinton's diplomacy, "told Tudjman that the [Croatian] offensive had great value to the negotiations" and "urged Tudjman" to extend it, he writes in his memoir, *To End a War,* driving out another 90,000 Serbs. Secretary of State Warren Christopher explained that "we did not think that kind of attack could do anything other than create a lot of refugees and cause a humanitarian problem. On the other hand, it always had the prospect of simplifying matters" in preparation for Dayton. Clinton commented that Croatia's ethnic cleansing operation could prove helpful in resolving the Balkan conflict, though it was problematic because of the risk of Serbian retaliation. As reported at the time, Clinton approved a "yellow-light approach" or "an amber light tinted green," which Tudjman took to be tacit encouragement for the "crowning achievement." The massive ethnic cleansing was unproblematic, merely a "humanitarian problem," apart from the risk of reaction.[28]

Reviewing the Croatian operations in a scholarly journal, Binder observes that "what struck me again and again ... was the almost total lack of interest in the US press and in the US Congress" about the US involvement: "Nobody, it appears, wanted even a partial accounting" of the role of "MPRI mercenaries" (retired US generals sent to train and advise the Croatian army under State Department contract) or "the participation of US military and intelligence components."[29] Direct participation included: bombardment of Krajina Serbian surface-to-air missile sites by US naval aircraft to eliminate any threat to Croatian attack planes and helicopters, Binder reports, citing US military journals; the supply of sophisticated US technology and intelligence; a "key role" in arranging the transfer to Croatia of 30 percent of the Iranian weapons secretly sent to Bosnia; and apparently the planning of the entire operation.

The International War Crimes Tribunal did investigate the offensive, producing a 150-page report with a section headed: "The Indictment. Operation Storm, A Prima Facie Case."[30] The tribunal concluded that the "Croatian Army carried out summary executions, indiscriminate shelling of civilian populations, and 'ethnic cleansing,' " but the inquiry was hampered by Washington's "refusal to provide critical evidence requested by the tribunal," and appears to have languished. The "almost total lack of interest" in ethnic cleansing and other atrocities committed by the right hands persists, illustrated once again at Tudjman's death, while we ponder the problem of our consistency in upholding the "new doctrine," revealed by the Chechnya quandary.

One of those allegedly under investigation by the International War Crimes Tribunal for Operation Storm atrocities is Agim Ceku, "a former brigadier in the Croatian army who emerged as commander of the Kosovo Liberation Army (KLA)" during the NATO bombings and was then designated by the occupying forces (KFOR) as "commander of the Kosovo Protection Force (TMK)," set up in September 1999 "to help police the war-torn province." UN and Western sources confirmed that Ceku is under investigation and "could be indicted for war crimes allegedly committed during the ethnic cleansing of Serbs by Croatian soldiers." "Sources familiar with the investigation into Ceku said the most serious crimes with which he had been linked were committed" in

Krajina in 1993, when he "was commanding the fledgling Croatian army's 9th Brigade." "Boosted by notorious mercenaries, the brigade was feared as one of the most ruthless in an area where Croatian nationalism was combined with the thuggish corruption of a mafia underworld." Ceku was also "one of the commanders trained by American forces before the infamous Operation Storm of August 1995, which pushed most of Croatia's rebellious Serbs from Krajina and into Serbia proper," an operation in which "about 300,000 Serbs were 'cleansed' " with unknown numbers killed and hundreds "still missing." "American diplomats, who have been the most supportive of the creation of the TMK, have suggested any indictment of Ceku would most likely be 'sealed' and thereby kept out of the public domain."[31]

Ceku also "comes in for fierce criticism" in a confidential UN report that covers the period January 21–February 29, 2000, and accuses the force that he commands of "criminal activities — killings, illtreatment/torture, illegal policing, abuse of authority, intimidation, breaches of political neutrality, and hate-speech." Set up by NATO to provide "disaster response services," and drawn primarily from the KLA, the TMK is instead "murdering and torturing people" while the UN is "paying the salaries of many of the gangsters." It has also "been running protection rackets across Kosovo ... demanding 'contributions' from shopkeepers, businessmen, and contractors," and perhaps prostitution rackets, resorting to terror and death threats and forcing the release of arrested criminals.[32]

It seems likely that Ceku's role here too will be "sealed." " 'If we lose him it will be a disaster,' said a diplomat close to Bernard Kouchner, the UN's special representative. 'When you get to the second level of the TMK, you're down to a bunch of local thugs.' "[33]

A still "harsher test" of the new doctrine was the reaction to the acceptance of Turkey as a candidate for membership in the European Union in December 1999. The ample coverage succeeded in overlooking the obvious issue: the huge terror operations, including massive ethnic cleansing, conducted with decisive US aid and training, increasing under Clinton as atrocities peaked to a level vastly beyond the crimes that allegedly provoked the NATO bombing of Serbia. True, some questions were raised: a *New York Times* headline read: "First Question for Europe: Is Turkey Really European?"[34] The US-backed atrocities merit a phrase: Turkey's "war against Kurdish rebels has subsided" — just as Serbia's far lesser pre-bombing "war against Albanian rebels" would have "subsided" had the US provided Belgrade with a flood of high-tech weapons and diplomatic support while the press and the intellectual community looked the other way. Shortly before, Stephen Kinzer had described how "Clinton Charm Was on Display in Turkey" (as the headline put it) as he visited earthquake victims, staring soulfully into the eyes of an infant he held tenderly, and demonstrating in other ways too his "legendary ability to connect with people" — revealed so graphically in the huge terror operations that continue to elicit "almost total lack of interest" while we admire ourselves for a dedication to human rights that is unique in history.[35]

An explanatory footnote was added quietly in mid-December. Turkish and Israeli naval forces, accompanied by a US warship, undertook maneuvers in the Eastern Mediterranean, a none-too-subtle warning to "prod Syria to negotiate with Israel" under US auspices.[36]

Appropriately, the president of Turkey was one of the few heads of state who attended Tudjman's funeral. Others stayed away because of objections to "Mr. Tudjman's authoritarian rule and his reluctance to cooperate" with UN war crimes tribunals,[37] but ethnic cleansing and other atrocities conducted by Tudjman and his Turkish friends do not reach the radar screen. That makes good sense when events are perceived "through the prism of our own values," given that the crimes of the Turkish and Croatian governments were sponsored by the Clinton administration.

Another test of the "new doctrine" was offered in mid-November, the 10th anniversary of the assassination of six leading Latin American intellectuals (along with many others), including the rector of El Salvador's leading university, in the course of yet another murderous rampage by an elite battalion of the US-run terrorist forces (called "the Salvadoran army"), fresh from another training session by Green Berets, capping a decade of horrendous atrocities. The names of the murdered Jesuit intellectuals did not appear in the US press. Few would even recall their names, or would have read a word they had written, in sharp contrast to dissidents in the domains of the monstrous enemy — who suffered severe repression, but, in the post-Stalin era, nothing remotely like that meted out regularly under US control. Like the events themselves, the contrast raises questions of no slight import, but these too are off the agenda.

Little need be said about the two examples offered as the demonstration of our commitment to high principles: East Timor and Kosovo. As for the Portuguese-administered territory of East Timor, there was no "intervention"; rather, dispatch of an Australian-led UN force after Washington at last agreed to signal to the Indonesian generals that the game was over, having supported them through 24 years of slaughter and repression, continuing through the atrocities of 1999 — again far beyond anything attributed to Milosevic in Kosovo before the NATO bombings. After finally withdrawing his support for Indonesian atrocities under mounting domestic and international (mainly Australian) pressure, with the country mostly destroyed, 85 percent of the population expelled from their homes, and unknown numbers killed, Clinton continued to stand aside. There were no air-drops of food to hundreds of thousands of refugees starving in the mountains, nor anything more than occasional rebukes to the Indonesian military, who continued to hold hundreds of thousands more in captivity in Indonesian territory, where many still remain. Clinton also refuses to provide meaningful aid, let alone the huge reparations that would be called for if the fine principles were meant at all seriously.[38]

That performance is now presented as one of Clinton's great moments and a prime example of the stirring "new doctrine" of intervention in defense of human rights, ignoring sovereignty (which did not exist). Here amnesia is not really selective: "total" would be closer to accurate.

On Kosovo, the current version in the media and much of scholarship is that NATO "reacted to the deportation of more than a million Kosovars from their homeland" by bombing so as to save them "from horrors of suffering, or from death."[39] The timing is crucially reversed in a manner that has been routine from the outset. In a detailed year-end review, the *Wall Street Journal* dismisses the stories of "killing fields" that were crafted to prevent "a fatigued press corps [from] drifting towards the contrarian story [of] civilians killed by NATO's bombs," but concludes nonetheless that the expulsions and other atrocities that did take place "may well be enough to justify the [NATO] bombing campaign" that precipitated them, as anticipated.[40]

The reasoning is by now standard: the US and its allies had to abandon the options that remained available (and were later pursued) and bomb, with the expectation — quickly fulfilled — that the result would be a major humanitarian catastrophe, which retrospectively justifies the bombing. Furthermore, it was necessary for the CIA to assist KLA guerrillas in their openly declared effort to elicit a harsh and brutal Serb response to the killing of Serb police and civilians, thus arousing Western opinion to support the planned bombing; the CIA, it seems, operated under the cover of the international monitors, thus subverting their mission, as in the case of Iraqi weapons monitors at the same time.[41] A further justification is that if NATO hadn't bombed, maybe something similar would have happened anyway.[42] That is the "new doctrine" in its most admired form, and perhaps the most exotic justification for state violence on record — even putting aside other consequences, including the effects of the bombardment of civilian targets in Serbia, the "cleansing" of Kosovo under the eyes of the NATO occupying forces, and the refusal of the US to help clear the more than 25,000 unexploded cluster bombs that are killing survivors in Kosovo,[43] with worse to come, very possibly.

The record does seem to reveal remarkable consistency, as one might expect. Why should we expect inconsistency when the institutional factors that undergird policy remain intact and unchanged, to bring up the forbidden question? Talk of a "double standard" is simply evasion; in fact, cowardly evasion when we consider what is omitted under the principle of selective amnesia.

13

Power in the Domestic Arena

The focus on the United States is distorting, and we should compensate for it: the US is powerful, but not all-powerful. It is the richest country in the world, it has unparalleled advantages, and has had for several hundred years, but the global economy has been what is called tripolar for almost 30 years, with intricate alliances and conflicts, and there are other power centers.

In 1945 the structure of world power was unusually clear by historical standards. A half-century before that, the United States had become by far the world's greatest economic power, but it was a relatively small player on the world scene. By 1945 that had radically changed, for obvious reasons: the industrial societies had been seriously damaged or destroyed, while the US economy had flourished through the war; the US had literally half the world's wealth, incomparable military power, and security; and it was in a position to organize much of the world, and did so with the assistance of its "junior partner," as the British Foreign Office ruefully described the new reality of the time.

The general point was put accurately enough by a leading diplomatic historian, Gerald Haines (also the senior historian of the CIA), in a recent book.[1] He observes that after World War II the United States "assumed, out of self-interest, responsibility for the welfare of the world capitalist system," which is a fair enough formula, but to understand it we have to carry out a few translations. The first is that the word "capitalist" doesn't mean capitalist. Rather, what it refers to are state-subsidized and protected private power centers — "collectivist legal entities," as they are called by legal historians — internally tyrannical, unaccountable to the public, granted extraordinary rights by US courts in radical violation of classical liberal ideals. That's why the corporatization of America, as it's called, early in this century was bitterly condemned by conservatives, a breed that has since vanished, aside from the name. The corporatization was condemned as "a form of communism," a return to "feudalistic" structures, and not without reason. Progressive intellectuals, who generally supported the process, gave a rather similar assessment, among them Woodrow Wilson.[2] Apart from their "power and control over the wealth and business opportunities of the country," he wrote, they are becoming "rivals of the government itself." More accurately, these corporations were casting over society the shadow that we call politics, as John Dewey put it a little later, making obvious points about the extreme limitations on democracy when "the life of the country," the production and information systems and so on, are ruled by private tyrannies, in a system that he described as industrial "feudalism" — the contemporary system.[3]

The corporatization process was in large part a reaction to great market failures of the late 19th century, and it was a shift from something you might call proprietary capitalism to administration of markets by collectivist legal entities — mergers, cartels, corporate alliances — in association with powerful states and by now international bureaucracies, which regulate and support private power. The primary task of the states — bear in mind that with all the talk about minimizing the state, in the OECD countries the state continues to grow relative to GNP, notably in the '80s and '90s — is essentially to socialize risk and cost, and to privatize power and profit. These are tendencies that have moved forward under Reaganite, Thatcherite, and New Democrat doctrines.

Well, going back to Haines's formula, it's not false, but we have to understand "capitalism" as referring to social arrangements that would have scandalized Adam Smith or Ricardo or James Madison — or, for that matter, even the American Republican Party in the mid–19th century. It's hard to remember now, but at that time the Republican Party opposed even wage labor as not very different from the chattel slavery that had just been overthrown in the Civil War.[4] These ideas are deep in the American tradition, without the dubious benefit of radical intellectuals. We also have to understand the phrase "self-interest" in Haines's formula. It does not refer to the interest of the population, except by the remotest accident — that's a truism as old as Adam Smith.

With these translations in mind, we can accept the conventional view that after World War II the United States "assumed, out of self-interest, responsibility for the welfare of the world capitalist system." That responsibility devolved into several related programs: the first and most important had to do with the domestic society.

There is a conventional doctrine about the current domestic scene and what it implies for the rest of the world, which has yet to benefit from what are called America's "entrepreneurial values and rugged individualism." The standard picture of the domestic scene is given, for example, by a recent lead article in the *New York Times*. The headline is "America Is Prosperous and Smug," perhaps too much so, and it goes on to explain that Americans have "boundless confidence" and "expectations of unlimited economic success" in the "happy glow of the American boom," "the fairy tale US expansion since 1991," a "remarkable economic success" under the direction of "the saintly [Alan] Greenspan."[5] Another lead article in the *New York Times,* a front-page article, described what it called a "fat and happy America," enjoying the current economic boom, "one of the longest and healthiest in American history."[6] It has indeed been a fairy tale for some. Both of the articles I cited give one — the same — example, namely the stock market. There has been enormous asset inflation, which is certainly a fairy tale to the 1 per cent of households that own half the stocks and the 10 percent that own most of the rest. It has also been a fairy tale for corporations; the business press has been ecstatic about the profit growth in the last few years. It has been called "extraordinary," "stunning," "dazzling," "stupendous" — I think they have run out of adjectives.

But it's not unproblematic. *Business Week* did detect a problem; they had an article headlined "The Problem Now: What to Do With All That Cash," as "surging profits" are overflowing the coffers of corporate America. Shortly after it became even worse: "The liquid assets of non-financial corporations hit a staggering $679 billion," causing "vexing problems" for Boeing, Intel, General Motors and others like them.[7] Fortunately, there is a solution, and there is a bipartisan consensus on it: namely, to reduce taxes on capital gains. That is, for the benefit of everyone, not just the top 1 percent, for whom it's half their income. The purpose of this is to free funds for investment, because the staggering two-thirds of a trillion dollars that's causing such vexing problems is not enough. I should say, it takes a good education to keep all this in hand with proper sobriety.

What about the fairy-tale expansion since 1991? Well, it's true that it breaks new records; for one thing it's the first recovery in US history that has not been accompanied by increases in wealth and income, apart from the top few percent. It is also one of the weakest recoveries of the post-war period, similar to the anemic '70s and '80s. In fact, the per capita growth rate of the US economy through 1997 is approximately at the OECD average; it is well below the '50s and the '60s. It's also been a period of slower productivity growth, which is a portent for the future.

So that raises some questions. How can we have dazzling profit growth when the fairy-tale expansion is one of the weakest since the Second World War? Well, there's a simple answer to that: most of the population has been left out of the story. So, for two-thirds of workers, average incomes are below the late 1970s. In the late 1980s, which was a period of recovery, hunger in the US increased 50 percent, to about 30 million people. Around 1980 the US was rather similar to other industrial societies by what are called quality of life measures — things like poverty, child malnutrition, mortality, the proportion of the population in jail, inequality, and so on — now it's far in the lead. Working hours have gone way up — Americans apparently work about a month a year more than they did 25 years ago, wages have stagnated, support systems have gone down, working conditions have deteriorated. The decline of US labor costs to the lowest, second to England, in the industrial world was hailed by the *Wall Street Journal* as "a welcome development of transcendent importance," and that's part of the United States being happy and satisfied.

Illegal firing of union organizers tripled in the 1980s, along with other violations of law, which continue under Clinton. The Reagan administration essentially informed the business world it wasn't going to apply the laws, and this was reported rather accurately in the business press.[8] That's a big factor in the increase in inequality, the attack on wages and incomes. If you turn to the business pages of the *New York Times,* they tell the story pretty straight: for example, in a story headlined "America's Treadmill Economy," in which most people are "Going Nowhere Fast," with poor prospects.[9] Let's go back to the headline, "America is Prosperous and Smug," and so on. That all makes sense as long as we understand what the word "America" means: it doesn't refer to Americans, it refers to a small, privileged minority, which is in fact the constituency of the *New York Times* — those are the people you meet in elegant restaurants, boardrooms, and so on — and they are indeed smug and prosperous, happy and confident.

Let us turn our attention to Alan Greenspan, who presided over the miracle in the 1990s. He recently testified to the Senate Banking Committee on the miracle, which he attributed in part to "greater worker insecurity."[10] Workers are intimidated; they are afraid to ask for a living wage and benefits, and that's a good thing. It makes Americans confident and smug, if you understand the word "Americans" correctly. The latest economic report of the president also takes great pride in the fairy-tale economy, which it attributes to "significant wage restraint" that results from "changes in labor market institutions and practices."[11] That translates into English as things like non-enforcement of laws on illegal strike-breaking, allowing permanent replacement workers — the US has been cited by the ILO for that, but nobody pays any attention. And there are other factors in the fairy tale. Caterpillar, the construction producer, won a major strike in Illinois, seriously harming one of the major unions, United Auto Workers. How did they do it? Well, by hiring permanent replacement workers, considered illegal in most of the world, and also by using the dazzling profits that they shared with their associates to construct excess capacity abroad, from which they could supply their markets even with the Caterpillar plants in Illinois on strike. Notice that the use of profits to construct excess capacity abroad is not for profits and not for efficiency, but for class war: that is, it's a way of attacking US workers, and so it was used. Capital is mobile, labor is not, and, unfortunately, international links are quite weak.

Greenspan recently gave a talk to newspaper editors in the US. He spoke passionately about the miracles of the market, the wonders bought by consumer choice, and so on. He also gave some examples: the Internet, computers, information processing, lasers, satellites, transistors.[12] It's an interesting list: these are textbook examples of creativity and production in the public sector. In the case of the Internet, for 30 years it was designed, developed, and funded primarily in the public sector, mostly the Pentagon, then the National Science Foundation — that's most of the hardware, the software, new ideas, technology, and so on. In just the last couple of years it has been handed over to people like Bill Gates, whom, at least, you have to admire for his honesty: he attributes his success to his ability to "embrace and extend" the ideas of others, commonly others in the public sector.[13] In the case of the Internet, consumer choice was close to zero, and during the crucial development stages the same was true of computers, information processing, and all the rest — unless by "consumer" you mean the government; that is, public subsidy.

In fact, of all the examples that Greenspan gives, the only one that maybe rises above the level of a joke is transistors, and they are an interesting case. Transistors, in fact, were developed in a private laboratory — Bell Telephone Laboratories of AT&T — which also made major contributions to solar cells, radio astronomy, information theory, and lots of other important things. But what is the role of markets and consumer choice in that? Well, again, it turns out, zero. AT&T was a government-supported monopoly, so there was no consumer choice, and as a monopoly they could charge high prices: in effect, a tax on the public which they could use for institutions like Bell Laboratories, where they could do all of this work. So again, it's publicly subsidized. As if to demonstrate the point, as soon as the industry was deregulated, Bell Labs went out of existence, because the public wasn't paying for it any more: its successors work mostly on short-term applied projects. But that's only the beginning of the story. True, Bell Labs invented transistors, but they used wartime technology, which, again, was publicly subsidized and state-initiated. Furthermore, there was nobody to buy transistors at that time, because they were very expensive to produce. So, for 10 years the government was the major procurer, particularly for high-performance transistors. In 1958 the Bell Telephone supplier, Western Electric, was producing hundreds of thousands of these, but solely for military applications. Government procurement provided entrepreneurial initiatives and guided the development of the technology, which could then be disseminated to industry.[14] That's "consumer choice" and the "miracle of the market" in the one case that you can even look at without ridicule. And in fact that story generalizes. The dynamic sectors of the economy rely crucially on massive public subsidy, innovation, and creativity; the examples that Greenspan gave are mostly some of the most dramatic cases of this. It's a revealing set of choices. A lot of this is masked as defense, but that's not all — the same is true in biotechnology, pharmaceuticals, and so on.

Naturally, business is delighted with all of this: the public pays the costs and assumes the risks (a kind of "socialism for the rich"), and profit and power are privatized — that's really existing market theory. It goes back for centuries, but it is dramatically true now. Particular cases make it even more dramatic. Take the former leader of the conservative revolution in Congress, Newt Gingrich. He is a fount of very impressive rhetoric about the work ethic and getting off the cycle of dependency — how seven-year-old children have to learn responsibility, and that sort of thing. But, year after year, he held the championship in bringing home federal subsidies to his rich constituents, in a sector of Georgia where the economy is even more dependent on federal subsidies than in most places.[15] His favorite cash-cow was Lockheed-Martin. There is a $200 annual Lockheed-Martin tax per capita in the US. Sometimes, even with all that, Lockheed-Martin goes under; when it does, the government steps in, as under the Nixon administration, with a couple of hundred million dollars of guaranteed loans. It was that performance that led Senator Proxmire to coin the phrase "corporate welfare." So, that's conservatism in the House of Representatives. The Senate majority leader, Trent Lott, is the same. The *Financial Times* described him as "the most successful pork producer in 1997," which is quite accurate. So, that's conservatism in the Senate.[16]

And it continues — I will just give one last example. Here is a front-page story in the *New York Times* on "an economic miracle in the United States." They describe "the prosperous new economy" in "the nation's most Republican state," with its "deep-seated distrust of the Federal Government" and its "tradition of self-reliance," — it happens to be Idaho.[17] They point out, as is conventional, that there is downside to the economic miracle: Idaho also breaks national records in child abuse and imprisonment, the unions have been wiped out, reading scores are going down, and so on. But it's a prosperous new economy, and the most Republican state, and so on. From the article we don't learn anything about the economic miracle, so you look elsewhere. For example, you can look at the publications of the Idaho National Engineering and Environmental Lab. This is a national laboratory, managed jointly by the Department of Energy with the Lockheed-Martin Corporation —

that's the private contribution symbolizing self-reliance and distrust of the federal government. The publication opens by saying, "Americans have made a huge investment in the Idaho National Laboratory" since it was founded in 1949 to bring us nuclear energy and a nuclear navy. Last year the Department of Energy put $850 million into this single site, which is the "premier engineering lab in the DOE system of national laboratories." Its mission is to "move federally developed technologies into private industry and academia."[18] In academia, research and development is also federally funded, very substantially; its role is a kind of funnel for transferring public funds into private profits. Notice the phrase, "move federally developed technologies into private industry." That's the role of the government in a free-enterprise economy. In the Idaho DOE lab, it's not only nuclear energy; it's also radioactive waste disposal, chemical processing, "the world's most sophisticated materials and testing complex," a "rapid-tooling technology" laboratory that should "revolutionize the way automobiles and other products are built" — after the taxpayer gifts are handed over to the private sector — a supercomputer center to ensure that the United States stays at the forefront of computer development. To help out on that, the Clinton administration recently slapped a huge tariff on Japanese supercomputers, which were undercutting the US ones — a magnificent contribution to free trade. The Clinton administration's moves of that sort — tariff interventions — range from supercomputers to Mexican tomatoes, which were banned by tariffs because they were preferred by American consumers.[19] There are laws about this, but laws are not for rich and powerful people, they are for places like Haiti. The same DOE publication goes on to say that one of the purposes of the National Lab is to "assist start-up companies in attracting and securing state and federal grants and lines of credit" — that's what is known as entrepreneurial initiative and rugged individualism. In brief, the public invests massively, for 50 years, hands the gifts over to private power and profit, and we now admire this prosperous new economy, in the nation's most Republican state, with its deep-seated distrust of the federal government and its tradition of self-reliance.

Again, it takes a good education to handle all of this, but that is the way the real economy works, in accordance with really existing market theory. And of course it's not just the US; these are elementary facts about economic history since the 18th century, when England pioneered the way. And it's well understood in the business world, if not by ideologues — after all, they're the ones who designed it. The depression in the 1930s removed any lingering beliefs that real capitalism might be viable; the New Deal measures barely affected it, but World War II overcame it. World War II was a grand success economically; there was a kind of semi-command economy, directed by corporate executives who flocked to Washington to run it, and they learned the lessons. It was confidently predicted, across the board, that the US would go right back into depression after the war; therefore something had to be done. The business press was frank about it. *Fortune* and *Business Week* reported that high-tech industry cannot survive in a "pure, competitive, unsubsidized, 'free enterprise' economy" (specifically the aircraft industry, though the point was more general), and "the government is their only possible savior."[20]

The only question was how. Well, they understood perfectly well. There was an interesting discussion in the business press in the late '40s. They understood that social spending could serve to stimulate and sustain the economy, but they much preferred, and quickly hit upon, an alternative; namely, the Department of Energy, NASA, the Atomic Energy Commission — the whole Pentagon system. And there were good reasons, not economic reasons, but more important ones. Social spending has a downside: it has a democratizing effect. So, people have opinions about where you should put a hospital or a school or a road or something. But they have no opinions about what kind of jet plane to build, or what kind of lasers to build. So, you undercut the democratizing effect if you switch to the Pentagon system. Furthermore, social spending tends to be redistributive, whereas the Pentagon system is a pure gift to private power, with no negative side effects. It is also secret. It is easy to sell; you just make people cower in terror, and then they will pay for it, and meanwhile Alan Greenspan, and others like him, can spin fantasies for the public.

Just keeping to the present, the role of the state is not just to create and protect high-tech industry, it also has to intervene to overcome management failures — that was quite dramatic in the 1970s. At the time there was a lot of concern about the low level of productivity and investment growth, and the failure of incompetent US management to keep up with more advanced Japanese methods. There were public calls for what was called the re-industrialization of the US. Well, the Pentagon responded with a program called Mantech ("Manufacturing Technology"). The goals, as described by the Pentagon, were to design the "factory of the future," to integrate computer technology and automation in production and design, and to develop flexible manufacturing technology and management efficiency.[21] The goal was to boost the market share and industrial leadership of US industry in the traditional way, through state initiative and taxpayer funding. There was also a side benefit: the factory of the future can reduce and control the workforce. It's an old story — take automation. Automation was so inefficient that it had to be developed in the public sector for a long period, then finally handed over to private industry. When it was designed in the state sector it was designed in a very specific way, which is not inherent in the technology, and this topic has been rather well studied.[22] The system of computer-controlled machine tools could have been developed so as to empower mechanics and get rid of useless layers of management. But it was done the other way around: it was done to increase the layers of management and to de-skill workers. Again, that's not a technological or an economic decision, but it's a power decision — basically, part of class war. The same can be done with the factory of the future, when it is designed in the state sector — without anyone observing it, of course, except the business world, who are quite happy about it.

The Mantech program expanded rapidly under the Reagan administration, which actually went far beyond the norm in violating market principles for the rich, while being full of elevated rhetoric for the poor. Under Reagan the main research branch of the Pentagon, DARPA, actively promoted new technologies in a variety of fields, such as massively parallel computing — the source of the main technology in supercomputers and information technology, finishing up the work on the Internet, which they initiated in fact, and so on. And also in establishing start-up companies. *Science* magazine, the journal of the American Academy for the Advancement of Science, had an article in which they pointed out that "DARPA became a pivotal market force" under Reagan and Bush, transferring new technologies to "nascent industries" — it's a major source of Silicon Valley.[23] The Reagan administration also doubled protective barriers; it broke all post-war records in protectionism. The purpose was to keep out superior Japanese products — that was true of steel, automotive industries, semiconductors, computers — not only to save the industries but to place them in a dominant position for the triumph of the market, as it's called, in the 1990s, thanks in large measure to huge public subsidies, public sector innovation and development, protection, straight bailouts like Continental Illinois, and so on. It's amazing to watch the story transmuted into the politically correct terms that you read and hear.

14

Socioeconomic Sovereignty

In the past year, many global issues have been framed in terms of the notion of sovereignty, that is, the right of political entities to follow their own course — which may be benign or may be ugly — and to do so free from external interference. In the real world, that means interference by highly concentrated power, with its major center in the United States. This concentrated global power is called by various terms, depending on which aspect of sovereignty and freedom one has in mind. So sometimes it's called the Washington consensus, or the Wall Street/Treasury complex, or NATO, or the international economic bureaucracy (the World Trade Organization, World Bank, and IMF), or G-7 (the rich, Western, industrial countries) or G-3 or, more accurately, usually, G-1. From a more fundamental perspective, we could describe it as an array of megacorporations, often linked to one another by strategic alliances, administering a global economy which is in fact a kind of corporate mercantilism tending toward oligopoly in most sectors, heavily reliant on state power to socialize risk and cost, and to subdue recalcitrant elements.

In the past year, the issues of sovereignty have risen in two domains. One has to do with the sovereign right to be secure from military intervention. Here, the questions arise in a world order based on sovereign states. The second is the matter of sovereign rights in the face of socioeconomic intervention. Here, the questions arise in a world that's dominated by multinational corporations, especially financial institutions, and the whole framework that's been constructed to serve their interests — for example, the issues that arose dramatically in the anti-WTO protests in Seattle in November 1999.

Let me turn to the second topic, and that's the one I'll keep to for this discussion: the questions of sovereignty, freedom, and human rights that arise in the socioeconomic arena. First, a general comment: sovereignty is no value in itself. It's only a value insofar as it relates to freedom and rights, either enhancing them or diminishing them. I also want to take for granted something that may seem obvious, but is actually controversial: namely that, in speaking of freedom and rights, we have in mind human beings — that is, persons of flesh and blood, not abstract political and legal constructions like corporations, or states, or capital. If these entities have any rights at all, which is questionable, they should be derivative from the rights of people. That's the core classical liberal doctrine. It's also been the guiding principle for popular struggles for centuries, but it's very strongly opposed. It's opposed by official doctrine. It's opposed by sectors of wealth and privilege, and that's true both in the political and the socioeconomic realms.

The Political Realm

In the political realm, the familiar slogan is "popular sovereignty in a government of, by, and for the people," but the operative framework is quite different. The operative framework is that the people are considered a dangerous enemy. They have to be controlled for their own good. These issues go back centuries, to the earliest modern democratic revolutions in 17th-century England and in the North American colonies a century later. In both cases, the democrats were defeated — not completely, and certainly not permanently, by any means. In 17th-century England, much of the population did not want to be ruled by either king or parliament. Recall that those were the two contestants in the standard version of the civil war, but, as in most civil wars, a good part of the population wanted neither of them. As their pamphlets put it, they wanted to be governed "by countrymen like ourselves, that know our wants," not by "knights and gentlemen [that] make us laws, that are chosen for fear and do but oppress us, and do not know the people's sores."[1]

These same ideas animated the rebellious farmers of the colonies a century later, but the constitutional system was designed quite differently. It was designed to block that heresy. The goal was "to protect the minority of the opulent from the majority" and to ensure that "the country [is] governed by those who own it." Those are the words of the leading framer, James Madison, and the president of the Continental Congress and first chief justice of the Supreme Court, John Jay. Their conception prevailed, but the conflicts continued. They continually take new forms; they're alive right now. However, elite doctrine remains essentially unchanged.[2]

Fast forwarding to the 20th century (I'll keep here to the liberal, progressive side of the spectrum — it's harsher on the other side), the population are regarded as "ignorant and meddlesome outsiders" whose role is to be "spectators," not "participants," apart from periodic opportunities to choose among the representatives of private power.[3] These are what are called elections. In elections, public opinion is considered essentially irrelevant if it conflicts with the demands of the minority of the opulent who own the country. We're seeing that right now, in fact.

One striking example (there are many) has to do with the international economic order — what are called trade agreements. The general population, as polls make very clear, is strongly opposed to most of what's going on, but the issues don't arise in elections. They're not an issue in elections because the centers of power — the minority of the opulent — are unified in support of instituting a particular kind of socioeconomic order. What is discussed are things that they don't much care about, like questions of character or questions about reforms, which they know aren't going to be implemented. That's pretty typical, and it makes sense on the assumption that the role of the public — as the ignorant and meddlesome outsiders — is just to be spectators. If the general public, as it often does, seeks to organize and enter the political arena, to participate, to press its own concerns, that's a problem. It's not democracy; it's "a crisis of democracy" that has to be overcome.

These are all quotes from the liberal, progressive side of the modern spectrum, but the principles are quite widely held, and the past 25 years have been one of those regular periods when a major campaign has been conducted to try to overcome the perceived crisis of democracy and to reduce the public to their proper role of apathetic and passive and obedient spectators. That's the political realm.

The Socioeconomic Realm

In the socioeconomic realm there's something similar. There have been parallel, closely related conflicts for a long, long time. In the early days of the industrial revolution in the United States, in New England 150 years ago, there was a very lively, independent labor press run by young women from the farms and laborers from the towns. They condemned the "degradation and subordination" of the newly emerging industrial system, which compelled people to rent themselves to survive. It's worth remembering, and hard to remember, perhaps, that wage labor was considered not very different from chattel slavery at that time, not only by the workers in the mills, but right through much of the mainstream: for example, Abraham Lincoln, or the Republican Party, or even editorials in the *New York Times* (which they might like to forget). Working people opposed the return to what they called "monarchical principles" in the industrial system, and they demanded that those who work in the mills should own them — the spirit of republicanism. They denounced what they called the "new spirit of the age — gain wealth forgetting all but self," a demeaning and degrading vision of human life that has to be driven into people's minds by immense effort — which, in fact, has been going on over centuries.[4]

In the 20th century, the literature of the public relations industry provides a very rich and instructive store of information on how to instill the "new spirit of the age" by creating artificial wants or by "regimenting the public mind every bit as much as an army regiments the bodies of its soldiers" (Edward Bernays), and inducing a "philosophy of futility" and lack of purpose in life, by concentrating human attention on "the more superficial things that comprise much of fashionable consumption."[5] If that can be done, then people will accept the meaningless and subordinate lives that are appropriate for them, and they'll forget subversive ideas about taking control of their own lives.

This is a major social engineering project. It's been going on for centuries, but it became intense and enormous in the last century. There are a lot of ways of doing it. Some are the kind I just indicated, which are too familiar to illustrate. Others are to undermine security, and here, too, there are a number of ways. One way of undermining security is the threat of job transfer. One of the major consequences and, assuming rationality, one has to assume one of the major purposes of the mislabeled "trade agreements" (stress "mislabeled," because they're not about free trade: they have strong anti-market elements of a variety of kinds, and they're certainly not agreements, at least if people matter, since people are mostly opposed to them), is to facilitate the threat — it doesn't have to be reality, but just the threat — of job transfer, which is a good way of inducing discipline by undermining security.

Another device is to promote what's called "labor market flexibility." Let me quote the World Bank, who put the matter pretty plainly. They said, "Increasing labor market flexibility — despite the bad name it has acquired as a euphemism for pushing wages down and workers out [which is just what it is] — is essential in all the regions of the world .... The most important reforms involve lifting constraints on labor mobility and wage flexibility, as well as breaking the ties between social services and labor contracts."[6] That means cutting the benefits and the rights that have been won in generations of bitter struggle.

When they talk about lifting constraints on wage flexibility, they mean flexibility down, not flexibility up. The talk about labor mobility doesn't mean the right of people to move anywhere they want, as has been required by free market theory ever since Adam Smith, but rather the right to fire employees at will. And, under the current investor-based version of globalization, capital and corporations must be free to move, but not people, because their rights are secondary, incidental.

These "essential reforms," as the World Bank calls them, are imposed on much of the world as conditionalities for ratification by the World Bank and the IMF. They're introduced into the rich, industrial countries by other means, and they've been effective. Alan Greenspan testified before Congress that "greater worker insecurity" was an important factor in what's called the "fairy-tale economy." It keeps inflation down because workers are afraid to ask for wages and benefits. They're insecure. And that shows up pretty clearly in the statistical record. In the past 25 years, this period of rollback, of the crisis of democracy, wages have stagnated or declined for the majority of the workforce, for nonsupervisory workers, and working hours have increased very sharply — they've become the highest in the industrial world. This is noticed, of course, by the business press, which describes it as "a welcome development of transcendent importance," with working people compelled to abandon their "luxurious lifestyles," while corporate profits are "dazzling" and "stupendous."

There Is No Alternative

In the dependencies, less delicate measures are available. One of them is the so-called "debt crisis," which is largely traceable to World Bank/ IMF policy programs of the 1970s, and to the fact that the Third World rich are, for the most part, exempt from social obligations. That's dramatically true in Latin America, and one of its major problems. The "debt crisis" is not a simple economic fact, by any means. It is, to a large extent, an ideological construct. What's called the "debt" could be largely overcome in a number of elementary ways.[7]

But that's not to be. The debt is a very powerful weapon of control, and it can't be abandoned. For about half of the world's population right now, national economic policy is effectively run by bureaucrats in Washington. Also, half of the population of the world (not the same half, but overlapping) is subject to unilateral sanctions by the United States, which is a form of economic coercion that, again, undermines sovereignty severely and has been condemned repeatedly, most recently by the United Nations, as unacceptable, but it makes no difference.

Within the rich countries, there are other means of achieving similar results. Before getting to that, just a word about what we should never allow ourselves to forget, and that is that the devices that are used in the dependencies can be very brutal. There was a Jesuit-organized conference in San Salvador a couple of years ago, which considered the state terrorist project of the 1980s and its continuation since, by the socioeconomic policies imposed by the victors. The conference took special note of what it called the residual "culture of terror," which lasts after the actual terror declines and has the effect of "domesticating the expectations of the majority," who abandon any thought of "alternatives different to the demands of the powerful." They've learned the lesson that There Is No Alternative — TINA, as it's called — Maggie Thatcher's cruel phrase. The idea is that there is no alternative — that's now the familiar slogan of the corporate version of globalization. In the dependencies, the great achievement of the terrorist operations has been to destroy the hopes that had been raised in Latin America and Central America in the

1970s, inspired by popular organizing throughout the region and the "preferential option for the poor" of the Church, which was severely punished for that deviation from good behavior.

Sometimes the lessons about what happened are drawn rather accurately in measured tones. Right now there is a torrent of self-adulation about our success in inspiring a wave of democracy in our Latin American dependencies. The matter is put a little differently, and more accurately, in an important scholarly review by a leading specialist on the topic, Thomas Carothers, who, as he says, writes with an "insider's perspective," since he served in the State Department "democracy enhancement programs" of the Reagan administration, as they were called. He believes that Washington had good intentions, but he recognizes that in practice, the Reagan administration sought to maintain "the basic order of … quite undemocratic societies" and to avoid "populist-based change," and, like its predecessors, adopted "pro-democracy policies as a means of relieving pressure for more radical change, but inevitably sought only limited, top-down forms of democratic change that did not risk upsetting the traditional structures of power with which the United States has long been allied." It would be more accurate to say "the traditional structures of power with which the traditional structures of power within the United States had long been allied."

Carothers himself is dissatisfied with the outcome, but he describes what he calls the "liberal critique" as fundamentally flawed. This critique leaves the old debates "unresolved," he says, because of "its perennial weak spot." The perennial weak spot is that it offers no alternative to the policy of restoring the traditional structures of power, in this case by murderous terror that left a couple hundred thousand corpses in the 1980s and millions of refugees and maimed and orphaned people in the devastated societies. So, again, TINA — There Is No Alternative.[8]

The same dilemma was recognized at a different point on the political spectrum by President Carter's main Latin American specialist, Robert Pastor, who's quite far to the dovish, progressive end of the admissible spectrum. He explains in an interesting book why the Carter administration had to support the murderous and corrupt Somoza regime right to the bitter end, and then, when even the traditional structures of power turned against the dictator, the US had to try to maintain the National Guard that it had established and trained and that was then attacking the population "with a brutality a nation usually reserves for its enemy," as he puts it. This was all done with benign intent under the TINA principle—no alternative. Here's the reason: "The United States did not want to control Nicaragua or the other nations of the region, but it also did not want developments to get out of control. It wanted Nicaraguans to act independently, *except* [his emphasis] when doing so would affect US interests adversely."[9] So, in other words, Latin Americans should be free — free to act in accord with our wishes. We want them to be able to choose their own course freely, unless they make choices that we don't want, in which case we have to restore the traditional structures of power — by violence, if necessary. That's the more liberal and progressive side of the spectrum.

There are voices that are outside the spectrum — I don't want to deny that. For example, there's the idea that people should have the right "to share in the decisions, which often profoundly modify their way of life," not have their hopes "cruelly dashed" in a global order in which "political and financial power is concentrated" while financial markets "fluctuate erratically" with devastating consequences for the poor, "elections can be manipulated," and "the negative aspects on others are considered completely irrelevant" by the powerful. Those are quotes from the radical extremist in the Vatican whose annual New Year's message could scarcely be mentioned in the national press, and it's certainly an alternative that's not on the agenda.[10]

Why is there such broad agreement that Latin Americans — in fact, the world — cannot be allowed to exercise sovereignty, that is, to take control of their lives? It's the global analog to the fear of democracy within. Actually, that question has been frequently addressed in very instructive ways, primarily in the internal record, which we have (this is quite a free country — we have a rich record of declassified documents, and they're very interesting). The theme that runs through them is strikingly illustrated in one of the most influential cases, a hemispheric conference that the United States called in February 1945 in order to impose what was called the Economic Charter for the Americas, which was one of the cornerstones of the post-war world still firmly in place. The Charter called for an end to "economic nationalism [meaning sovereignty] in all its forms." Latin Americans would have to avoid what was called "excessive" industrial development that would compete with US interests, though they could have "complementary development." So Brazil could produce low-cost steel that the US corporations weren't interested in. Crucially, it was necessary to protect our resources, as George Kennan put it, even if that required "police states."

But Washington faced a problem in imposing the Charter. That was clearly explained internally in the State Department at the time in this way: Latin Americans were making the wrong choices. They were calling for "policies designed to bring about a broader distribution of wealth and to raise the standard of living of the masses," and they were convinced that "the first beneficiaries of the development of a country's resources should be the people of that country," not US investors. That's unacceptable, so sovereignty cannot be allowed. They can have freedom, but freedom to make the right choices.[11]

The same concerns lie in the background of the trade agreements — NAFTA, for example. At the time of NAFTA, you will recall, the propaganda was that it was going to be a wonderful boon to working people in all three countries — Canada, the United States, and Mexico. Well, that was quietly abandoned shortly after, when the facts were in, and what was obvious all along was in fact finally publicly conceded. The goal was to "lock Mexico into the reforms" of the 1980s, the reforms which had sharply reduced wages and enriched a small sector and foreign investors. The background concerns were articulated at a Latin American strategy development conference in Washington in 1990. It warned that "a 'democracy opening' in Mexico could test the special relationship by bringing into office a government more interested in challenging the US on economic and nationalist grounds." Notice that's the same threat as in 1945 and since, overcome, in this case, by locking Mexico into treaty obligations. These same reasons consistently lie behind a half a century of torture and terror, not only in the western hemisphere. And they're also at the core of the investor rights agreements that are being imposed under the specific form of globalization that's designed by state corporate power nexus.[12]

Corporatization

Let's go back to our point of departure: the contested issues of freedom and rights, hence sovereignty, insofar as it's to be valued. Do they inhere in persons of flesh and blood, or only in small sectors of wealth and privilege? Or even in abstract constructions like corporations, or capital, or states? In the past century the idea that such entities have special rights, over and above persons, has been very strongly advocated. The most prominent examples are Bolshevism, fascism, and private corporatism, which is a form of privatized tyranny. Two of these systems have collapsed. The third is alive and flourishing under the banner TINA — There Is No Alternative to the emerging system of state corporate mercantilism disguised with various mantras like globalization and free trade.

A century ago, during the early stages of the corporatization of the United States, discussion about these matters was quite frank. Conservatives a century ago denounced the procedure, describing corporatization as a "return to feudalism" and "a form of communism," which is not an entirely inappropriate analogy. There were similar intellectual origins in neo-Hegelian ideas about the rights of organic entities, along with the belief in the need to have a centralized administration of chaotic systems — like the markets, which were out of control. It's worth bearing in mind that in today's so-called "free-trade economy" a very large component of cross-border transactions (which are misleadingly called trade), probably about 70 percent of them, are actually within centrally managed institutions, within corporations and corporate alliances, if we include outsourcing and other devices of administration. That's quite apart from all kinds of other radical market distortions.

The conservative critique — notice that I am using the term "conservative" in a traditional sense; such conservatives scarcely exist any more — was echoed at the liberal/progressive end of the spectrum early in the 20th century, most notably perhaps by John Dewey, America's leading social philosopher, whose work focused largely on democracy. He argued that democratic forms have little substance when "the life of the country" — production, commerce, media — is ruled by private tyrannies in a system that he called "industrial feudalism," in which working people are subordinated to managerial control, and politics becomes "the shadow cast by big business over society."[13] Notice that he was articulating ideas that were common coin among working people many years earlier. And the same was true of his call for the replacement of industrial feudalism by self-managed industrial democracy.

Interestingly, progressive intellectuals who favored the process of corporatization agreed more or less with this description. Woodrow Wilson, for example, wrote that "most men are servants of corporations," which now account for the "greater part of the business of the country" in a "very different America from the old, ... no longer a scene of individual enterprise, ... individual opportunity, and individual achievement," but a new America, in which "small groups of men in control of great corporations wield a power and control over the wealth and business opportunities of the country," becoming "rivals of the government itself," and undermining popular sovereignty, exercised through the democratic political system.[14] Notice this was written in support of the process. He described the process as maybe unfortunate, but necessary, agreeing with the business world, particularly after the destructive market failures of the preceding years had convinced the business world and progressive intellectuals that markets simply had to be administered and that financial transactions had to be regulated.

Similar questions are very much alive in the international arena today: talk about reforming financial architecture, and that sort of thing. A century ago, corporations were granted the rights of persons by radical judicial activism, an extreme violation of classical liberal principles. They were also freed from earlier obligations to keep to specific activities for which they were chartered. Furthermore, in an important move, the courts shifted power upward from the stockholders in a partnership to the central management, which was identified with the immortal corporate person. Those of you who are familiar with the history of Communism will recognize that this is very similar to the process that was taking place at the time, very much as predicted, in fact, by left-Marxist and anarchist critics of Bolshevism. People like Rosa Luxemburg warned early on that the centralizing ideology would shift power from working people to the party, to the central committee, and then to the maximal leader, as happened very quickly after the conquest of state power in 1917, which at once destroyed every residue of socialist forms and principles. The propagandists on both sides prefer a different story for self-serving reasons, but I think that's the more accurate one.

In recent years, corporations have been granted rights that go far beyond those of persons. Under the World Trade Organization rules, corporations can demand what's called the right of "national treatment." That means that General Motors, if it's operating in Mexico, can de-

mand to be treated like a Mexican firm. Now that's only a right of immortal persons; it's not a right of flesh-and-blood persons. A Mexican
can't come to New York and demand national treatment and do very
well, but corporations can.

Other rules require that the rights of investors, lenders, and specula-
tors must prevail over the rights of mere flesh-and-blood people generally, undermining popular sovereignty and diminishing democratic
rights. Corporations are able in various ways to bring suits, bring actions, against sovereign states, and there are interesting cases. For example, Guatemala, a couple of years ago, sought to reduce infant mortality
by regulating the marketing of infant formula by multinationals. The
measures that Guatemala proposed were in conformity with World
Health Organization guidelines, and they kept to international codes, but
the Gerber Corporation claimed expropriation, and the threat of a World
Trade Organization complaint sufficed for Guatemala to withdraw, fearing retaliatory sanctions by the United States.

The first such complaint under the new World Trade Organization
rules was brought against the United States by Venezuela and Brazil,
who complained that EPA regulations on petroleum violated their rights
as petroleum exporters. Washington backed down that time, also allegedly in fear of sanctions, but I'm skeptical about that interpretation. I
don't think the US fears trade sanctions from Venezuela and Brazil.
More likely the Clinton administration simply saw no compelling reason to defend the environment and protect health.

These issues are arising very dramatically and, in fact, obscenely
right now. Tens of millions of people around the world are dying from
treatable diseases because of the protectionist elements written into the
World Trade Organization rules that grant private megacorporations
monopoly pricing rights. So Thailand and South Africa, for example,
which have pharmaceutical industries, can produce life-saving drugs at
a fraction of the cost of the monopolistic pricing, but they're afraid to do
so under threat of trade sanctions. In fact, in 1998 the United States even
threatened to withdraw funding if the World Health Organization even
monitored the effects of trade conditions on health.[15] These are very real
threats today.

All of this is called "trade rights." It has nothing to do with trade. It
has to do with monopolistic pricing practices enforced by protectionist

measures that are introduced into what are called free trade agreements. The measures are designed to ensure corporate rights. They also have the effect of reducing growth and innovation. And they are only part of the array of regulations introduced into these agreements which prevent development and growth. What is at stake is investor rights, not trade. And trade, of course, has no value in itself. It's a value if it increases human welfare, otherwise not.

In general the principle of the World Trade Organization, the primary principle, and related treaties, is that sovereignty and democratic rights have to be subordinated to the rights of investors. In practice that means the rights of the huge immortal persons, the private tyrannies to which people must be subordinated. These are among the issues that led to the remarkable events in Seattle. But in some ways, a lot of ways, the conflict between popular sovereignty and private power was illuminated more sharply a couple of months after Seattle, in Montreal, where an ambiguous settlement was reached on the so-called "biosafety protocol." There the issue was very clearly drawn. Quoting the *New York Times*, a compromise was reached "after intense negotiations that often pitted the United States against almost everyone else" over what's called "the precautionary principle." What's that? Well the chief negotiator for the European Union described it this way: "Countries must be able to have the freedom, the sovereign right, to take precautionary measures with regard" to genetically altered seed, microbes, animals, crops that they fear might be harmful. The United States, however, insisted on World Trade Organization rules. Those rules are that an import can be banned only on the basis of scientific evidence.[16]

Notice what's at stake here. The question that's at stake is whether people have the right to refuse to be experimental subjects. So, to personalize it, suppose the biology department at the university were to walk in and tell you, "You folks have to be experimental subjects in an experiment we're carrying out, where we're going to stick electrodes in your brain and see what happens. You can refuse, but only if you provide scientific evidence that it's going to harm you." Usually you can't provide scientific evidence. The question is, do you have a right to refuse? Under World Trade Organization rules, you don't. You have to be experimental subjects. It's a form of what Edward Herman has called "producer sovereignty."[17] The producer reigns; consumers have to somehow defend themselves. That works domestically, too, as he pointed out. It's not the responsibility, say, of chemical and pesticide industries to prove that what they're putting into the environment is safe. It's the responsibility of the public to prove scientifically that it's unsafe, and they have to do this through underfunded public agencies that are susceptible to industry influence through lobbying and other pressures.

That was the issue at Montreal, and a kind of ambiguous settlement was reached. Notice, to be clear, there was no issue of principle. You can see that by just looking at the lineup. The United States was on one side, and it was joined, in fact, by some other countries with a stake in biotechnology and high-tech agro-export, and on the other side was everybody else — those who didn't expect to profit by the experiment. That was the lineup, and that tells you exactly how much principle was involved. For similar reasons, the European Union favors high tariffs on agricultural products, just as the United States did 40 years ago, but no longer — and not because the principles have changed; just because power has changed.

There is an overriding principle. The principle is that the powerful and the privileged have to be able to do what they want (of course, pleading high motives). The corollary is that sovereignty and democratic rights of people must go, in this case — and that's what makes it so dramatic — their reluctance to be experimental subjects when US-based corporations can profit by the experiment. The US appeal to the World Trade Organization rules is very natural, since they codified that principle; that's the point.

These issues, although they're very real and are affecting a huge number of people in the world, are actually secondary to other modalities to reduce sovereignty in favor of private power. Most important, I think, was the dismantling of the Bretton Woods system in the early 1970s by the United States, Britain, and others. That system was designed by the US and Britain in the 1940s. It was a time of overwhelming popular support for social welfare programs and radical democratic measures. In part for those reasons the Bretton Woods system of the mid-'40s regulated exchange rates and allowed controls on capital flow. The idea was to cut down wasteful and harmful speculation, and to restrict capital flight. The reasons were well understood and clearly articulated — free capital flow creates what's sometimes called a "virtual parliament" of global capital, which can exercise veto power over government policies that it considers irrational. That means things like labor rights, or educational programs, or health, or efforts to stimulate the economy or, in fact, anything that might help people and not profits (and therefore is irrational in the technical sense).

The Bretton Woods system more or less functioned for about 25 years. That's what many economists call the "golden age" of modern capitalism (modern state capitalism, more accurately). That was a period, roughly up until about 1970, a period of historically unprecedented growth of the economy, of trade, of productivity, of capital investment, extension of welfare state measures, a golden age. That was reversed in the early '70s. The Bretton Woods system was dismantled, with liberalization of financial markets and floating exchange rates.

The period since has often been described as a "leaden age." There was a huge explosion of very short-term, speculative capital, completely overwhelming the productive economy. There was marked deterioration in just about every respect — considerably slower economic growth, slower growth of productivity, of capital investment, much higher interest rates (which slow down growth), greater market volatility, and financial crises. All of these things have very severe human effects, even in the rich countries: stagnating or declining wages, much longer working hours, particularly striking in the United States, cutback of services. Just to give you one example in today's great economy that everyone's talking about, the median income (half above, half below) for families has gotten back now to what it was in 1989, which is below what it was in the 1970s. It also has been a period of the dismantling of social democratic measures that had considerably improved human welfare. And in general, the newly imposed international order provided much greater veto power for the "virtual parliament" of private capital of investors leading to significant decline of democracy and sovereign rights, and a significant deterioration in social health.

While those effects are felt in the rich societies, they're a catastrophe in the poorer societies. These issues cut across societies, so it's not a matter of this society getting richer and that one getting poorer. The more significant measures are sectors of the global population. So, for example, using recent World Bank analyses, if you take the top 5 percent of the world's population and compare their income and wealth to the bottom

5 percent, that ratio was 78 to 1 in 1988 and 114 to 1 in 1993 (that's the last period for which figures are available), and undoubtedly higher now. The same figures show the top 1 percent of the world's population has the same income as the bottom 57 percent — 2.7 billion people.[18]

It's quite natural that dismantling of the post-war economic order should be accompanied by a significant attack on substantive democracy — freedom, popular sovereignty, and human rights — under the slogan TINA (There Is No Alternative). It's kind of a farcical mimicry of vulgar Marxism. The slogan, needless to say, is self-serving fraud. The particular socioeconomic order that's being imposed is the result of human decisions in human institutions. The decisions can be modified; the institutions can be changed. If necessary, they can be dismantled and replaced, just as honest and courageous people have been doing throughout the course of history.

Notes

South End Press would like to thank the following people and organizations for their assistance with *Rogue States:* David Barsamian and Alternative Radio, Rami Elkhatib and the MIT Arab Students Organization, Helena Feder, the Interhemispheric Resource Center, Roger Leisner and Radio Free Maine, Mobilization for Survival, Eduardo Monteverde, Doug Morris, Pastors for Peace, *Peacework,* Gillian Russom, Beverly Stohl, *Z Magazine,* and ZNet.

List of Abbreviations

AFP	*Agence-France Presse*
AP	Associated Press
BG	*Boston Globe*
BW	*Business Week*
CSM	*Christian Science Monitor*
GW	*Guardian Weekly*
NYT	*New York Times*
WP	*Washington Post*
WSJ	*Wall Street Journal*

Books by Noam Chomsky Cited

After the Cataclysm: Postwar Indochina and the Reconstruction of Imperial Ideology, The Political Economy of Human Rights: Volume II, with Edward Herman. Cambridge, MA: South End Press, 1979.

The Culture of Terrorism. Cambridge, MA: South End Press, 1988.

Deterring Democracy. New York: Verso, 1991; expanded edition, New York: Hill & Wang, 1992.

Fateful Triangle: The United States, Israel, and the Palestinians. Cambridge, MA: South End Press, 1983; Updated Edition, 1999.

For Reasons of State. New York: Pantheon, 1973.

Necessary Illusions: Thought Control in Democratic Societies. Cambridge, MA: South End Press, 1989.

A New Generation Draws the Line: Kosovo, East Timor and the Standards of the West. New York: Verso, 2000.

The New Military Humanism: Lessons From Kosovo. Monroe, ME: Common Courage Press, 1999.

The Political Economy of Human Rights, volumes I and II *(The Washington Connection and Third World Fascism* and *After the Cataclysm: Postwar Indochina and the Reconstruction of Imperial Ideology),* with Edward Herman. Cambridge, MA: South End Press, 1979.

Profit over People: Neoliberalism and Global Order. New York: Seven Stories, 1998.

Pirates and Emperors: International Terrorism in the Real World. Claremont, 1986; Montreal, Quebec: Black Rose Books, 1987; Amana, 1988.

Powers and Prospects: Reflections on Human Nature and the Social Order. Cambridge, MA: South End Press, 1996.

Rethinking Camelot: JFK, the Vietnam War, and US Political Culture. Cambridge, MA: South End Press, 1993.

Towards a New Cold War: Essays on the Current Crisis and How We Got There. New York: Pantheon, 1982.

Turning the Tide: US Intervention in Central America and the Struggle for Peace. Cambridge, MA: South End Press, 1985.

The Washington Connection and Third World Fascism, The Political Economy of Human Rights: Volume I, with Edward Herman. Cambridge, MA: South End Press, 1979.

World Orders Old and New. New York: Columbia Univ. Press, 1996.

Year 501: The Conquest Continues. Cambridge, MA: South End Press, 1993.

1. Rogues' Gallery

A shorter version of this article was published in *Harvard International Review,* Summer 2000.

1. *American Society of International Law (ASIL) Newsletter* (March–April 1999). Detlev Vagts, "Taking Treaties Less Seriously," "Editorial Comments," *American Journal of International Law* 92:458 (1998).

2. *Proceedings of the American Society of International Law* 13, 14 (1963), cited by Louis Henkin, *How Nations Behave* (Council on Foreign Relations, Columbia Univ., 1979), 333–34; 1961 Acheson Report (Kennedy Library), cited by Marc Trachtenberg, "Intervention in Historical Perspective" in Laura Reed and Carl Kaysen, eds., *Emerging Norms of Justified Intervention* (American Academy of Arts and Sciences, 1993).

3. "American Republics," vol. XII of *Foreign Relations of the United States* (US Dept. of State, 1961–63), 13f., 33. See chap. 6, in this volume.

4. Daniel Patrick Moynihan, *A Dangerous Place* (Little, Brown, 1978).

5. See chap. 4, in this volume, and expanded versions, " 'Green Light' for War Crimes," in R. Tanter, M. Selden, and S. Shalom, eds., *East Timor, Indonesia, and the World Community* (Rowman & Littlefield, 2000), and my *A New Generation Draws the Line.*

6. George Shultz, "Moral Principles and Strategic Interests," address at Kansas State University, April 14, 1986, reprinted in US Dept. of State, Bureau of Public Affairs, *Current Policy* 820; Sofaer, "The United States and the World Court" (statement before the Senate Foreign Relations Committee, Dec. 1985), reprinted in *Current Policy* 769. See my " 'Consent Without Consent': Reflections on the Theory and Practice of Democracy," *Cleveland State Law Review* 44.4 (1996).

7. On the International Court of Justice decision, the reactions, and the aftermath, see my *Necessary Illusions,* chap. 4.

8. Bill Clinton, speech before the UN General Assembly, Sept. 27, 1993; William Cohen, *Annual Report to the President and Congress: 1999* (US Dept. of Defense, 1999), cited by Jonathan Bach and Robert Borosage, in Martha Honey and Tom Barry, eds., *Global Focus* (St. Martin's, 2000), 180, 10. Madeleine Albright's statement that the US will act "multilaterally when we can, and unilaterally as we must" in areas "we recognize ... as vital to US national interests," cited by Jules Kagian, *Middle East International,* Oct. 21, 1994.

9. For more detail, see my *Deterring Democracy,* chap. 11, and sources cited.

10. On Lebanon, see my *Fateful Triangle.* On Turkey, see my *The New Military Humanism,* chaps. 3 and 5.

11. See my *World Orders Old and New,* chap. 1; and my *Rethinking Camelot.*

12. Audrey Kahin and George Kahin, *Subversion as Foreign Policy* (New Press, 1995).

13. Michael Glennon, "The New Interventionism," *Foreign Affairs* (May–June 1999).

14. *The Second World War,* vol. 5 (Houghton Mifflin, 1951), 382.

15. See my *The New Military Humanism,* chap. 6, for sources and more extensive quotes. See also *Defense Monitor* (Washington, DC: Center for Defense Information), XXIX.3, 2000.

16. See my *Powers and Prospects,* chap. 7.

17. See my *For Reasons of State* for a review from the Pentagon Papers, one of their few surprises.

18. For fuller discussion, see my *World Orders Old and New,* chap. 1.

19. For more extensive quotes from the official record, see my *Necessary Illusions,* 263–64, and *Deterring Democracy,* 262–63.

20. Cited by Piero Gleijeses, *Shattered Hope* (Princeton, 1991), 365.

21. See my *Year 501,* chap. 8; and my *Profit Over People,* chap. 4; and sources cited.

22. On Lebanon, see my "International Terrorism: Image and Reality," in A. George, ed., *Western State Terrorism* (Polity-Blackwell, 1991). On Sudan, see Colum Lynch, *BG,* Sept. 24, 1998; Patrick Wintour, *London Observer,* Dec. 20, 1998; *NYT,* Aug. 28, 1998.

23. Anthony Lewis, *NYT,* April 21 and 24, 1975; Dec. 27, 1979. On McNamara's *In Retrospect* and the reactions to it, see my "Memories," *Z* magazine, July–Aug. 1995; and my "Hamlet Without the Prince," *Diplomatic History* 20:3 (1996).

24. Glennon, "New Interventionism"; Sebastian Mallaby, *NYT Book Review,* Sept. 21, 1997; David Fromkin, *Kosovo Crossing* (Free Press, 1999), 196.

2. Rogue States

This article originally appeared in *Z Magazine,* April 1998.

1. Mark Curtis, *The Ambiguities of Power* (Zed, 1995), 146.

2. Jules Kagian, *Middle East International,* Oct. 21, 1994; Kagian, *FT,* Feb. 19, 1998; Steven Erlanger and Philip Shenon, *NYT,* Feb. 23, 1998; Clinton press conference, *NYT,* Feb. 24, 1998; R.W. Apple, *NYT,* Feb. 24, 1998; Aaron Zitner, *BG,* Feb. 21, 1998.

3. Colum Lynch, *BG,* March 3, 1998; Weston, Costa Rica, *BG,* March 3, 1998; *WSJ,* March 3, 1998; Barbara Crossette, *NYT,* March 3, 1998; Laura Silber and David Buchan,

FT, March 4, 1998; Steven Lee Myers, *NYT,* March 4, 1998; R.W. Apple, *NYT,* Feb. 24, 1998 (Lott); Steven Erlanger and Philip Shenon, *NYT,* Feb. 23, 1998 (McCain, Kerry); Aaron Zitner, "A Visible Kerry Turns Tough on Crisis," *BG,* Feb. 21, 1998.

4. Editorial, *BG,* Feb. 27, 1998; William Pfaff, *BG,* Feb. 23, 1998; Ronald Steel, *NYT,* March 1, 1998.

5. Nov. 29, 1990.

6. Aug. 2, 1990.

7. Editorial, *FT,* March 2, 1998.

8. See chap. 1, p. 4, in this volume.

9. See my *Culture of Terrorism,* 67f.; and my *Necessary Illusions,* 82f., 94f., 270.

10. National Security Council 5429/2; my emphasis.

11. See my *For Reasons of State,* 100ff.; *Pirates and Emperors,* 140; UN Ambassador Thomas Pickering and Justice Dept., cited in my *Deterring Democracy,* 147; and *World Orders Old and New,* 16f.; George Kahin, *Intervention* (Knopf, 1986), 74.

12. Steven Donziger, ed., *The Real War on Crime: The Report of the National Criminal Justice Commission* (HarperCollins, 1996); Nils Christie, *Crime Control as Industry* (Routledge, 1993); Michael Tonry, *Malign Neglect: Race, Crime, and Punishment in America* (Oxford, 1995); Randall Shelden and William Brown, *Criminal Justice* (Wadsworth, forthcoming). See chap. 5.

13. "Irrationality Suggested to Intimidate US Enemies," AP, *BG,* March 2, 1998. See chaps. 1, 7, and 8, in this volume, for further details. On the Israeli theory, see my *Fateful Triangle,* 464ff.

14. George Bush, *National Security Strategy of the United States,* White House, March 1990; for more extensive quotations, see my *Deterring Democracy,* chap. 1.

15. On these matters and what follows, see my articles in *Z* magazine in 1990–91; *Deterring Democracy* (chaps. 4–6, afterword); *Powers and Prospects,* chap. 6; my article in Cynthia Peters, ed., *Collateral Damage: The "New World Order" at Home and Abroad* (South End, 1992). Also Dilip Hiro, *Desert Shield to Desert Storm* (Routledge, 1992); Douglas Kellner, *The Persian Gulf TV War* (Westview, 1992); Miron Rezun, *Saddam Hussein's Gulf Wars* (Praeger, 1992); and a number of useful collections. There is also a much (self)-praised "scholarly history" by Lawrence Freedman and Efraim Karsh, which contains useful information but with serious omissions and errors: *The Gulf Conflict 1990–1991: Diplomacy and War in the New World Order* (Princeton, 1992). See my *World Orders Old and New,* chap. 1, note 18; and my "World Order and Its Rules," *Journal of Law and Society* (Cardiff, Wales), Summer 1993.

16. Ronald Steel, *NYT,* March 1, 1998.

17. Cited by Charles Glass, *Prospect* (London), March 1998.

18. See chaps. 1 and 4, in this volume.

19. See my articles in *Z* magazine from the Madrid conference in 1991 through the Oslo conference in 1993, and beyond. Also *Deterring Democracy,* chap. 6 and afterword; *Powers and Prospects,* chap. 6; *World Orders Old and New,* chap. 3 and epilogue; and sources cited. For further update, see my "The 'Peace Process' in US Global Strategy," address at Ben-Gurion University conference, June 1997, in Haim Gordon, ed., *Looking Back at the June 1967 War* (Praeger, 1999); and my *Fateful Triangle.*

20. Serge Schmemann and Douglas Jehl, *NYT,* Feb. 27, 1998.

21. See sources cited earlier. Albright, Cohen, CNN live report, Ohio State Univ.,

Feb. 18, 1998; partial transcript (omitting the interchange quoted), *NYT*, Feb. 19, 1998. Trent Lott, *BG*, Feb. 26, 1998. Charles Glass, *New Statesman*, Feb. 20, 1998. Bill Blum, *Consortium*, March 2, 1990. William Broad and Judith Miller, *NYT*, Feb. 26, 1998. Scott Inquiry Report, Feb. 1996. Gerald James, *In the Public Interest* (London: Little, Brown, 1996). Alan Friedman, *Spider's Web: The Secret History of How the White House Illegally Armed Iraq* (Bantam, 1993). Mark Phythian, *Arming Iraq: How the US and Britain Secretly Built Saddam's War Machine* (Northeastern Univ. Press, 1997).

22. David Korn, ed., *Human Rights in Iraq* (Human Rights Watch, Yale, 1989); CARDRI (Committee Against Repression and for Democratic Rights in Iraq), *Saddam's Iraq* (Zed, 1986, 1989), 236f.; Dilip Hiro, *The Longest War* (Routledge, 1991), 53; Rezun, *Saddam Hussein's Gulf Wars,* 43f.; Darwish and Gregory Alexander, *Unholy Babylon* (St. Martin's, 1991), 78f.; John Gittings, "How West Propped Up Saddam's Rule," *GW*, March 10, 1991.

23. Andy Thomas, *Effects of Chemical Warfare* (Stockholm International Peace Research Institute [SIPRI], Taylor & Francis, 1985), chap. 2. See my *Turning the Tide,* 126; and *Deterring Democracy*, 181f.

24. On Vietnam, see my *Necessary Illusions*, 38f. On Cuba, see Chomsky and Edward Herman, *Political Economy of Human Rights,* vol. I, 69; and much subsequent material, including Alexander Cockburn, *Nation*, March 9, 1998.

25. *The Struggle* (New Haven), Feb. 21, 1998; Maggie O'Kane, *Guardian*, Feb. 19, 1998; Scott Peterson, *CSM*, Feb. 17, 1998; Roula Khalaf, *FT*, March 2, 1998. The impact of the bombing and sanctions was known at once; see Jean Drèze and Haris Gazdar, *Hunger and Poverty in Iraq 1991*, London School of Economics, Sept. 1991. For extensive review, see Geoff Simons, *The Scourging of Iraq* (London: Macmillan, 1996).

26. Hiro, *Longest War*, 239f.

27. AP, *NYT*, May 26, 1993.

28. *NYT*, July 7, 1991; June 28, 1993. On Kubba, Chalabi, see my article in Peters, *Collateral Damage.*

29. David Marcus, *BG*, Feb. 18, 1998; Roula Khalaf, Mark Suzman, David Gardner, *FT*, Feb. 23, 1998; *FT*, Feb. 9, 1998; Robin Allen, *FT*, March 3, 1998; Steven Lee Myers, *NYT*, Feb. 9, 1998; Douglas Jehl, *NYT*, Feb. 9, 1998; Charles Sennott, *BG*, Feb. 18, 1998, Feb. 19, 1998; Daniel Pearl, *WSJ*, Feb. 25, 1998.

30. David Fairhall and Ian Black, *GW*, Feb. 8, 1998; Reuters, *BG*, March 3, 1998; Douglas Jehl, *NYT*, Feb. 22, 1998; Jimmy Burns, *FT*, Feb. 15, 1998.

31. Peterson, *CSM*, Feb. 17, 1998 .

32. David Gardner, *FT*, Feb. 28, 1998; Robin Allen, *FT*, March 3, 1998.

3. Crisis in the Balkans

This article originally appeared in *Z Magazine,* May 1999. See also my *The New Military Humanism* and my *A New Generation Draws the Line.*

1. Ann Scales and Louise Palmer, Kevin Cullen, *BG,* March 25, 1999; Bill Clinton, *NYT*, May 23, 1999.

2. "Overview," *NYT*, March 27, 1999. Also *Sunday Times* (London), March 28, 1999: "NATO's supreme commander, Wesley Clark, was not surprised at the retaliatory

upsurge. 'This was entirely predictable at this stage,' he said," referring to the "horrific" impact on civilians.

3. *BG,* April 4, 1999.

4. James Hooper, "Kosovo: America's Balkan Problem," *Current History,* April 1999. A strong advocate of NATO military action, Hooper is executive director of the Balkan Action Council in Washington, having served in the State Department as deputy director responsible for Balkan affairs, then deputy chief of mission in Warsaw.

5. Hooper, "Kosovo: America's Balkan Problem."

6. Colum Lynch, *BG,* Oct. 8, 1998; Susan Milligan, *BG,* Oct. 9, 1998.

7. Jane Perlez, "Trickiest Divides Are Among Big Powers at Kosovo Talks," *NYT,* Feb. 11, 1999. Kevin Cullen, "US, Europeans in Discord over Kosovo," *BG,* Feb. 22, 1999.

8. See chap. 2, note 15, in this volume.

9. Serge Schmemann, "The Critics Now Ask: After Missiles, What?," *NYT,* Dec. 18, 1998. Colum Lynch, "In the End, US Urged a Change," *BG,* May 21, 1998. See chap. 1, in this volume.

10. Steven Erlanger, "Belgrade 'Targets' Find Unity 'From Heaven,' " *NYT,* March 30, 1999; Veran Matic, op-ed, *NYT,* April 3, 1999; Randolph Ryan, "NATO Bombs Raze Dreams of Democracy," *BG,* April 4, 1999

11. Barton Gellman, William Drozdiak, *WP Weekly,* March 29, 1999.

12. William Glaberson, *NYT,* March 27, 1999.

13. See my *World Orders Old and New,* and sources cited, particularly Amnesty International, Human Rights Watch, and the Washington Office on Latin America. See chap. 5, in this volume.

14. See my *The New Military Humanism,* chap. 3.

15. Ibid.

16. Kevin Cullen and Anne Kornblut, *BG,* April 4, 1999; Clinton speech, April 1, 1999, at Norfolk Air Station , in *NYT,* April 2, 1999.

17. Colum Lynch, "US Seen Leaving Africa to Solve Its Own Crises," *BG,* Feb. 19, 1999.

18. Lesley Stahl interview with Madeleine Albright, *60 Minutes,* May 12, 1996.

19. Columbia University professor of preventive diplomacy David Phillips, cited by Ethan Bronner, "The Scholars: Historians Note Flaws in President's Speech," *NYT,* March 26, 1999.

20. Sean Murphy, *Humanitarian Intervention: The United Nations in an Evolving World Order* (Univ. of Pennsylvania Press, 1996). Citations are from his 1994 doctoral dissertation of the same title. For review, see *American Journal of International Law,* vol. 92 (1998), 583f. On Japan's actions and rhetoric in Manchuria as compared with those of the US in Vietnam, see my "Revolutionary Pacifism of A.J. Muste," reprinted in *American Power and the New Mandarins: Historical and Political Essays* (Pantheon, 1969), 323–66.

21. Gaddis, "The Old World Order," *NYT Book Review,* March 21, 1999.

22. See chap. 1, in this volume.

23. Samuel Huntington, *Foreign Affairs,* March–April 1999.

24. Kevin Done, *FT,* March 27 and 28, 1999.

25. For details on the documentary record and coverage, see my *The New Military Humanism,* chap. 5.

26. Henry Kissinger, "Commentary," *BG,* March 1, 1999.

27. Tony Judt, "Tyrannized by Weaklings," op-ed , *NYT,* April 5, 1999.

28. Serge Schmemann, "A New Collision of East and West," *NYT,* April 4, 1999.

29. Cohen, Federal News Service, April 1, 1999.

30. Adam Clymer, *NYT,* March 29, 1999.

31. Clinton speech, *NYT,* April 2, 1999; Bob Hohler, *BG,* April 3, 1999.

32. Jane Perlez, *NYT,* March 28, 1999, and many others.

33. Hedley Bull, "Justice in International Relations," Hagey Lectures, University of Waterloo, Ontario, 1983, 1–35. Louis Henkin, *How Nations Behave* (Council on Foreign Relations, Columbia Univ., 1979), 144–45; also cited in Murphy, *Humanitarian Intervention,* as being of particular significance.

4. East Timor Retrospective

Portions of this article originally appeared as ZNet commentaries, Oct. 4, 1999, and Oct. 23, 1999, and in "Western 'Green Light' for Massacres," *Le Monde diplomatique,* Oct. 1999. For further detail, update, and sources, see references of chap. 1, note 5, in this volume.

1. Report of the Security Council Mission to Jakarta and Dili, Sept. 8–12, 1999.

2. *NYT,* op-ed, Sept. 15, 1999.

3. *BG,* Sept. 15, 1999. Later UN estimates were that 85 percent of the population had been expelled.

4. Benedict Anderson, statement before the Fourth Committee of the UN General Assembly, Oct. 20, 1980. For fuller quotes and context, see my *Towards a New Cold War.*

5. David Briscoe, AP online, Sept. 8, 1999.

6. For review and sources, see my *Year 501.*

7. Alan Nairn, *The Nation,* Sept. 27, 1999.

8. Elizabeth Becker, *NYT,* Sept. 14, 1999.

9. Sander Thoenes, *FT,* London, Sept. 8, 1999; *CSM,* Sept. 14, 1999.

10. Guy Alcorn, *Sydney Morning Herald,* Aug. 25, 1999, citing US State Dept. spokesman James Foley. Defense Secretary William Cohen, press briefing, Sept. 8, 1999.

11. Elizabeth Becker and Philip Shenon, *NYT,* Sept. 9, 1999. Steven Mufson, Sept. 9, 1999.

12. Peter Hartcher, *Australian Financial Review* (Sydney), Sept. 13, 1999.

13. Daniel Patrick Moynihan, *A Dangerous Place* (Little, Brown, 1978).

14. Arnold Kohen, *WP,* Sept. 5, 1999.

15. Philip Shenon, *NYT,* Sept. 13, 1999.

16. *The Observer* (London), Sept. 13, 1999.

17. Becker and Shenon, *NYT,* Sept. 9, 1999.

18. Jenkins, *Sydney Morning Herald,* July 8, 1999. Anderson, *New Left Review* 235, May/June 1999.

19. Brian Toohey, *Australian Financial Review,* Aug. 14, 1999, referring to a radio interview "earlier this year."

20. *The Observer,* Sept. 13, 1999.

21. Mark Dodd, *Sydney Morning Herald,* July 26, 1999.

22. For sources below, see my *A New Generation Draws the Line.*

5. The Colombia Plan

This article originally appeared in *Z Magazine,* June 2000.

1. Arms transfers, Adam Isacson and Joy Olson, *Just the Facts: A Citizen's Guide to US Defense and Security Assistance to Latin America and the Caribbean* (Latin America Working Group and Center for International Policy, Washington DC, 1999). For background and sources not cited here, see my *Deterring Democracy,* chaps. 4 and 5; and my *World Orders Old and New,* chaps. 1 and 2. See also Javier Giraldo, S.J., *Colombia: The Genocidal Democracy* (Common Courage, 1996). On the correlation, see Lars Schoultz, chap. 10, p. 127, in this volume. For broader confirmation and inquiry, which helps explain the reasons, see Noam Chomsky and Edward Herman, *Political Economy of Human Rights,* vol. I, chap. 2.1.1; Herman, *The Real Terror Network* (South End, 1982), 126ff. There is a substantial literature of case studies.

2. Martin Hodgson, "The coca leaf war," *Bulletin of the Atomic Scientists,* May/June 2000. Officially, Colombia states that "Plan Colombia will cost a total of $7.3 billion, of which $4.2 billion will be financed by the Colombian Government, and $3.1 billion contributed by the international community," with $1.08 billion for "a counter-narcotics strategy." Press release, Colombian Embassy, Washington, DC, June 2, 2000. "Intentional ignorance" is the phrase used by human rights monitors Donald Fox and Michael Glennon, commenting on Washington's decision "not to see" the terror it was carrying out, through proxies, in Central America. "Report to the International Human Rights Law Group and the Washington Office on Latin America," Washington DC, April 1985, 21. Also Glennon, "Terrorism and 'intentional ignorance,' " *CSM,* March 20, 1986. See my *Necessary Illusions,* 78.

3. Fiscal years. On US arms transfers, see Tamar Gabelnick, William Hartung, and Jennifer Washburn, *Arming Repression: US Arms Sales to Turkey During the Clinton Administration* (World Policy Institute and Federation of American Scientists, Oct. 1999). For review of US-Turkey counterinsurgency programs, see my *The New Military Humanism.*

4. Judith Miller, *NYT,* April 30, 2000. The other great achievers in the war against terrorism are Spain (at least, those members of the government who have not yet been jailed for torture and atrocities for their counterterrorism activities) and Algeria, a reference that surpasses comment. The report and review merit much more extensive discussion.

5. Reuters, May 9, 2000 (datelined Ankara); *AFP,* May 26, 2000. AP, *BG,* Chicago Tribune, *WP* (brief excerpt), May 27, 2000. Anne Kornblut, "Congress sees differences on China, Cuba," *BG,* May 27, 2000. Kinzer, "Turkey Reviews the Darkest Hours in Its Painful Past," *NYT,* May 28, 2000. Kinzer, "Turkish Study Finds Torture of Prisoners Is Widespread," *NYT,* June 4, 2000, noting that "the mostly Kurdish population has long complained of bad treatment by police" in the southeast; not quite the full story. On Kinzer's rendition of Turkey's massive ethnic cleansing and terror operations of the '90s, and of the Clinton administration's contribution to them, see my *The New Military Humanism.* For review of his impressive feats of suppression of US atrocities and undermining of diplomacy in his previous post in Nicaragua, see my *Necessary Illusions.*

6. Merely to illustrate, as the April military assaults were being organized, editors of eight newspapers in a Kurdish province were facing possible three-year prison sentences if found guilty of spelling a Kurdish festival *Newroz* instead of *Nevroz,* as in Turkish orthog-

raphy (AP Worldstream, March 25, 2000).

7. Ferit Demer, Reuters, datelined Tunceli, Turkey, April 1, 2000. Chris Morris, *Guardian* (London), April 3, 2000. "Arab League Denounces Turkish Incursion into Iraq," *Mena* (Cairo), April 4, 2000; *Kurdish News Bulletin,* April 1–16, 2000. A US database search found only AP, *Los Angeles Times,* April 2, 2000, 326 words. Rubin, US Dept. of State daily press briefing, April 4, 2000; M2 Presswire.

8. Federal News Service, Defense Dept. Briefing, Secretary of Defense William Cohen, "Turkey's Importance to 21st Century International Security," Grand Hyatt Hotel, Washington, DC, March 31, 2000; Charles Aldinger, "US Praises Key NATO Ally Turkey," Reuters, March 31, 2000.

9. Human Rights Watch, *The Ties That Bind: Colombia and Military-Paramilitary Links,* Feb. 2000. Martin Hodgson, *CSM,* April 26, 2000 (UN Report). State Dept. *Country Reports on Human Rights Practices,* 1999 and 1998. 1999 report cited by Hodgson, "coca leaf war." Swedish director quoted by Ana Carrigan, "Dogs of war are loose in Colombia," *Irish Times,* May 6, 2000.

10. Winifred Tate, Washington Office on Latin America (WOLA), Oct. 6, 1999. Comisión Colombiana de Juristas, "Panorama de los derechos humanos y del derecho humanitario en Colombia: 1999," Sept. 1999; see *Colombia Update* 11:3–4 (Winter/ Spring 2000). Bland, "Colombia: Don't forget the lesson of Salvador," *LAT,* April 10, 2000. UNICEF, CODHES, cited by Maurice Lemoine, "The Endless Undeclared Civil War," *Le Monde diplomatique,* May 2000.

11. Federal News Service, May 1, 2000, State Dept. Briefing.

12. Lindsay Murdoch, *The Age* (Australia), April 8, 2000; Barry Wain, Asia editor, *WSJ* (Asia edition), April 17, 2000. On East Timor and Kosovo, see my essays "In Retrospect" and " 'Green Light' for War Crimes," published in several languages and versions in 1999–2000, updated in my *A New Generation Draws the Line.*

13. Ibid., and *The New Military Humanism* for details and sources.

14. AFL-CIO, "Statement on the Situation of Labor in Colombia and US Policy," Feb. 17, 2000, distributed by WOLA. Human Rights Watch, *World Report 2000* (Human Rights Watch, Dec. 1999).

15. In April 2000, the FARC announced the formation of a new political party, the Bolivarian Movement for a New Colombia, calling for "a new political, social, and economic environment ... that would make the use of arms unnecessary." AP, April 30, 2000, *Miami Herald* Web site, and Reuters, *El Nuevo Herald* (Miami), cited in *Weekly News Update on the Americas* 535 (April 30, 2000). The new party "will, however, remain clandestine for now to prevent its leaders from being slaughtered, said FARC commanders." Vivian Sequera, AP, *BG,* April 30, 2000.

16. Steven Greenhouse, *NYT,* March 15, 1994. See my *World Orders Old and New* for further quotes and comment.

17. Arlene Tickner, general coordinator of the Center for International Studies at the University of the Andes, Bogota, "Colombia: Chronicle of a Crisis Foretold," *Current History,* Feb. 1998.

18. Lars Schoultz, *Human Rights and United States Policy toward Latin America* (Princeton, 1981), 7. Vázquez Carrizosa, and further background, see references of note 1.

19. Michael McClintock, "American Doctrine and Counterinsurgent State Terror," in A. George, ed., *Western State Terrorism* (Polity-Blackwell, 1991), 139; McClintock, *Instruments of Statecraft* (Pantheon, 1992), 222.

20. Ibid., 227.

21. On the programs of the guerrillas, see Andrés Cala, "The Enigmatic Guerrilla: FARC's Manuel Marulanda," *Current History,* Feb. 2000; Karen DeYoung, "Colombia's Non-Drug Rebellion," *WP National Weekly,* April 17, 2000. See also the FARC "agenda for negotiations," in Adam Isacson, "The Colombian Dilemma," *International Policy Report* (Washington, DC: Center for International Policy), Feb. 2000.

22. James Wilson, "Rebels tax plan outrages Colombia," *FT,* April 28, 2000. Also Carrigan, op. cit.

23. Larry Rohter, "Colombia Agrees to Turn Over Territory to Another Rebel Group," *NYT,* April 26, 2000; Alma Guillermoprieto, *New York Review,* May 11, 2000. For analysis in more depth, see Lemoine, op. cit., discussing the appeal of the FARC to many peasants and working people who see it as "the army of the poor," and particularly to women, who now constitute one-third of its forces, because of its break from oppressive and degrading practices that are particularly harsh at the depths of poverty and desperation.

24. James Wilson, "Colombia's citizens get the chance to confront rebels," *FT,* April 26, 2000.

25. *La Prensa Gráfica* (San Salvador), April 28, 2000; cited in *Weekly News Update on the Americas* 535, April 30, 2000; also earlier updates cited there. Kintto Lucas, Interpress Service (Quito, Ecuador), March 23, 2000.

26. For background and analysis, see particularly Arnold Chien, Margaret Connors, and Kenneth Fox, "The Drug War in Perspective," in J.Y. Kim, J. Millen, A. Irwin, and J. Gershman, eds., *Dying for Growth* (Institute for Health and Social Justice/Partners in Health, Cambridge MA [Common Courage, 2000]).

27. General Accounting Office, *Drug Control: Narcotics Threat from Colombia Continues to Grow,* June 1999.

28. Alan Feuer, "US Colonel Is Implicated in Drug Case," *NYT,* April 4, 2000.

29. John Donnelly, *BG,* March 9, 2000. See "Paramilitary Leader Goes Public," *Latinamerica Press* (Peru), March 20, 2000.

30. DeYoung, "Colombia's Non-Drug Rebellion."

31. Cala, "Enigmatic Guerrilla." Ricardo Vargas Meza, *The Revolutionary Armed Forces of Colombia (FARC) and the Illicit Drug Trade* (Acción Andina [Bolivia], TNI [Netherlands], WOLA [Washington, DC]), June 1999.

32. Ibid. Also Vargas, "Drug Cultivation, Fumigation, and the Conflict in Colombia" (TNI and Acción Andina Colombia), Oct. 1999; Hodgson, "coca leaf war." Also Larry Rohter, "Colombia Tries, Yet Cocaine Thrives," *NYT,* Nov. 20, 1999, on opposition by the Colombian government and farmers to the US insistence on crop-destruction programs rather than the crop-substitution programs they prefer. On current plans for the use of biological in addition to the usual chemical weapons, see "UN to Unleash Biowar Against Colombian Cocaine Plant," *AFP,* March 8, 2000, reporting an article in the British journal *New Scientist* (March 9, 2000) on a plan funded by the US and UN to conduct open field trials of a fungus *(Fusarium oxysporum)* so far tested only in US government greenhouses. "The biowar tactic is being considered because of the failure of crime busters to stamp out

the coca crop," *AFP* reports. Farmers in Peru claim that a fungus that has sharply reduced coca production there "has also mutated and is killing many traditional crops, including bananas, cacao, coffee, corn, lemon grass, papaya, and yucca," but "US government officials insist that charges that they are connected in some way to the fungus are groundless." Eric Lyman, "US Accused of Creating Blight Killing Coca Plants and Harming Other Crops," *San Francisco Chronicle,* Nov. 4, 1999.

33. Walter LaFeber, "The Alliances in Retrospect," in A. Maguire and J.W. Brown, eds., *Bordering on Trouble: Resources and Politics in Latin America* (Adler & Adler, 1986). Joseph Treaster, "Coffee Impasse Imperils Colombia's Drug Fight," *NYT,* Sept. 24, 1988. On Food for Peace and the effects of US "export subsidies" and on the use of counterpart funds, see William Borden, *The Pacific Alliance: United States Foreign Economic Policy and Japanese Trade Recovery, 1947–1955* (Univ. of Wisconsin Press, 1984), 182f. For more general information, see Tim Barry and Deb Preusch, *The Soft War* (Grove, 1988). On the background, see also Chien et al., "The Drug War in Perspective," in *Dying for Growth.*

34. Susan Strange, *Mad Money: When Markets Outgrow Governments* (Univ. of Michigan, 1998), 127.

35. See chap. 10, in this volume.

36. Tim Weiner, "Congress Agrees to $7.1 Billion in Farm Aid," *NYT,* April 14, 2000; Nicolas Kristof, "As Life for Family Farmers Worsens, the Toughest Wither," *NYT,* April 2, 2000; Laurent Belsie, "Collapse of Free-Market Farm Economy?," *CSM,* March 23, 2000. For detail and informative analysis, see National Farmers Union (Saskatoon, SK, Canada), *The Farm Crisis, EU Subsidies, and Agribusiness Market Power,* report presented to Canadian Senate Standing Committee on Agriculture and Forestry, Ottawa, Feb. 17, 2000.

37. One current illustration is the reaction to the Declaration of the South Summit in the Havana meeting of April 2000. It condemned the Western-instituted forms of "globalization" and called for "an international economic system which will be just and democratic," emphasizing the "right to development" that the US rejects, also condemning "the so-called 'right' of humanitarian intervention" and any military or economic intervention to prevent countries from developing their own "political, economic, social, and cultural systems," with many specific charges and proposals. As is customary, the declaration of countries accounting for 80 percent of the world's population was unreported and ignored.

38. Adam Isacson, "Getting in Deeper," Center for International Policy, *International Policy Report* (Feb. 2000); Linda Robinson, *World Policy Journal* (Winter 1999–2000); Cala, "Enigmatic Guerrilla." Larry Rohter, *NYT,* Nov. 20, 1999, reporting the "dismay" of Colombian officials, who are overruled; Rohter, "To Colombians, Drug War Is Toxic Foe," *NYT,* May 1, 2000, on the effects of spraying in violation of regulations (applied in the US), and US Embassy denials. See note 32.

39. Gwen Robinson and James Wilson, *FT,* March 30, 2000; Michael Isikoff, Gregory Vistica, Steven Ambrus, "The Other Drug War," *Newsweek,* April 3, 2000.

40. AP, *NYT,* April 10, 2000; Peter McFarren, AP, *BG,* April 10, 2000; Reuters, AP, April 18, 2000; Richard Lapper, "Anger in the Andes," *FT,* April 26, 2000; Francis McDonagh, *National Catholic Reporter,* April 28, 2000.

41. Jim Schultz, The Democracy Center, Bogotá, April 9, 2000; *San Jose Mercury News,* April 8, 2000; Democracy Center, April 13, 2000; Pacific News Service, April 13, 2000; *San Francisco Examiner,* April 19, 2000; *In These Times,* May 15, 2000.

42. Kirk Semple, "Antidrug Efforts Sowing Fear in Colombia," *BG*, April 10, 2000.

43. Alvin Winder, Ted Chen, and William Mfuko, "Influence of American Tobacco Imports on Smoking Rates Among Women and Youth in Asia," *International Quarterly of Community Health Education* 14:4 (1993–94), 345–59; Chen and Winder, "APACT: Its Organization and Impact on Resistance to US Tobacco Imperialism," *International Quarterly of Community Health Education* 12:1 (1991–92), 59–67. See also chap. 10, p. 150, in this volume. On the USTR hearings that forced Asian countries to open their doors to US lethal drugs and aggressive advertising at exactly the time when George Bush announced the new "drug war," and the astonishing media reaction to these two simultaneous events, see my *Deterring Democracy*, chap. 4. On Colombian vs. US deaths, see Peter Bourne, *World Development Forum* 6 (June 1988), cited by Joyce Millen and Timothy Holtz, "Transnational Corporations and the Health of the Poor," in Kim et al., *Dying for Growth.*

44. Stephen Bezruchka, "Is globalization dangerous to our health?," *Western Journal of Medicine* 172:332-334, May 2000.

45. Colin Nickerson, "A Northern Border Menace," *BG*, April 26, 2000. UN International Drug Control Programme, *World Drug Report* (Oxford, 1997). See my *Deterring Democracy* for some of the interesting record on banks and chemical corporations, and Washington's reaction.

46. Linda Greenhouse, "Excerpts From [Supreme Court] Opinions," *NYT*, March 22, 2000. Peto, see chap. 10, note 94, in this volume.

47. John Donnelly, *BG*, March 22, 2000.

48. Dissenting Views of Hon. Nancy Pelosi and Hon. David Obey in House Committee Report 106-521 on H.R. 3908, March 14, 2000, distributed by WOLA.

49. John Donnelly, *BG*, Feb. 21, 2000.

50. Michael Tonry, *Malign Neglect: Race, Crime, and Punishment in America* (Oxford, 1995). See Juan Pablo Ordoñez, *No Human Being Is Disposable* (Columbia Human Rights Committee, Washington, DC, 1995). Ordoñez is another human rights activist who was compelled to flee the country under death threats. On policy consequences for the US population, see Marc and Marque-Luisa Miringoff, *The Social Health of the Nation* (Oxford, 1999), the latest Index of Social Health report of the Fordham Institute for Innovation in Social Policy, which monitors social indicators (as is done by government bodies in other industrial countries). Their most striking conclusion is that social indicators tracked GDP closely until the mid-1970s, and have since declined, leaving the US below the level of 1959, in what they call a "social recession." The shift coincides with the onset of official "globalization" and the domestic version of selective "neoliberal reforms."

51. Chien et al., "The Drug War in Perspective," in Kim et al., *Dying for Growth*. On the criminal justice system past and present, see Randall Shelden, *Controlling the Dangerous Classes: A Critical Introduction to the History of Criminal Justice* (Allyn and Bacon, forthcoming).

6. Cuba and the US Government

This is an edited version of an address given at the Old South Church, Boston, June 1, 1999, sponsored by Pastors for Peace.

1. See chap. 1, p. 2 and note 3, in this volume.

7. Putting on the Pressure

This is excerpted from an address given at Cuyahoga Community College in Cleveland, OH, on March 14, 1999. The talk was sponsored by the Interreligious Task Force on Central America.

1. Christian Tomuschat, the German law professor who chaired the Historical Clarification Commission, cited by Edward Hegstrom, *Houston Chronicle*, Feb. 26, 1999.

2. Steven Greenhouse, *NYT*, Feb. 28, 1999.

3. "Memorandum by the Director of Central Intelligence (Smith) to the Under Secretary of State (Bruce), Dec. 12, 1952; NIE-84, May 19, 1953. *Foreign Relations of the United States* 1952–1954, vol. IV, 1055ff.

4. Ibid. For further discussion and documentation, see my *Necessary Illusions*, app. V.1; and *Deterring Democracy*, chaps. 3, 8, and 12.

5. See chap. 1, note 20, in this volume.

6. Bryce Wood, *The Dismantling of the Good Neighbor Policy* (Univ. of Texas, 1985), 177. See my *Deterring Democracy*, chap. 3, for further discussion.

7. *Latinamerica Press* (Peru), Feb. 22, 1999.

8. See chap. 8, in this volume.

9. Joel Millman, "Is the Mexico Model Worth the Pain?," *WSJ*, March 8, 1999.

10. Dan McCosh, *El Financiero*, Jan. 3 and Dec. 20, 1998.

11. Minutes of the Latin American Strategic Development Workshop (Sept. 26–27, 1990), 3.

8. Jubilee 2000

Excerpts of this piece appeared in the *Guardian* (London), May 15, 1998, in a series on Jubilee 2000.

1. Jeffrey Sachs, *FT*, Nov. 5, 1998. On the techniques that effectively rewarded the banks for unwise Latin American lending that would have ruined them, see Karin Lissakers, *Banks, Borrowers, and the Establishment* (Basic Books, 1991), and Susan Strange, *Mad Money* (Univ. of Michigan Press, 1998).

2. Lissakers, *Banks, Borrowers;* Cheryl Payer, *Lent and Lost* (Zed, 1991).

3. Indonesia specialist Benedict Anderson estimated the Suharto family fortune at $30 billion, not far below the scheduled IMF rescue package (*London Review of Books*, April 16, 1998). Indonesian economist Kwik Kian Gie, cited by Gerry van Klinken, *Inside Indonesia*, April–June 1998. Robison, director of Murdoch University's Asian Research Center in Perth, cited in "Stalinist State," *Far Eastern Economic Review*, April 16, 1998.

4. Lissakers, *Banks, Borrowers;* Payer, *Lent and Lost.* For government spending growth under Reagan, see Fred Block, *Vampire State* (New Press, 1996). Current programs of cancellation of debt (recognized to be unpayable) for the "Highly Indebted Poor Countries" (HIPC) are conditioned on their acceptance of IMF structural adjustment programs, renamed "Poverty Reduction and Growth Facility" (PRGF).

5. Peter Cowhey and Jonathan Aronson, *Managing the World Economy* (Council on Foreign Relations, Columbia Univ., 1993).

6. Eric Helleiner, *States and the Reemergence of Global Finance* (Cornell Univ. Press, 1994).

7. Patricia Adams, *Odious Debts* (Earthscan, 1991); Lissakers, *Banks, Borrowers. Witness for Peace, A Bankrupt Future: The Human Cost of Nicaragua's Debt* (WFP, 2000); *Envío* (Managua, Nicaragua: UCA), 18.220, Nov. 1999.

8. Payer, *Lent and Lost;* Emma Rothschild, *NYT Magazine,* March 13, 1977.

9. Walter Laqueur, *NYT Magazine,* Dec. 16, 1973.

10. Lissakers, *Banks, Borrowers.* On the background, see, inter alia, David Felix, "Asia and the Crisis of Financial Globalization," in D. Baker, G. Epstein, and R. Pollin, eds., *Globalization and Progressive Economic Policy* (Cambridge Univ. Press, 1998).

11. Payer, *Lent and Lost;* Philip Wellons, *Passing the Buck* (Harvard Business School Press, 1987).

12. Mexican economist Alejandro Nadal, "*World Investment Report 1999* Flawed on Many Fronts," *Third World Economics,* Nov. 16–30, 1999.

13. Felix, "Asia and the Crisis of Financial Globalization"; "Globalizing Financial Capital Mobility: The Empire's New Clothes?," Working Paper No. 213, Washington University, June 1998, to appear in *CEPAL Review.* On the decline of macroeconomic indicators since the onset of financial liberalization ("globalization"), see Baker et al., *Globalization and Progressive Economic Policy;* Robin Hahnel, *Panic Rules!* (South End, 1999), John Eatwell and Lance Taylor, *Global Finance at Risk* (New Press, 2000).

14. Jeffrey Sachs, "International Economics: Unlocking the Mysteries of Globalization," *Foreign Policy* (Spring 1998); Paul Krugman, "Cycles of Conventional Wisdom on Economic Development," *International Affairs* 71:4 (Oct. 1995). Joseph Stiglitz, "Some Lessons from the East Asian Miracle," *World Bank Research Observer* 11:2 (Aug. 1996). Stiglitz was soon to be appointed chief economist of the World Bank. For his reflections on the East Asian crisis, see his WIDER Annual Lectures 2, UN University, 1997; "An Agenda for Development in the Twenty-First Century," Annual World Bank Conference on Development Economics 1997, IBRD, 1998.

15. David Felix, "The Tobin Tax Proposal: Background, Issues, and Prospects," Working Paper No. 191, Washington University, June 1994; see his and other papers in Mahbub Ul Haq, Inge Kaul, Isabelle Grunberg, *The Tobin Tax: Coping with Financial Volatility* (Oxford, 1996).

16. Argentine political scientist Atilio Boron, "Democracy or Neoliberalism?," *Boston Review,* Oct.–Nov. 1996; see his *State, Capitalism, and Democracy in Latin America* (Lynne Rienner, 1996).

9. "Recovering Rights"

This is excerpted from an address given at the Oxford Amnesty Lectures, "Globalizing Rights," Feb. 9, 1999. The full series of lectures is to be published in *Globalizing Rights,* ed. Matthew Gibney, forthcoming.

1. Reuters, "UN Agencies Tell of Damage in Iraq," *NYT,* Jan. 7, 1999; Betsy Pisik, "Strikes Hit Iraqi Schools, Hospitals," *Washington Times,* Jan. 8, 1999.

2. *New Republic,* editorials, May 2, 1981; April 2, 1984. Tom Wicker, *NYT,* March 14, 1986; editorial, *WP National Weekly,* March 1, 1986. For reviews of the spectrum that reached the general public, see my *Necessary Illusions* and *Deterring Democracy.*

3. Juan Hernández Pico, *Envío* (UCA, Jesuit Univ., Managua), March 1994. See chaps. 1, 5, 6, and 7, in this volume, on the historical context.

4. Ruben Ricupero; statement published in *Third World Resurgence* (Penang) 95 (1998).

5. Paul Jeffrey, *National Catholic Reporter*, Dec. 11, 1998, citing Honduran bishop Angel Garachana. On effects of deforestation and US development programs, see also Sara Silver, "Coffee Growers Find Less Is More," *Austin American-Statesman*, Dec. 27, 1998; Dudley Althaus, "Deforestation Contributed to Tragedy by Mitch in Honduras, Experts Claim," *Houston Chronicle*, Dec. 30, 1998 (*Central America NewsPak* 13:23, Dec.–Jan. 1999).

6. Nitlapán-Envío team, "A Time for Opportunities and Opportunists," *Envío* 17:209 (Dec. 1998). See also David Gonzales, "Mitch Who? US Stalls Mercy Flights; Aid to Contras by Express, Disaster Relief by Boat," *NYT*, Dec. 16, 1988, New York City Section, 27.

7. Reuters, "French to Clear Unearthed Land Mines," *Peacework* (Cambridge, MA: AFSC), Dec. 1998.

8. Mary Ann Glendon, "Knowing the Universal Declaration of Human Rights," 73 *Notre Dame Law Review* 1153 (1998). Paine, *Rights of Man*, Part II (1792). Bruce Kucklick, ed., *Thomas Paine: Political Writings* (Cambridge Univ. Press, 1989).

9. *The United Nations and Human Rights 1945–1995*, Volume VII, UN Blue Books Series (UN New York: Dept. of Public Information, 1995).

10. "Respect for Human Rights, the Secret of True Peace." See Arthur Jones, "Pope Blasts Consumerism as Human Rights Threat," *National Catholic Reporter*, Jan. 8, 1999. In the national press, the message was briefly reported, but its content was largely ignored (*WP* and *NYT*, Jan. 2, 1999; the last sentence of the *New York Times* report alluded to the content). The Vatican message had received some limited earlier mentions. A database search found scattered references, including one in the national press: Reuters, *NYT*, Dec. 16, 1998, 19. The general issues received some coverage when the Pope visited Mexico a few weeks later. See Alessandra Stanley, "Pope Is Returning to Mexico with New Target: Capitalism," *NYT*, Jan. 22, 1999; also Jan. 24, 1999. Richard Chacón and Diego Ribadeneira, *BG*, Jan. 24 and 25, 1999.

11. Stanley, *NYT,* Jan. 22, 1999.

12. Vyshinsky quoted by David Manasian, "Human-Rights Law: The Conscience of Mankind," *Economist*, Dec. 5, 1998; Kirkpatrick quoted by Joseph Wronka, "Human Rights," in R. Edwards, ed., *Encyclopedia of Social Work* (Washington, DC: NASW, 1995), 1405–18. See also Wronka, *Human Rights and Social Policy in the 21st Century* (Univ. Press of America, 1992), and "A Little Humility, Please," *Harvard International Review* (Summer 1998). Morris Abram, statement to UN Commission on Human Rights re: Item 8, "The Right to Development," Feb. 11, 1991.

13. Amnesty International–London, *United States of America: Rights for All* (Oct. 1998). See interview with Pierre Sané, secretary-general of AI, by Dennis Bernstein and Larry Everest, *Z* magazine (Jan. 1999), a rare departure from the general dismissal, far at the dissident extreme.

14. Lawrence Mishel, Jared Bernstein, John Schmitt, *The State of Working America 1998–1999* (Cornell Univ. Press, 1999). On inequality, working hours, legal mandate, see *State of Working America* and Phineas Baxandall and Marc Breslow, *Dollars and Sense,* Jan.–Feb. 1999 (citing OECD, *Annual Employment Outlook*, 1998). Second decile, Edward Wolff's research cited by Aaron Bernstein, "A Sinking Tide Does Not Lower All Boats," *BW,* Sept. 14, 1998. On Reaganite criminality, see chap. 10, pp. 137–38, in this

volume. On corporate manslaughter in England and its impunity, see Gary Slapper, *Blood in the Bank* (Ashgate, 1999).

15. Among many recent examples, Gerald Baker, *FT,* Dec. 14, 1998, who also notes potential flaws in the miracle; Reed Ableson, *NYT,* Jan. 2, 1999.

16. James Bennet, "At a Conference on Wall Street Diversity, the President Finds His Own Stock Soaring," *NYT,* Jan. 16, 1999.

17. Alan Greenspan quoted by Edward Herman from July 22, 1997, congressional hearings, "The Threat of Globalization," *New Politics* 26 (Winter 1999). Gene Koretz, "Which Way Are Wages Headed," *BW*, Sept. 21, 1998. 1994 survey, Robert Pollin and Stephanie Luce, *The Living Wage* (New Press, 1998). On unionization and wages, see Mishel et al., *State of Working America,* and earlier studies in this biennial series of the Economics Policy Institute.

18. Louis Uchitelle, "The Rehabilitation of Morning in America," *NYT,* Feb. 23, 1997.

19. Joseph Stiglitz, "Some Lessons from the East Asian Miracle," *World Bank Research Observer* 11:2 (Aug. 1996); "An Agenda for Development in the Twenty-First Century," *Annual World Bank Report on Development Economics* (World Bank, 1998); WIDER Annual Lectures 2, UN University and World Institute for Development Economics Research, May 1997. David Felix, "Is the Drive Toward Free-Market Globalization Stalling?" *Latin American Research Review* 33:3 (1998).

20. Eichengreen, *Globalizing Capital: A History of the International Monetary System* (Princeton Univ. Press, 1996).

21. *Survey of Current Business* 76:12 (Washington, DC: US Dept. of Commerce, Dec. 1996).

22. Morton J. Horwitz, *The Transformation of American Law 1870–1960* (Oxford, 1992).

23. "Looking for New Leadership," *Newsweek International*, Feb. 1, 1999.

24. On the interesting MAI record, see my *Profit Over People.*

25. Alan Story, "Property in International Law," *Journal of Political Philosophy* 6:3 (1998), 306–33.

26. Christopher Hill, *Liberty Against the Law* (Penguin, 1996), 229.

27. Center for Responsive Politics, cited in *Dollars and Sense* (Jan.–Feb. 1999).

28. Bernays, *Propaganda* (Liveright, 1928). See Alex Carey, *Taking the Risk Out of Democracy* (Univ. of New South Wales Press, 1995, and Univ. of Illinois Press, 1997); Elizabeth Fones-Wolf, *Selling Free Enterprise: The Business Assault on Labor and Liberalism, 1945–1960* (Univ. of Illinois Press, 1995); Stuart Ewen, *PR!: A Social History of Spin* (Basic Books, 1996). On the general context, see my "Intellectuals and the State," reprinted in *Towards a New Cold War* (Pantheon, 1982), and "Force and Opinion," reprinted in my *Deterring Democracy.*

29. Hutchins Commission, quoted in William Preston, Edward Herman, and Herbert Schiller, *Hope and Folly: The United States and UNESCO 1945–1985* (Univ. of Minnesota Press, 1989). Human Rights Watch, *The Limits of Tolerance: Freedom of Expression and the Public Debate in Chile* (Nov. 1998).

30. Stuart Ewen, *Captains of Consciousness: Advertising and the Social Roots of the Consumer Culture* (McGraw-Hill, 1976); Bagdikian, *The Media Monopoly* (fifth ed., Beacon, 1997).

31. Bruce Knecht, "Magazine Advertisers Demand Prior Notice of 'Offensive' Articles," *WSJ*, April 30, 1997.

32. Dan Schiller, *Digital Capitalism* (MIT Press, 1999).

33. Preston, in Preston et al., *Hope and Folly.*

34. Herbert Schiller, *Information Inequality: The Deepening Social Crisis in America* (Routledge, 1996); Edward Herman and Robert McChesney, *The Global Media* (Cassell, 1997); Schiller, *Digital Capitalism;* McChesney, *Rich Media, Poor Democracy* (Univ. of Illinois Press, 1999).

35. Marshall Clark, "Cleansing the Earth," *Inside Indonesia*, Oct.–Dec. 1998. MAI, see my *Profit Over People.*

10. The United States and the "Challenge of Relativity"

This article originally appeared in Tony Evans, ed., *Human Rights Fifty Years On: A Reappraisal* (Manchester Univ. Press, 1999). Parts of this article appeared in *Index on Censorship,* July/August 1994.

1. Historian David Fromkin, *NYT Book Review,* May 4, 1997, summarizing recent work. Thomas Friedman, *NYT,* Jan. 12, 1992.

2. Bernard Crick, *Times Literary Supplement,* Sept. 15, 1972; reprinted in Everyman's Library edition of *Animal Farm.*

3. Howard, "The Bewildered American Raj," *Harper's,* March 1985.

4. William Earl Weeks, *John Quincy Adams and American Global Empire* (Univ. Press of Kentucky, 1992), 193.

5. Kahin and Kahin, *Subversion as Foreign Policy,* 30. On the British analogue, see John Saville, *The Politics of Continuity* (London: Verso, 1993), 156f.; and for the broader context, Mark Curtis, *The Ambiguities of Power* (Zed, 1995).

6. US Commerce Dept., 1984, cited by Howard Wachtel, *The Money Mandarins* (M.E. Sharpe, 1990), 44.

7. *BW,* April 7, 1975.

8. Helleiner, *States and the Reemergence of Global Finance* (Cornell Univ. Press, 1994), 58–62. His emphasis.

9. *Comparative Politics,* Jan. 1981.

10. Chomsky and Herman, *After the Cataclysm,* chap. 2.1.1. Herman, *The Real Terror Network* (South End, 1982), 126ff.

11. Wronka, *Human Rights and Social Policy in the 21st Century,* citing the judgment in *Filartiga v. Peña* (1980). For additional cases see Wronka's "Human Rights," in Edwards, ed., *Encyclopedia of Social Work,* 1405–18 (see chap. 9, note 12, in this volume).

12. Elaine Sciolino, *NYT,* June 15, 1993.

13. Alan Riding, *NYT,* June 26, 1993.

14. William Hartung, *And Weapons for All* (HarperCollins, 1994); Hartung, *Nation,* Jan. 30, 1995. The Congressional Research Service reported that the US was responsible for 57 percent of arms sales to the Third World in 1992; *FT,* July 23, 1993. The CRS reports further that among the 11 leading arms suppliers to the "developing countries" from 1989 to 1996, the US provided over 45 percent of the arms flow and Britain 26 percent.

Richard Grimmett, "Conventional Arms Transfers to Developing Nations, 1989–1996" (Washington, DC: CRS); Jim Mann, *Los Angeles Times,* Oct. 8, 1997.

15. On the sharp increase of British arms sales to Indonesia under Thatcher as atrocities continued in East Timor (and in Indonesia as well), see John Taylor, *Indonesia's Forgotten War: The Hidden History of East Timor* (Zed, 1991), 86, and John Pilger, *Distant Voices* (Vintage, 1992), 294–323. Thatcherite policy was explained by "defense procurement minister" Alan Clark: "My responsibility is to my own people. I don't really fill my mind much with what one set of foreigners is doing to another" (Pilger, 309). By 1998, Britain had become the leading supplier of arms to Indonesia, not for defense, and over the strong protests of Amnesty International, Indonesian dissidents, and Timorese victims. Arms sales are reported to make up at least a fifth of Britain's exports to Indonesia (estimated at one billion pounds), led by British Aerospace (Martyn Gregory, "World in Action," Granada production for ITV, June 2 and 9, 1997). On Rwanda, see *Rwanda: Death, Despair, and Defiance* (London: African Rights, 1994).

16. Jeff Gerth and Tim Weiner, "Arms Makers See a Bonanza in Selling NATO Expansion," *NYT,* June 29, 1997.

17. International Court of Justice Year 1986, June 27, 1986, General List No. 70.

18. *NYT,* Oct. 29, 1990; *DC,* Nov. 4, 1996; *Extra!* (FAIR), Dec. 1987.

19. Panama, *Central America Report* (Guatemala), Feb. 4, 1994. The US also vetoed (with Britain and France) a Security Council resolution (Dec. 23, 1989) condemning the invasion and voted against a General Assembly resolution demanding the withdrawal of the "US-armed invasion forces from Panama" and calling the invasion a "flagrant violation of international law and of the independence, sovereignty, and territorial integrity of states" (Sean Cronin, *Irish Times,* Aug. 11, 1990). The Church estimates that more than 650 victims of the intensive bombing of the poor El Chorrillo district of Panama City died in hospitals, along with unknown numbers of others. US-installed President Endara went on a hunger strike in March 1990 to protest the US failure to deliver promised economic aid. Inhabitants of El Chorrillo are suing the US for damages before the Inter-American Human Rights Court. *Central America Report,* March 19, 1998.

20. For a review of recently declassified and other evidence, and the interpretive reaction throughout, see my *Rethinking Camelot,* and references of chap. 1, note 23, in this volume.

21. Assistant Secretary of State for Human Rights John Shattuck, cited by Joseph Wronka, "Toward Building Peace/Human Rights Cultures: Why Is the United States So Resistant?," American Society of International Law, Interest Group of the UN Decade of International Law Newsletter, vol. 13 (Feb. 1997).

22. Resolution of the UN General Assembly condemning "Terrorism Wherever and by Whomever Committed," passed 153 to 2 (US and Israel opposed, Honduras abstained); UN Press release GA/7603, Dec. 7, 1987. For discussion, see my *Necessary Illusions,* 84f., 269ff. For more on these matters, see my *Pirates and Emperors;* Alexander George, ed., *Western State Terrorism* (Polity, 1991).

23. Chomsky and Herman, *The Washington Connection and Third World Fascism,* The Political Economy of Human Rights, vol. II, chap. 3.4.4; Chomsky, *Towards a New Cold War;* Taylor, *Indonesia's Forgotten War.*

24. Peter Kornbluh, *Nicaragua: The Price of Intervention* (Institute for Policy Studies, 1987), chap. 1; Walter LaFeber, *Inevitable Revolutions* (Norton, 1983), 239. On

the bloody Carter/Christopher record in El Salvador, see my *Towards a New Cold War,* 35ff.; Herman, *Real Terror Network,* 181ff.; Chomsky, *Turning the Tide,* 14f., 101ff. US-backed state terrorism in the region mounted sharply under Reagan, as is well known (see my *Turning the Tide* and numerous other sources).

25. For some scattered exceptions, see note 65.

26. Patrick Low, *Trading Free* (Twentieth Century Fund, 1993), 70ff., 271. Shafiqul Islam, "Capitalism in Conflict," *Foreign Affairs,* special issue on "America and the World" (Winter 1989–90).

27. For discussion, keeping to the special case of protectionism, see Paul Bairoch, *Economics and World History* (Univ. of Chicago Press, 1993). Among many other sources, see Frederic Clairmont's classic study, *The Rise and Fall of Economic Liberalism* (Asia Publishing House, 1960; reprinted and updated, Third World Network, 1996). On the general picture, see my *World Orders Old and New,* chap. 2. On the historic role of the state system (often military) in economic development in the US, see Nathan Rosenberg, *Inside the Black Box* (Cambridge Univ. Press, 1982); John Tirman, ed., *The Militarization of High Technology* (Ballinger, 1984); Merritt Roe Smith, ed., *Military Enterprise and Technological Change* (MIT Press, 1985); Richard Nelson, ed., *National Innovation Systems* (Oxford Univ. Press, 1993); and numerous special studies. On the growing First World–Third World gap, see UNDP, *Human Development Report,* 1992, 1994. For discussion, see my *World Orders Old and New,* chap. 2; Eric Toussaint and Peter Drucker, eds., *IMF/World Bank/WTO, Notebooks for Study and Research* 24:5 (Amsterdam: International Institute for Research and Education, 1995). On the situation internal to the US, see particularly the biennial publication, *The State of Working America,* of the Economic Policy Institute. The latest edition is Lawrence Mishel, Jared Bernstein, and John Schmitt, *The State of Working America 1998–1999* (Cornell Univ. Press, 1999).

28. Women's International League for Peace and Freedom (Geneva) and International Institute for Human Rights, Environment, and Development (Kathmandu), *Justice Denied!* (Kathmandu: Karnali Offset Press, 1994).

29. Jules Kagian, *Middle East International,* Dec. 17, 1993; *Middle East Justice Network,* Feb.–March 1994. On the background and status of UN 194, see Thomas and Sally Mallison, *The Palestine Problem in International Law and World Order* (Longman, 1986), chap. 4.

30. Reuters, "Haiti Peasant Group Backs UN Sanctions," *BG,* June 18, 1993, 68.

31. On Carter policies, see Chomsky and Herman, *After the Cataclysm,* 54f. On subsequent years, see Americas Watch, National Coalition for Haitian Refugees, Jesuit Refugee Service/USA, *No Port in a Storm* 5:7 (Sept. 1993). For Haitian background see, inter alia, Amy Wilentz, *The Rainy Season* (Simon & Schuster, 1989); my *Year 501,* chap. 8; Paul Farmer, *The Uses of Haiti* (Common Courage, 1994); Deidre McFadyen, Pierre LaRamée, and North American Congress on Latin America (NACLA), eds., *Haiti: Dangerous Crossroads* (South End, 1995).

32. Americas Watch et al., *No Port in a Storm,* 1.

33. Amy Wilentz, *New Republic,* March 9, 1992; see my *Year 501,* chap. 8, for further details.

34. Larry Rohter, *NYT,* April 19, 1997.

35. Wronka, "Human Rights."

36. Statement, UN Commission on Human Rights, on Item 8, "The Right to Development," Feb. 11, 1991.

37. Joseph Wronka, "Human Rights Postscript," American Society of International Law: Human Rights Interest Group Newsletter (Fall 1995).

38. Mishel et al., *The State of Working America 1996–1997* (M.E. Sharpe, 1997).

39. *Observer,* Jan. 12, 1997; *Independent,* Nov. 24 and 25, 1996; *GW,* Jan. 5, 1997; *Observer,* Jan. 19, 1997.

40. John Plender, "An Accidental Revolution," *FT,* Jan. 17, 1997 (42.25 percent of GDP, he reports, in 1978–79 and 1995–96). According to the *World Bank Development Report, 1996,* UK central government budget as percent of GNP (current) increased by close to 10 percent from 1980 to 1994. Comparative statistics in Gail Omvedt, *Bulletin of Concerned Asian Scholars* 29:4 (Oct.–Dec. 1997).

41. Chomsky, *World Orders Old and New,* chap. 2, and *Powers and Prospects,* chap. 5. UNICEF, *The State of the World's Children 1997* (Oxford Univ. Press, 1997).

42. UNICEF, *The Progress of Nations 1996* (UNICEF House, 1996).

43. The second-ranking recipient, Egypt, is granted aid to ensure its adherence to the US-Israel alliance, a core part of the system of control of the oil-producing regions, also a factor in Turkey's regular place among the top aid recipients.

44. Despouy, *The Realization of Economic, Social, and Cultural Rights,* Commission on Human Rights, Economic and Social Council, e/CN.4/Sub.2/1996/13, June 28, 1996.

45. Elizabeth Olson, "West Hinders Inquiry on Dumping as Rights Issue," *NYT,* April 5, 1998.

46. John Hoerr, *American Prospect,* Summer 1992. See my *Year 501,* chap. 11.

47. Keith Harper, *Guardian,* May 24, 1994; see same issue on the onerous "check off" law and other devices to undermine labor rights.

48. "The Workplace: Why America Needs Unions, But Not The Kind It Has Now," *BW,* May 23, 1994.

49. Fones-Wolf, *Selling Free Enterprise.* For background, see Alex Carey, *Taking the Risk Out of Democracy* (Univ. of Illinois Press, 1996), a collection of pioneering essays on these topics.

50. *World Labour Report 1994* (Geneva: ILO Publications, 1994).

51. *In the National Interest: 1996 Quadrennial Report on Human Rights and US Foreign Policy* (New York and Washington, DC: Lawyers Committee for Human Rights, 1996).

52. Annan, "The Unpaid Bill That's Crippling the UN," *NYT,* March 9, 1998.

53. Barbara Crossette, *NYT,* March 27, 1998.

54. *BW;* see note 48.

55. *WSJ,* Sept. 13, 1993. On persistence of the process through the recovery of the 1990s, see Mishel et al., *State of Working America.*

56. Editorial, *Multinational Monitor,* March 1997.

57. Bronfenbrenner, "We'll Close," *Multinational Monitor,* March 1997, based on the study she directed: "Final Report: The Effects of Plant Closing or Threat of Plant Closing on the Right of Workers to Organize."

58. Paul Wright, "Making Slave Labor Fly," *Prison Legal News,* March 1997; *CovertAction Quarterly,* Spring 1997.

59. Alex Lichtenstein, "Through the Rugged Gates of the Penitentiary," in Melvyn Stokes and Rick Halpern, *Race and Class in the American South Since 1890* (Berg, 1994).

60. Robert Taylor, *FT*, June 13, 1997.

61. John Cassidy, "Who Killed the Middle Class?," *New Yorker*, Oct. 16, 1995.

62. John Liscio, *Barron's*, April 15, 1996.

63. Youssef Ibrahim, *NYT*, July 3, 1997.

64. Lawrence Mishel and Jared Bernstein, *The State of Working America: 1994–95* (M.E. Sharpe, 1994).

65. During the Vienna conference, see Alan Riding, "Human Rights: The West Gets Some Tough Questions," *NYT*, June 20, 1993, and particularly Beth Stephens of the Center for Constitutional Rights, "Hypocrisy on Rights," *NYT*, op-ed, June 24, 1993.

66. Barbara Crossette, "Snubbing Human Rights," *NYT*, April 28, 1996; "For the US, Mixed Success in UN Human Rights Votes," *NYT*, Dec. 18, 1995.

67. Editorial, "The New Attack on Human Rights," *NYT*, Dec. 10, 1995.

68. Seth Faison, "China Turns the Tables, Faulting US on Rights," *NYT*, March 5, 1997.

69. *Torture and Ill-Treatment: Israel's Interrogation of Palestinians from the Occupied Territories* (Human Rights Watch, 1994).

70. Moshe Reinfeld, *Ha'aretz*, March 5, 1998. Amnesty International lists 21 Lebanese prisoners in Israeli jails, secretly brought to Israel from Lebanon from 1986 to 1994, most held without charge, the others sentenced in Israeli military courts but kept in prison after serving their sentences.

71. *Torture and Ill-Treatment: Human Rights and UN Security Assistance* (Amnesty International, May 1996).

72. Amnesty International, *Torture and Ill-Treatment.*

73. Mark Sommers, "Sanctions Are Becoming 'Weapon of Choice,' " *CSM*, Aug. 3, 1993. Richard Garfield, Julia Devin, and Joy Fausey, "The Health Impact of Economic Sanctions," *Bulletin of the New York Academy of Medicine* 72:2 (Winter 1995).

74. Jim Morrell, Center for International Policy, *Inquiry*, April 17, 1978.

75. Gay McDougall and Richard Knight, in Robert Edgar, ed., *Sanctioning Apartheid* (Africa World Press, 1990). Garfield et al., "Health Impact of Economic Sanctions."

76. For review, see my *Year 501*, chap. 5. See Kahin and Kahin, *Subversion as Foreign Policy*, on the 1958 operations, still largely concealed in the declassified record.

77. Reuters, *NYT*, Dec. 8, 1993, a few lines on an inside page.

78. Irene Wu, *Far Eastern Economic Review*, June 30, 1994. Other forms of chicanery were revealed in 1998: Tim Weiner, "US Training of Indonesian Troops Goes On Despite Ban," *NYT*, March 17, 1998; and for fuller detail, Alan Nairn, "Indonesia's Killers," *Nation*, March 30, 1998. On what followed, see chap. 4, in this volume, and sources cited.

79. *Economist*, April 2, 1994. *Counterpunch* (Institute for Policy Studies), Feb. 15 and March 15, 1994.

80. Barbara Crossette, *NYT*, Feb. 5, 1992.

81. Kenneth Roth, executive director of Human Rights Watch, Letter, *NYT*, April 12, 1997. On trade, see my *World Orders Old and New*, chap. 1.

82. John Solomon, AP, Sept. 18, 1994 (lead story), ignored by the major journals. For a detailed record, see my " 'Democracy Restored,' " *Z* magazine, Nov. 1994.

83. National Security Advisor Anthony Lake, *NYT*, Sept. 26, 1993; Sept. 23, 1994. On the measures used to impose on the "restored democracy" the programs of Washington's defeated candidate, see my " 'Democracy Restored' " and *Powers and Prospects*, chap. 5. And for extensive detail, Lisa McGowan, *Democracy Undermined, Economic Justice Denied* (Development Gap, 1997); Laurie Richardson, *Feeding Dependency, Starving Democracy* (Grassroots International, 1997).

84. Thomas Kamm and Robert Greenberger, *WSJ*, Nov. 15, 1995.

85. *Denial of Food and Medicine: The Impact of the US Embargo on Health and Nutrition in Cuba* (American Association for World Health, Executive Summary, 1997).

86. Garfield et al., "The Health Impact of Economic Sanctions." Wayne Smith, *In These Times*, Dec. 9, 1996. Anthony Kirkpatrick, "Sanctions on Health in Cuba," *The Lancet* 348/9040 (Nov. 30, 1996); *Cuba Update*, Winter 1997. David Marcus, "EU Backs Off on US-Cuba Trade Law," *BG*, April 12, 1997. See also Joanne Cameron, "The Cuban Democracy Act of 1992: The International Implications," *Fletcher Forum*, Winter–Spring 1996; Peter Morici, "The United States, World Trade, and the Helms-Burton Act," *Current History*, Feb. 1997.

87. Morris Morley and Chris McGillion, *Washington Report on the Hemisphere* (Council on Hemispheric Affairs), June 2, 1997.

88. Letter, *NYT*, Feb. 26, 1997.

89. See chap. 1, note 3, in this volume.

90. Resolution proposed to the UN Security Council by the US and other countries. Cited in *Denial of Food and Medicine*.

91. Richard Smith, "Creative Destruction: Capitalist Development and China's Environment," *New Left Review* 222 (March–April 1997). The record is similar elsewhere in the region.

92. Thomas Friedman, *NYT*, Jan. 21 and Jan. 23, 1993.

93. Sheila Tefft, *CSM*, Dec. 22, 1993. Reese Erlich, *CSM*, Feb. 9, 1994. See note 58.

94. Philip Shenon, *NYT*, May 15, 1994; Sheila Tefft, Fazlur Rahman, *CSM*, May 25, 1994; *Multinational Monitor*, June 1994. Frank Chaloupka and Adit Laixuthai, *US Trade Policy and Cigarette Smoking in Asia* (National Bureau of Economic Research, April 1996). See my *Deterring Democracy*, chaps. 4–5, for details on 1989–90. See chap. 5, in this volume.

95. Ibid. Amnesty International, *Amnesty Action: The Colombia Papers* (Winter 1997).

96. *Human Rights Violations in the United States* (Human Rights Watch/American Civil Liberties Union, Dec. 1993). On the Convention on Rights of the Child, see Steven Ratner, *Foreign Policy* (Spring 1998).

97. For other examples, see note 44. See also chap. 9, note 13, in this volume.

98. UNICEF, *State of World's Children; Lynching in All but Name* (Amnesty International, Jan. 1994). AP, *BG*, June 2, 1994. Human Rights Watch Children's Project, *United States: A World Leader in Executing Juveniles* (Human Rights Watch, March 1995).

99. "US Executions Tainted by Bias, Says UN Report," *Los Angeles Times; BG*, April 4, 1998.

100. Wronka, *Human Rights and Social Policy*, 5n.

101. *Cruel and Usual* (Human Rights Watch, March 1997). Steven Donziger, ed., *The Real War on Crime: Report of the National Criminal Justice Commission*

(HarperCollins, 1996). Reuters, *NYT,* June 23, 1997.

102. Randall Shelden and William Brown, *Criminal Justice* (Wadsworth, forthcoming), chap. 12; their emphasis. By the new millennium, the number of prisoners was approaching 2 million.

103. Donziger, *Real War on Crime.*

104. Ibid. Christie, *Crime Control as Industry.* Tonry, *Malign Neglect.* On the traditional use of the criminal justice system to control the "dangerous classes," see also Richard Bonnie and Charles Whitebread, *The Marihuana Conviction* (Univ. Press of Virginia, 1974).

105. Christie, *Crime Control as Industry.*

106. Paulette Thomas, *WSJ,* May 12, 1994. Christie, *Crime Control as Industry;* Donziger, *Real War on Crime,* on "the prison-industrial complex"; Randall Shelden, "The Crime Control Industry and the Management of the Surplus Population," paper read at Western Society of Criminology annual meeting, Feb.–March 1997, in Honolulu.

107. Wronka, "Human Rights Postscript."

108. See Harry Kalven, *A Worthy Tradition: Freedom of Speech in America* (Harper & Row, 1988).

109. *HRW World Report 1997* (Human Rights Watch, 1997).

11. The Legacy of War

This is an edited and updated version of an address given on April 13, 1997, as part of the 14th annual Hanna Lectures on Philosophy at Hamline University.

1. Peter Waldman, "In Vietnam, the Agony of Birth Defects Calls an Old War to Mind," *WSJ,* Feb. 18, 1997.

2. Barbara Crossette, *NYT,* Aug. 18, 1992, Science section.

3. *NYT,* Oct. 24, 1992.

12. Millennium Greetings

Portions of this article originally appeared as a ZNet commentary, Jan. 12, 2000.

1. Alan Ryan, "The Evil Empire," *NYT Book Review,* Jan. 2, 2000.

2. For a sample of the highly revealing material that is standardly — perhaps invariably — ignored, see my *Deterring Democracy,* chap. 1.

3. Michael Wines, *NYT Week in Review,* lead story, June 19, 1999.

4. John Burns, "Methods of the Great Leader," *NYT Book Review,* Feb. 6, 2000. See Letters, *NYT Book Review,* Feb. 27, 2000.

5. Jean Drèze and Amartya Sen, *Hunger and Public Action* (Oxford, 1989), chap. 11. They estimate famine deaths at 16.5 million to 29.5 million. See also Sen, "Indian Development: Lessons and Non-Lessons," *Daedalus* 118 (1989).

6. Drèze and Sen, *Hunger and Public Action.*

7. Sen, op. cit.

8. Drèze and Sen, *Hunger and Public Action.*

9. Amartya Sen, "Women's Survival as a Development Problem," *Bulletin* of the American Academy of Arts and Sciences (Nov. 1989); Drèze and Sen, *Hunger and Public Action.*

10. Sen, "Women's Survival"; Drèze and Sen, *Hunger and Public Action.*

11. Sen, "Women's Survival."

12. Sen, "Indian Development."

13. Quoted by Joseph Stiglitz, recently resigned chief economist of the World Bank, "Who Will Guard the Guardians?," *Challenge* (Nov–Dec. 1999).

14. "We had all seen the broken eggs, but nobody had ever seen the omelet," Ryan observes, expanding his apparent conclusion that conditions in Russia in 1989 were as bad as or worse than before World War I; "Mao broke an awful lot of eggs to make his omelet" (Burns, "Methods of a Great Leader").

15. Ryan, "Evil Empire." For review, see "The Victors," in my *Deterring Democracy;* and "The Colossus of the South," in my *Year 501.*

16. See chaps. 7 and 8, in this volume. The term *reform* is also an ideological construction. One does not refer to Pol Pot's measures as *reforms* — only those measures that are by definition "good" because they conform to the demands of Western power.

17. Brooke Schoepf, Claude Schoepf, and Joyce Millen, "Theoretical Therapies, Remote Remedies: SAPs and the Political Ecology of Poverty and Health in Africa," in Kim et al., *Dying for Growth.*

18. For a sample, see my *The New Military Humanism.*

19. Whitney, "The No-Man's-Land in the Fight for Human Rights," *NYT,* Week in Review, Dec. 12, 1999.

20. It might perhaps be added that the horrifying photographs of the remnants of devastated Grozny immediately brought to mind what I saw in Thanh Hoa province near Hanoi in 1970, including the provincial capital. The destruction was vastly worse farther south, below the 20th parallel, and in South Vietnam; and in all of the countries subjected to murderous US aggression, it was the rural areas that suffered most.

21. "Clinton's Words to Press," *NYT,* Dec. 9, 1999; excerpts from news conference of Dec. 8, 1999.

22. "UN Rebuffs US Again on Cuba," Reuters, *International Herald Tribune,* Nov. 11, 1999; six lines. The vote was taken on Nov. 9, 1999.

23. Someshwar Singh, "Half the World Hit by US Unilateral Sanctions," *Third World Economics* (Jan. 16–31, 2000). See also W. Bowman Cutter, Joan Spero, and Laura D'Andrea Tyson, *Foreign Affairs* (March–April 2000). The authors note that "during the last several years, America has imposed some form of unilateral economic sanctions against ... half the world's population," and object to them because the sanctions "have not achieved their goals" and "often harm exactly those they seek to help"; the latter objective is axiomatic, requiring no evidence, and remaining axiomatic in the face of overwhelming evidence that the sanctions harm the alleged beneficiaries but not the official target, as in the notorious case of Iraq.

24. Singh, "Half the World Hit." On the Cuba sanctions, their background, their motivations, and their effects, see "The Passion for Free Markets," in my *Profit Over People.* See chaps. 6, 8, and 10, in this volume.

25. "UN Condemns US Embargo Against Cuba for Eighth Year," *AFP,* Nov. 10, 1999. Separately, the 21 Ibero-American nations called on the US to terminate the Helms-Burton Act, again declaring it to be in violation of UN resolutions. Malaysia condemned the embargo for having "caused enormous economic damage and untold suffering to Cubans," as well as violating trade regulations. Patricia Grogg, Inter Press Service, Nov. 9, 1999; Bernama, Malaysian national news agency, Nov. 10, 1999. The embargo has been

condemned as being in violation of international law by virtually every relevant body.

26. Michael Jordan, *CSM,* Dec. 13, 1999 — fairly typical.

27. "Tudjman Is Dead: Croat Led Country Out of Yugoslavia," *NYT,* Dec. 11, 1999. See also Zoran Radosavljevic, *BG,* Dec. 24, 1999, noting the criticisms of Tudjman for supporting Bosnian Croat separatists and reviving symbols of Croatia's pro-Nazi past, but not for ethnic cleansing and other atrocities.

28. "Report of the Secretary-General Pursuant to General Assembly Resolution 53/55, The Fall of Srebrenica," Nov. 15, 1999, pp. 95ff. Christopher, Tim Judah, *The Serbs* (Yale Univ. Press, 1997), 301. David Binder, "The Role of the United States in the Krajina Issue," *Mediterranean Quarterly* (1997).

29. Binder, "Role of US in Krajina Issue."

30. Ray Bonner, *NYT,* March 21, 1999.

31. Tom Walker, *Sunday Times* (London), Oct. 10, 1999.

32. John Sweeney and Jens Holsoe, "Kosovo 'Disaster Response Service' Stands Accused of Murder and Torture," *Observer* (London), March 12, 2000.

33. Walker, *Sunday Times.*

34. Stephen Kinzer, *NYT,* Dec. 9, 1999.

35. Kinzer, *NYT,* Nov. 20, 1999.

36. Louis Meixler, "Turkey, Israel Join in Show of Might," AP, *BG,* Dec. 16, 1999.

37. Steven Erlanger, "Snubbed by the West, Tudjman Receives a Posthumous Rebuke," Dec. 14, 1999.

38. See chap. 4, in this volume, and references cited.

39. Historian David Fromkin, *Kosovo Crossing* (Free Press, 1999).

40. See chap. 3, in this volume, and references cited.

41. Alan Little, "How Nato Was Sucked into Kosovo Conflict," *Sunday Telegraph* (London), Feb. 27, 2000; Tom Walker and Aidan Laverty, "CIA Aided Kosovo Guerrilla Army," *Sunday Times* (London), March 12, 2000; Alan Little, *Moral Combat: NATO at War*, BBC documentary, March 12, 2000.

42. See chap. 3, in this volume.

43. Jonathan Steele, "US Refuses to Remove Cluster Bombs in Kosovo, Death Lurks in the Fields," *Guardian* (London), March 14, 2000.

13. Power in the Domestic Arena

This is excerpted from the 2nd Barry Amiel and Norman Melburn Trust Memorial Lecture given May 5, 1998, at the Institute of Education, London. A much longer version originally appeared in *New Left Review* 230 (July–Aug. 1998).

1. Gerald Haines, *The Americanization of Brazil* (Scholarly Resources, 1989).

2. See chap. 14, p. 209 and note14, in this volume.

3. See chap. 14, p. 208 and note 13, in this volume.

4. See Michael Sandel, *Democracy's Discontent* (Harvard Univ. Press, 1996).

5. David Sanger, "America Is Prosperous and Smug, Like Japan Was," *NYT,* Week in Review, April 12, 1998; Gerald Baker, "Is This Great, Or What?," *FT,* March 31, 1998.

6. Sylvia Nasar, "Unlearning the Lessons of Econ 101," *NYT,* Week in Review, May 3, 1998.

7. "The Problem Now: What to Do With All That Cash," *BW*, Dec. 12, 1994; "An Enormous Temptation to Waste," *BW*, Feb. 10, 1997.

8. *BW*, March 23, 1994.

9. Louis Uchitelle, "America's Treadmill Economy: Going Nowhere Fast," *NYT*, Money and Business section, March 8, 1998.

10. Alan Greenspan, testimony before the Senate Banking Committee, Feb. 1997: the "sustainable economic expansion" was thanks to "atypical restraint on compensation increases [which] appears to be mainly the consequence of greater worker insecurity."

11. "Economic Report of the President," Feb. 1997. Both this and the foregoing Greenspan quotation are cited in "Editorial," *Multinational Monitor*, March 1997.

12. "Remarks by Alan Greenspan, Chairman, Board of Governors of the Federal Reserve System, at the Annual Convention of the American Society of Newspaper Editors, Washington, DC," April 2, 1998.

13. Cited in "Microsoft Researches Its Future," *Science*, Feb. 27, 1998.

14. Thomas Misa, "The Development of the Transistor," in Merritt Roe Smith, ed., *Military Enterprise and Technological Change: Perspectives on the American Experience* (MIT Press, 1985).

15. See my *Powers and Prospects*, chap. 5

16. See William Hartung and Jennifer Washburn, "Lockheed Martin: From Warfare to Welfare," *Nation*, March 2, 1998. Gerard Baker, *FT*, March 11, 1998.

17. Timothy Egan, "As Idaho Prospers, Prisons Fill Up While Spending on the Poor Lags," *NYT*, April 16, 1998.

18. *Inside INEEL* (Idaho National Engineering and Environmental Laboratory), Sept. 1997.

19. Bob Davis, "In Effect, ITC's Steep Tariffs on Japan Protect US Makers of Supercomputers," *WSJ*, Sept. 29, 1997; David Sanger, *NYT*, Oct. 12, 1996.

20. Cited in Frank Kofsky, *Harry Truman and the War Scare of 1948* (St. Martin's, 1993). For the business press generally on military *vs.* social spending, see my *Turning the Tide;* and my *Deterring Democracy*, 49.

21. Tom Schlesinger, "Labor, Automation, and Regional Development," in John Tirman, ed., *The Militarization of High Technology* (MIT Press, 1984); James Cypher, "Military Spending, Technical Change, and Economic Growth: A Disguised Form of Industrial Policy?," *Journal of Economic Issues* 21:1 (March 1987).

22. See David Noble, *Forces of Production: A Social History of Industrial Automation* (Oxford Univ. Press, 1986).

23. Elizabeth Corcoran, *Science*, April 2, 1993. For general background, see my *World Orders Old and New*, chap. 2.

14. Socioeconomic Sovereignty

This is excerpted from an address given in Albuquerque, NM, on Feb. 26, 2000, on the 20th anniversary of the Interhemispheric Resource Center.

1. See my *Deterring Democracy*, chap. 12.

2. Madison, see my *Powers and Prospects*, chap. 5; for further discussion, see my " 'Consent Without Consent': Reflections on the Theory and Practice of Democracy," *Cleveland State Law Review* 44.4 (1996). Jay, Frank Monaghan, *John Jay* (Bobbs-Merrill,

1935), 323.

3. Walter Lippmann. For more extensive discussion, see my *Towards a New Cold War*, chaps. 1 and 2; *Necessary Illusions*, chap. 1; *Deterring Democracy*, chap. 12. For general background, see the pioneering work of Alex Carey, essays reprinted in *Taking the Risk Out of Democracy* (Univ. of Illinois Press, 1997).

4. See my *Powers and Prospects*, chap. 4.

5. Bernays, see chap. 9, p. 120 and note 28, in this volume. Stuart Ewen, *Captains of Consciousness* (McGraw-Hill, 1976).

6. World Bank, *World Development Report*, 1995. Cited with discussion by Jerome Levinson, "The International Financial System: A Flawed Architecture," *Fletcher Forum* 23:1 (Winter–Spring 1999).

7. See chap. 8, in this volume.

8. Carothers, "The Reagan Years, " in Abraham Lowenthal, ed., *Exporting Democracy* (Johns Hopkins Univ. Press, 1991); *In the Name of Democracy* (Univ. of California Press, 1991); "Dithering in Central America," *NYT Book Review*, Nov. 15, 1998.

9. *Condemned to Repetition* (Princeton, 1987).

10. See chap. 9, p. 111, in this volume.

11. See my *Turning the Tide*, chap. 2; and *Year 501*, chap. 2.

12. See my *Profit Over People*, chap. 4; see chap. 7, in this volume, note 11 and text.

13. Cited in Robert Westbrook, *John Dewey and American Democracy* (Cornell, 1991).

14. Cited in Martin Sklar, *The Corporate Reconstruction of American Capitalism, 1890–1916* (Cambridge Univ. Press, 1988), 413–14.

15. Shawn Crispin, "Global Trade: New World Disorder," *Far Eastern Economic Review* (Bangkok), Feb. 17, 2000.

16. Montreal Meeting (First Extraordinary Meeting of the Conference of Parties to the UN Convention on Biological Diversity to Finalize and Adopt a Protocol on Biosafety — Resumed Session) (2000), Andrew Pollack, "130 Nations Agree on Safety Rules for Biotech Food," *NYT*, Jan. 30, 2000; Pollack, "Talks on Biotech Food Turn on a Safety Principle," *NYT*, Jan. 28, 2000.

17. Edward Herman, "Corporate Junk Science in the Media," *Z* magazine, Jan. and Feb. 1999.

18. World Bank economist Branko Milanovic, cited in Doug Henwood, *Left Business Observer* 93, Feb. 2000.

Index

T

Taft, William Howard, 103

Tegucigalpa conference, 97

Teicher, Howard, 28

Thailand, 18, 150, 210

Thatcher, Margaret, 75, 107, 204, 232n15; and economic/social/cultural rights, 135, 141–42

TINA (There Is No Alternative) principle, 75, 107, 204–6, 214

Tobacco trafficking, 78–80, 150–51

Tokyo fire-bombing, 162–63

Tonry, Michael, 81, 154

"Trade rights." *See* International socioeconomic order

Tudjman, Franjo, 36, 182, 185, 239n27

Turkey, 32, 234n43; ethnic atrocities, 5, 41–42, 62–64, 184–85, 222–23n6

Twain, Mark, 86, 179

U

UD. *See* Universal Declaration of Human Rights

UN Charter: and human rights, 116; and "humanitarian intervention," 40, 45; and Iraq crisis, 12–13, 14, 15, 17–18; and Vietnam War, 164

UN Commission on Human Rights, 180

UN Conference on Trade and Development (UNCTAD), 75–76

UNESCO, 122

Unions. *See* Labor rights

United Arab Emirates, 30

United Fruit Company, 95

United Nations: deliberate US incapacitation, 2, 3, 8, 23, 55–56; US Security Council vetoes, 3, 4, 17, 24. *See also* UN Charter; *specific countries and issues*

US aid to repressive countries, 5, 127, 143; Croatia, 35–36, 182–84; El Salvador, 108, 185; Guatemala, 93–97; Iraq, 3, 21–22, 25, 28, 29, 37–38, 90;

Israel, 5; official counterterrorism reports, 63, 66, 222n4; Turkey, 5, 42, 62–64, 184–85; and Universal Declaration of Human Rights, 128. *See also* East Timor atrocities; Nicaragua; US Colombia policies

US Colombia policies, 62, 64–81, 182, 222n2; crop destruction, 74, 76, 78, 224–25n32; and drug war, 80–81; extent of atrocities, 41, 64, 65–66; Food for Peace program, 74–75; guerrilla countermeasures, 70–72, 224n23; Kennedy administration, 5, 68–70, 88; and political system, 67–68, 224n15; and refugees, 67; and socioeconomic conditions, 68–69, 74, 77–78; UNCTAD proposals, 75–76; and US tobacco trafficking, 78–80, 151. *See also* Colombian drug trafficking

US Constitution, 12, 15

US Cuba policies, 82–92; biological weapons, 27; and Cuban influence on Latin America, 2, 89–90, 92, 148; and democracy, 91–92; and end of Cold War, 2, 84, 91, 146–47, 148, 180; and foreign debt, 102–3; and international law, 1–2, 82–83, 118–19; Kennedy administration, 2, 83, 84, 148; missile crisis, 88; 19th century, 85, 86–88; and official counterterrorism reports, 63, 66; and "rogue state" term, 29; sanctions, 1–2, 63, 82–84, 91, 143, 146–49, 180–81, 238–39n25; US public opinion, 83, 92

US economy, 106, 135, 188–98, 226n50; and democracy, 196, 208; and drug war, 81; industrial revolution, 202; and labor rights, 114, 115, 137–41, 191, 192, 202–4, 240n10; postwar corporatization, 188–89; prosperity reports, 114–15, 190–92,